A VOICE

CRYING

IN

THE

WILDERNESS

BY

LESLIE MELVILLE

Published by Richter Publishing LLC www.richterpublishing.com

Formatted by Ke'Shawnda Chambers

ISBN:0692461922
ISBN-13:9780692461921

CONTENTS

PREFACE

<u>Paper 1 – Contemporary Labor Relations and Prospects for a National Tripartite Social Partnership Agreement in the Caribbean – 1968</u>

I was invited to deliver this paper by the ILO's Regional Office in Trinidad. My paper was delivered in two parts 1) The formulation of our contemporary tripartite system, and 2) Prospects for tripartite social partnerships in Guyana.

In preparing this paper, I utilized the work of three of the leading contributors to the study of modern industrial relations, E. White Bakke – Mutual Survival The Goal of Union and Management, John Dunlop's watershed work – Industrial Relations System, and Alton W.J. Craig – Industrial Relations and the Wider Society. I also used Isaac Dookhan's – Pre-Emancipation History of the West Indies to advance my theory that the development of the Industrial Relations System in the English Speaking Caribbean commenced with the enactment of the Emancipation Act in the British Parliament in 1833 since by granting freedom to the slave, it established the employer/employee relationship in the English Speaking Colonies of the Caribbean, thereby creating a relationship governed by rules, one in which its citizens in the workplace should never experience the anxiety or despair of *A Voice Crying In The Wilderness.*

<u>Paper 2 – With Independence in Sight: A New Look for the Trade Union Movement - 1964:</u>

It was while on holiday in Trinidad and greatly concerned over the racial conflict then raging at home that I began writing this Paper. The reason for my writing was my strong belief that the Trade Union Movement could not be exculpated from the sad event then occurring. The Paper was completed on my return home and delivered to the General

Secretary of the Trade Union Congress at that time, J.H. Pollydore. Unfortunately my effort was not even worthy of an acknowledgement of receipt. It was a lot later in my career after many battles in conference rooms that I realized that my work was that of *A Voice Crying In The Wilderness*.

Paper 3 – The Modern Supervisor - 1967:

This Paper was submitted to the National Efficiency Committee of the Ministry of Works and Hydraulics where I was employed as a Draughtsman in the Hydraulics Division as my contribution to the Year of Efficiency program. As with Paper 1, I did not receive an acknowledgement from the committee. I was once again *A Voice Crying In The Wilderness.*

Paper 4 – The reasons for Low Production and Measures for Improvement:

This Paper was prepared and submitted to the Minister of Labor & Social Security, Mr. Rudy Kendall, and copied to the Prime Minister, Forbes Burnham. This Paper did receive attention. About one week after submitting the paper, I was on my way home when I noticed that the car directly behind me seemed to be changing direction with my every change. I stopped out of concern and the car drove slowly pass me and stopped about 15 feet ahead. Out came Mr. Kendall who hastened towards me and embraced me fondly saying "Mattie Berbician, you mek me proud today. Your paper was read today at the Cabinet and the Prime Minister has directed that action be taken on your paper". There followed several interviews with the Chief Publicity Officer that were aired on the State Owned Radio Station. Unfortunately nothing further developed and I continued to be *A Voice Crying In The Wilderness.*

<u>Paper 5 – Towards Greater Production – 1967:</u>

This Paper was submitted to the National Efficiency Committee on October 25th, 1967. I did get an acknowledgement from the Secretary of the Committee, Mr. Douglas Delph, on November 3rd with a request that if I were interested, "the committee is in the process of compiling a list of topics to review and perhaps you would not be averse to having your name put on such a list". I submitted my agreement on November 9th. Sadly, "Efficiency Year" ended on December 31st, 1967, and so it would appear did the work of the committee since I received no further communication. I often wondered what became of the "list" compiled by the Committee and whether there were other presenters who were experiencing my emotions of being *A Voice Crying In The Wilderness.*

<u>Paper: 6A– The Scope for establishing new relationships between the Trade Union Youth Movement (TUYM) and the Guyana Trades Union Congress (TUC) – 1974</u>

<u>Paper 6B – Youth and the Changing Society – 1975</u>

These papers were prepared for presentation to two Annual Conferences of the TUYM in the seventies. It was in 1965 when at a seminar for young workers held at Camp Kayuka, about one mile off the now Soesdyke/Linden Highway, that a committee was appointed to draft a constitution for a TUYM – one year after I delivered Paper 1 to the General Secretary of the Trade Union Congress, J.H. Pollydore stating "there is a great need for the establishment of a Youth Arm of the Movement in order to establish continuity of leadership and to rally the workers of the future in this struggle that must end in their emancipation. It is in my view that our greatest omission to date, is that we have so far failed a Youth Arm of the Movement."

While I noted earlier that I did not receive an official acknowledgement of Paper 1, and reflected that the non-response supported my self-description as *A Voice Crying In The Wilderness,* I would be remiss if I did not mention that in 1965, Owen Cato was sent to a Young Workers Conference in Mexico. Upon his return, we worked together to establish the TUYM. Whereas I was never recognized for conceptualizing the development of a Trade Union Youth Movement, I comforted myself in the knowledge that the birth of this Youth Movement gave us all hope of continued leadership in the fight to remove the despair felt by those of us who considered ourselves *A Voice Crying In The Wilderness.*

Paper 7 – The Role of the Branch, Branch Officer and Shop Stewards in the Changing Society

This paper was prepared in response to the need for a text that could be used in the TUC Education Program of the Critchlow Labor College following a decision of the PNC Ruling Party that Guyana was a country in transition to socialism and will be changing its name to Cooperative Socialist Republic of Guyana. It was in conformity with this decision that the Board of Directors of the College decided to introduce the teaching of Socialism in the curriculum. At the time I was employed as the Registrar of the College. It was this decision that led me to prepare this paper. This paper was one of the few articles I have written that for a brief period, gave me hope that we were on the right path to growth and reduced the feeling of *A Voice Crying In The Wilderness.*

Paper 8 – Trade Unions and Living Standards - 1983

This paper was presented to a seminar for the second tier leadership of the Public Service Union. The real wages of the public service employees were then in serious decline, a result of the 1983 global oil crisis. The paper advanced that the decline in the real value of an employee's salary between January 1973 and January 1983 was a huge 72% and the Government was then resisting all increases in salary and wages. As the paper further advanced, during the period of March 1981- June 1982, of four Caricom countries, Guyana, Jamaica, Trinidad and Barbados, Guyana had the highest increase in its CPI, 28.8%. Consequently as the paper seemed to have suggested, there was obviously something wrong with the management of the Guyana economy. That unfortunately would earn me hostility from the Government and further entrench me as *A Voice Crying In The Wilderness.*

Paper 9 – The scope of Collective Bargaining in Central Planning – 1986

This paper was presented to a special meeting of the TUC held at Critchlow Labor College. The basis of the paper was to alert the Congress of the responsibilities that would befall the TUCs' representatives on several councils created to form the State Planning Commission. The paper contended that this was especially a concern for the current format of collective bargaining since there was a potential that it would give-way to a specialized Council of the commission, whose responsibility in the new Socialist Environment would change to determine how the accumulated wealth created by society is to be distributed. The paper contended that the TUC representative would require new knowledge along with the skill of advocacy, both of which were lacking in most TUC representatives. Again I was a *A Voice Crying In The Wilderness.*

Paper 10 – The Trade Union Movement – A Way Forward - 1985

This paper was presented to the Teaching Staff of the University of Guyana on the invitation of the Staff Association on February 26th. The paper raised many controversial issues, which many of my colleagues claimed to be too radical. One year after presentation, a long standing colleague, Kenneth Denny, would, no doubt in jest, inform me that it was my essay that was responsible for the death of the President, Forbes Burnham, some six months after its presentation, August 6th 1985. I must admit that I had deliberately set out to be controversial and strongly felt that the University was the ideal setting.

My reception from the students was so invigorating; it provided me the energy for the next five papers as I started to feel a reduction in the loneliness associated with being _A Voice Crying In The Wilderness_.

Paper 11 – The Role and Development Strategy of Trade Unions in a Third World Environment - 1986

This paper was presented to a group of female trade unionists at a seminar held at Critchlow Labor College. The participants were from member states of Caribbean Common Market (CARICOM) affiliated with the Caribbean Congress of Labor and sponsored by the International Labor Organization. In the introduction to the paper, I stated, "it is my firm conviction that the end objective of the Trade Union Movement can only be the economic emancipation of the working man and woman". The paper emphasized E. Wright Bakke's statement in his book The Concept of Social Organizations where he defines a social organization as "A continuing system of differentiated and coordinated human activities utilizing, transforming and welding together a specific set of human material, capital, ideational and natural resources into a unique problem solving whole, engaged in satisfying particular human need in interaction with other systems of human activities...."

The paper was well received, and as one of the participants would later report, it was the first time she had been given such an in-depth look of a trade union giving me once again hope for the future and for a brief moment reduced the anxiety of _A Voice Crying In The Wilderness._

Paper 12 – Trade Union Unity for Progress – Workers Stand Up for Guyana – 1986

This paper is my May-Day Address given in Linden, the hub of the Bauxite Mining Committee, as the representative of the TUC on the BIDCO Board - the management body of the industry. When I was told that the Government speaker at the Rally would be the Prime Minister, Hamilton Green, I decided to focus my address on beliefs expressed by both the management of the industry and the political establishment, that it was the Trade Union militancy that was responsible for the levels of decline in the industry – 54% decline in the production of dried bauxite and 43.4% decline in the calcite bauxite between 1972 and 1983. Unfortunately it seemed that the Prime Minister was unprepared to address the issues presented and instead resorted to character assassination in which he described me, and the leadership of the unions as "Enemies of the State". He had nothing to say, yet still said it. The Prime Ministers' actions were prevalent in our society resulting in several citizens opting to flee the country rather than continue to live the life of *A Voice Crying In The Wilderness.*

Paper 13 – Contemporary Labor Relations and Prospects for a National Tripartite Social Partnership Agreement in the Caribbean – 1968

I was invited to deliver this paper by the ILO's Regional Office in Trinidad. My paper was delivered in two parts 1) The formulation of our contemporary tripartite system, and 2) Prospects for tripartite social partnerships in Guyana.

In preparing this paper, I utilized the work of three of the leading contributors to the study of modern industrial relations, E. White Bakke – Mutual Survival The Goal of Union and Management, John Dunlop's watershed work – Industrial Relations System, and Alton W.J. Craig – Industrial Relations and the Wider Society. I also used Isaac Dookhan's –

Pre-Emancipation History of the West Indies to advance my theory that the development of the Industrial Relations System in the English Speaking Caribbean commenced with the enactment of the Emancipation Act in the British Parliament in 1833 since by granting freedom to the slave, it established the employer/employee relationship in the English Speaking Colonies of the Caribbean, thereby creating a relationship governed by rules, one in which its citizens in the workplace should never experience the anxiety or despair of *A Voice Crying In The Wilderness.*

Paper 14 – Trade Unions – What they are and What they do – 2003

This paper was prepared at the request of the General Secretary of the TUC, Linculd Lewis, for use as a 3-day seminar for Shop Stewards. Unfortunately, the seminar was never held due to the existing divisions within the TUC that led to several of the affiliates withdrawing and forming a counter federation. This division in our Movement that was created to unite the worker, now stood divided, *A Voice Crying In The Wilderness.*

Paper 15 – Unity Towards Improved Workers Welfare - 2001

This paper was prepared at the request of the General Secretary of the TUC, Linculd Lewis, as a 4-week training course for Senior Trade Unionists. The course was never scheduled. It had become obvious to all that even the educators of the leadership had become *A Voice Crying In The Wilderness.*

CONTEMPORARY LABOUR RELATIONS AND PROSPECTS FOR NATIONAL TRIPARTITE/SOCIAL PARTNERSHIP AGREEMENTS IN GUYANA/CARIBBEAN
1998

PART 1

None can deny that in the context of the changing world environment conditioned by what is being acclaimed as the "globalization of the Market Place", there is a tremendous need for a common understanding between capital and labor, about a strategy for ensuring what E. Wright Bakke termed – "their mutual survival". (Mutual Survival The Goal of the Union and Management).

However, before proceeding with the subject matter for discussion – "Contemporary Labor Relations and Prospects for National Tripartite/Social Partnership Agreements in Guyana/Caribbean", I must first establish that Industrial Relations, that "complex of private and public activity, operating in an environment which is concerned with the allocation of rewards to employees for their services and the conditions under which services are rendered," as Alton, W.J. Craig describes it, takes place within an Industrial Relations System.

Now John Dunlop in his watershed publication – INDUSTRIAL RELATIONS SYSTEMS, sets out what I will term the features of an Industrial Relations System when he posited:

"An Industrial Relations System at any one time in its development is regarded as comprised of certain actors, certain contexts, an ideology which binds the system together and a body of rules created to govern the actors at the workplace and work community".

The above is what I will term the features of a contemporary Industrial Relations System. I am submitting therefore, that before we can meaningfully discuss the National Tripartite/Social Partnership Agreements aspect of my presentation, it is first necessary that I look at how our Industrial Relations System developed into what it is today and some of the negatives that contributed to what some may term the unsatisfactory relationships that now exists within the system.

It is my submission that the fashioning of the Industrial Relations System of Guyana and the other English speaking countries in the Caribbean commenced as early as the 1st August, 1834 following the enactment of the Emancipation Bill in 1833 in the British Parliament.

THE ACTORS

It is to be remembered, that as a condition of the Act, the slaves who did not acquire their full freedom were considered as being apprenticed to their former masters.

Conditionally, they were expected, as Isaac Dookhan said in his PRE EMANCIPATION HISTORY OF THE WEST INDIES, " to work three quarters of the working week free for their masters, for the remainder of the week they could labor for their own benefits, or if they preferred, for their masters but for agreed wages. (See Annex 1 for more details).

The Emancipation Act as Dookhan further said made provision for the appointment of Stipendary Magistrates. They, as he said, were "expected to administer justice and prevent social and economic disturbance......... They were to ensure that both owner and apprentice secure their respective rights under the law."

What we were beginning to witness was the formulation of an industrial relations system. In the embryonic system of 1834, we can recognize those who will work for a wage (worker), those who managed the plantation, and the embryo of a Specialized Government Agency in the person of the Stipendary Magistrate. The actors, as Dunlop termed them, had begun to emerge.

THE CONTEXTS

Relative to the "context: as defined by Dunlop, and which he termed – "three sets of givens", the first - "technological characteristics of the workplace and work-community" – could be recognized in the technology utilized in the production of sugar. It was that technology that dictated a large and regular supply of labor and which was responsible for slavery and indentureship, which I will later discuss, and definitely, the presence of all who are seated this morning in the comfortable surroundings of the Le Meridien (Pegasus). As I have so often said, no matter how far up we may be on the social ladder, as Caribbean people, we all have our roots in some sugar plantation or former sugar plantation somewhere in Guyana or other parts of the Region.

The second of the contexts, as stated by Dunlop – "the markets and budgetary constraints, which impinge on the actors" – was definitely a major issue. This is so, since as many have argued; slavery was not abolished solely for altruistic reasons but due also to the fact that as a mode of production, it had become uneconomical. Further, the market for cane sugar was in decline due to reduced demand. It should be expected also, that the plantation had to be managed in keeping with some form of budgetary controls due to the "absentee ownership" of the period.

The third context – "locus and distribution of power in the wider society" was a definite given in 1834. Obviously, the former slaves wielded little power as their status dictated. The plantation owners did possess considerable power, as attested to in the slave lobby they maintained. It was that lobby in England which was successfully used to prolong and justify the abhorrent slave system in spite of its many critics. However, it was at Whitehall where ultimate power resided, and

would remain throughout the colonial period. Ultimate power, though, while residing at Whitehall, was often transferred to the Governors of the colonies, as the history of the respective nation states of the English speaking Caribbean can attest.

BODY OF RULES

Now, before discussing the emerging ideology of the I.R.S., it is first necessary for me to briefly consider the "body of rules" as stated by Dunlop. This is necessary since it would be the fashioning of the ideology of our Industrial Relations Systems that would be responsible for the bloody conflicts and animosities bordering on hatred that was a major feature during the colonial period and so would need a more lengthy discussion.

Having accepted that the fashioning of the Industrial Relations Systems of Guyana/Caribbean commenced on 1st August, 1834, I would advance that the first set of rules would be the conditions as set out in the Emancipation Act, some of which I have already referred to and others listed in Annex 1. It would be expected also that the plantation managements would, of necessity, have introduced work-rules of their own. Yet as history attests, many conflicts arose out of "the Rules" which necessitated the Colonial office bringing the period of apprenticeship to an end in 1838, two years before the scheduled date.

A significant event that coincided with the end of the period of apprenticeship was the arrival of the first batch of East Indian indentured labor to be bonded to respective plantations. This occurred mainly in Trinidad and British Guiana. They arrived under specific terms of service. They were to be paid for their services, provided with housing and free medical attention, so again we can see the presence of rules. These rules I know have been a subject of great controversy, which it is not my intention to discuss in this presentation. (See Annex II for additional information).

The indentureship system of labor supply, also introduced the third-party, in the person of the Indian Immigration Agent whose function, like that of the Stipendary Magistrate, was to regulate the relationship between the indentured immigrants and the plantation management.

The arrival of the East Indian immigrants, however, introduced some negatives. Their arrival led to competition for jobs in the sugar industry, a situation that the plantation management exploited much to their advantage, but unfortunately, to the disadvantage of the blacks that were now free men and women. Here, it must not be overlooked that the indentured immigrant spoke a language, possessed different religions and even their mode of dress was different. The Blacks, on the other hand, had been steeped in the European culture for nearly two hundred years.

It should not be surprising, therefore, that as the European management exploited the situation in which the freed Blacks found themselves, the attitudes of the Blacks towards the new arrivals had to be negative. Prejudices had started to develop. It should not be overlooked also, that the freed blacks had no cause to love the Europeans who had enslaved them in the first place, and were now denying them jobs which they had no doubt come to believe, were rightfully theirs.

However, as history informs us, many of the freed Blacks, denied employment on the plantation, had turned to self-employment in agriculture. But, problems with the plantation management over drainage and irrigation made their efforts uneconomical. Consequently, it left them little choice other than employment in the sugar industry, and it was there where the early seeds of inter-racial conflict were sown.

As a result of the steady flow of East Indian immigrant labor (1838 – 1917), employment opportunities dwindled for the Blacks in the sugar industry. That commenced the acceleration of the drift of the Blackman to the townships seeking the menial jobs that were available. The

Blacks who remained were the skilled factory workers who could not be easily replaced, and other skilled shovel men, etc.

The drift of the Blackman to the townships and villages they built, created a dichotomous situation. Two distinct societies had started to emerge. That of the society away from the plantation where the culture was predominantly European and that of the plantation where the East Indians preserved the culture which they brought with them from their homeland.

It was in such a dichotomy that our Industrial Relations System had begun to develop.

THE IDEOLOGY

It is now necessary that I look, as stated above, at the development of the ideology of our contemporary Industrial Relations System.

John Dunlop in speaking of an ideology in the context of industrial relations identified it as – "a set of ideas and beliefs commonly held by the actors that help to bind or to integrate the system together as an Entity". Dunlop also advanced that an ideology "involves a congruence or compatibility among these views and the rest of the systems".

Even under a microscope it would be difficult to identify an existing ideology in 1834. I would argue, however, that the fashioning process of an ideology had begun, and it would be the fashioning process of that ideology that would be the root cause of the bloody conflicts and animosities bordering on hatred to which I have earlier referred.

The problem throughout the fashioning process would be one of attitudes that influence the perception that individuals and groups would have of each other. The bugbear would be the perception of the plantocracy and the white ruling class, of the former slaves and the East Indian indentured immigrants throughout the fashioning process. Here Walter Rodney's – A

HISTORY OF THE GUYANESE WORKING PEOPLE, 1881 – 1905 must be mentioned. Especially the Chapters – "Struggles of the Indian Immigrant Work Force 1884 –1903, and "Industrial and Social Struggles of the Creole Working People".

The attitudes of the ruling class are further captured in statements attributed to Governors Hodgson and Jackson in 1905 and 1944.

In Rodney's work already mentioned, and Ashton Chase's – A HISTORY OF TRADE UNIONISM IN GUYANA, 1905 –1962, Governor Hodgson was recorded as saying during the 1905 Riots here in the then British Guiana in reference to the striking workers, that:

> "if you break the law in connection with your
> grievance, as Governor of the Colony and as the
> person who has to protect the lives and interests –
> more particularly the mercantile interests of the
> Colony, it is my duty to see that no one breaks
> The law."

There were no doubts on whose side Governor Hodgson would have stood in industrial disputes. Rodney's account of Governor Hodgson's actions during the strike made it quite clear. Interestingly, however, one Guyanese did make a statement to a British soldier after British troops had been summoned to the colony following the riots? As the Guianese informed the soldier – "The people are doing nothing. It is the Government who are rioting and shooting down people."

The other statement attributed to Governor Jackson is recorded in Harold Lutchman's – INTEREST REPRESENTATION IN THE PUBLIC SERVICE. Governor Jackson was then referring to the organizing efforts of the Manpower Citizen's Association following the gunning down of sugar workers during a strike in 1938 and the subsequent granting of recognition to the MPCA. As Governor Jackson had said in 1942:

"I have the strongest sympathies with the difficulties which the estate staff has to encounter in the delicate task of adjusting their ways and methods to meet the changing conditions of these times and in endeavoring to maintain control over an ignorant and easily influenced body of laborers..."

There is no doubt that the fashioning of an ideology for our Industrial Relations System was a long and painful one. It took riots, strikes and no doubt industrial sabotage to convince our managers that the workers of our country and Region had the right to have a say in the conditions under which they had to sell their labor.

Further, as I would later discuss, it was a change in the political culture, which would delay the fashioning process.

The development of an ideology proceeded slowly as I have said. However, by the 1940's a semblance of what some writer's term "volunteerism" could be recognized. Volunteerism as an ideology of an industrial relations system advances that the principal actors (employer/employee) have a preference for their relationship being guided by voluntary agreements and not dictated by statutory regulations. They also possess a preference for keeping the courts of law out of the decision making process.

The process of volunteerism accelerated on the introduction of the Ministerial form of Government in 1953 and continued until about the mid 1970's here in Guyana. From there on, following the nationalization process of the Burnham Government it was difficult to identify a clear-cut ideology. It was not until the late 1980s and following the divestment policy of the Hoyte Administration that the re-emergency of the ideology began. Since then it has continued to develop but recent legislations tend to suggest that the relationship is becoming more legalistic and less voluntary.

THE FASHIONING OF OUR CONTEMPORARY I.R.S.

I have already spoken of the two distinct societies that began to emerge as from 1838. By the turn of the century, the social structures away from the plantations were well established. At the apex stood the Europeans. They manned the colonial administration, the top managerial positions in the sugar industry, and other expatriate businesses. Below the Europeans were the Portuguese who controlled a large part of the commercial sector. They had arrived in the colony as indentured immigrants prior to the arrival of the East Indians, but had proven unfit for the rigorous plantation life, and so they later gravitated to commerce. Below the Portuguese stood the mulattoes who occupied positions in the civil service and junior managerial positions in the larger business enterprises. The Chinese, who like the Portuguese, had also arrived as indentureship immigrants, occupied a position that equated, to some extent with the Mulattoes. They had also proven unfit for the arduous plantation life, and like the Portuguese, many had gravitated to commerce and other white-collar jobs. Below the Mulattoes and the Chinese were the Blacks of varying hues with those of the darker hue, standing above the East Indians, still "quarantined" on the sugar plantation.

It was in such a social structure that final fashioning process of the Industrial Relations System of Guyana away from the plantations was taking place.

Starting with the 1905 strike which ended in rioting as already alluded to, there was yet another strike in 1906. The two strikes are significant, for as Rodney argued:

> "Small qualitative changes in the consciousness of workforce were registered, and after 1906 these changes became operational in the form of attempt at the organization of the working class for industrial and trade union struggle".

Rodney was right. In 1906, an informal organization "with norms of conduct and attitudes towards the hierarchy of managers" had definitely emerged. Hubert Nathaniel Critchlow was soon to occupy the center stage, on which the actors of the I.R.S. will be performing.

On the employer side, a Chamber of Commerce established in 1889, was soon to play an important role in employer/employee relations.

There was still no specialized Government Agency in 1906 as we know it today but the Indian Immigration Agent still played a significant role in industrial relations matters on the sugar plantations, and in the strike/riots of 1905, a Stipendary Magistrate, William Payne was quoted by Rodney as leading a "vigilante citizens" force to patrol the street. But what were their functions at that time is unclear.

In 1916 we can recognize the first attempt at collective bargaining when the Chamber of Commerce agreed to meet with a delegation of workers led by Critchlow during a strike.

In 1919 we had our first trade union, and in 1921 the Trade Union Ordinance, now an Act, came into being, and by the end of the 1930's there were at least seven registered trade unions.

In 1942 the Labor Ordinance was enacted following the Moyne Commission of 1938 which was appointed "to investigate social and economic conditions" in the English speaking Caribbean. The Commission, according to Prof. Nettleford in a paper kindly supplied by Mr. Goolsarran, recommended and obtained acceptance for the incorporation of labor into the formal process of governance in the old British West Indies".

Another result of the visit by the Moyne Commission was the registration of the first Trade Union Council here in Guiana in 1941. The founding and registration of the British Guiana Trades Union Congress was definitely due to the presence of Sir Walter Citrine, later Lord Citrine, who was then General Secretary of the British T.U.C, and a member of the Commission. Yet another organization to emerge was the Sugar Producers Association in 1942, and it would later play a significant role in the micro industrial relations system of the sugar industry. Yet, notwithstanding the changes, the Labor Ordinance through legislative action, had introduced some important "rules" in the I.R.S.

Finally in 1962, we saw the founding of CAGI, the Consultative Association of Guyanese Industry, and the Employer counterpart of the workers Trades Union Congress.

It can be said, therefore that all of the features of our contemporary Industrial Relations System were in place by the mid 1960's

To conclude this aspect of my presentation, i.e. PART I, it is necessary that I discuss how the various stages of the development of the IRS impacted on what, in industrial relations terminology we term the outputs of system, which Craig describes as "wages, hours, fringe benefits and working conditions," broadly described by Dunlop, as Rules.

If we should begin at the turn of the century, we can say with certainty that the Rules were definitely to the disadvantage of the workers throughout the Region. This is verified, in Guyana, by the bitter strike of 1905, and the lengths to which the workers were prepared to go to address their grievances. Rodney captured this in his work already referred to in a statement attributed to the Inspector General of Police while commenting on the behavior of one of the "rioters" in Cummingsburg, a ward of the city.

As he said:

> "A man whose courage could not be questioned ventured to within a short distance of the police while shooting was going on. He was a dangerous fellow at close quarters and he was ordered to be shot but notwithstanding that he was so near, shot after shot was discharge at him without harming him.

Standing face to face with the police he braved the
Desperate situation, striking himself on the chest and
Inviting the police to kill him. It was only when it
Seemed likely that he would be charged at that he
desisted and cleared out. Although I was bound to
order him to be fired at, personally I felt glad that the
pluckly fellow managed to escape."

By 1919 the workers were definitely better organized here in
Guyana and we saw the birth of our first union – the British
Guiana Labor Union. The better organizing had brought some
improvement in their bargaining position and so modest gains
were made as history attests. Among the gains was a shorter
workday. Yet, notwithstanding, their better bargaining
positions, the employers due to their much stronger financial
position, were nonetheless the stronger of the two. Of much
more importance, the employer still had the backing of the
state apparatus. Twenty-three years later, the role of the state
was unchanged as affirmed by the statement of Governor
Jackson, already quoted. It must be mentioned, however, that
Governor Jackson was referring to conditions within the
plantation society where changes were not keeping pace with
the society away from the plantation. By the 1940's the
workers hierarchy had grown much stronger for reasons already
advanced. Further, by the establishment of the Labor
Ordinance in 1942, the workers and their unions had access
through the conciliatory function of the Labor Department and
the provision for arbitration, to a source, which closed the
power gap between employer and employee. Generally,
however, though the sympathies of the state were still with the
employer, we can say that conditions of work had become
much improved.

Here, it is important that I refer to what Professor Nettleford
termed "political unionism". As he said, it was a "modality in

the fight for self-government". Unlike many of the other Caribbean countries, politics did not play a significant role in the development of trade unionism in Guyana until the mid- 1940's. This does not say that politicians did not evince an interest in the early movement, for they did. It was in the mid-1940's however, when a kind of fusion would commence and it was destined to later have serious consequences for the Movement. The fusion, as Prof. Nettleford rightly said, was the result of the struggle for self-government.

It was out of the struggle for self-government that a major change in the power-relationship in the I.R.S. would result. Self-government started with Jamaica, then with Trinidad and Tobago, Guyana, Barbados and the other member states of CARICOM. What this meant, was that for the first time total support of the state apparatus was no longer on the side of the employer. Ministerial Government, which came with internal self-government, saw persons from working-class political parties taking up positions as Ministers of Labor, all of whom would have possessed working-class sympathies.

It cannot be said, however, that the employer group was at a total disadvantage, for their individual financial strength still made them a formidable group.

Yet, notwithstanding the advent of the ministerial system of government, ultimate power still resided at Whitehall. This was made placidly clear in 1953 when British might was used to, what they claimed, "prevent a communist subversion of government." I speak here of the suspension of constitution of British Guiana. I am nonetheless contending that the suspension of the constitution was no more than a pretext to prevent the Guiana Industrial Workers Union from replacing the MPCA as bargaining agents for sugar workers. Sugar had again proven that it was still King and its lobby still effective. The suspension of the Constitution nonetheless confirmed where ultimate power resided.

Earlier, I referred to the "serious consequence" of political unionism. Very often it tends to take decision making out of the hands of union officialdom and places it in hands of the politician. The Guyana experience may have been necessary in the struggle for self-government and then independence. After those goals are achieved, it is my submission, that political unionism tends to be divisive, as it fosters inter-union rivalry of a political nature that can be counterproductive. Further, it is my experience that in most cases, it is the politicians who benefit and not the workers over the long term.

THE PLANTATION SOCIETY

As I have stated before, as from 1838 two distinct societies had begun to emerge. On the plantations, what was taking place was passing unnoticed by the wider society. There were reports of the many disturbances, which were occurring, but those of the wider society paid little heed. Baboo's problems were Baboo's problems. It was not until the 1920's and 1930's when the excess labor from the plantations started to drift away from the plantations to the wider society that notice had to be taken of this almost forgotten group of emerging Guyanese.

By the 1940's, it was no longer a drift since it had reached flood proportions. It was the Enmore strike of 1948, which clearly indicated, that conditions, as they existed on the individual sugar estates could not be again "swept under the carpet." It was the bold decision to bring the bodies of the five slain sugar worker/martyrs for burial in the La Pepentir Cemetery in Georgetown, that would introduce measures that commenced the fusion process of the two emerging societies. The workers as it was in 1938, were shot and killed during the strike at

Enmore, 12 miles beyond the city, "along the red, red road"
(Martin Carter's ENMORE: Poem of Resistance.)

Resulting from the Enmore strike was the Venn Commission and
the introduction of a set of rules that would improve the
working lives of the mainly East Indian Sugar workers.

POLITICAL UNIONISM

Here in Guyana, the struggle for self-government through
political unionism bore fruit when the People's Progressive
Party led by two charismatic young Guianese won a landslide
victory in the 1953 General Elections, held under the system of
universal adult suffrage. That victory, though short-lived, was
destined to change the country and later introduced problems
for which the society is still seeking solutions.

Though the PPP had won a resounding victory, internal divisions
developed even before they took office. The constitution was
suspended four months after they took office and it was not
surprising when a split occurred 1955. The victory of the PPP in
1953 is significant, for it had brought the two societies that
were emerging under a common banner, if not for a common
purpose. Tragically, one of the leaders – L.F.S. Burnham was a
product of the wider society and the other, C.B. Jagan, a
product of the plantation society. One a descendant of an
African slave, the other a descendant of an East Indian
immigrant. On their parting company, the result was inevitable.

The consequence of the split was that it polarized the two
emerging groups. Unfortunately, the division was not just
political, since it also had consequences for the Industrial
Relations System.

As we now look at our contemporary Industrial Relations

System it is not difficult to distinguish the problem as it exists. First, the former African slaves, as a necessity to survive, had to leave the plantation as a result of the competition the arriving East Indian Immigrants provided in the manipulative labor market that was the plantation. On leaving the plantation, they created most of our coastal villages. From the villages they trekked to the city and town, which together comprised the wider society.

Over time, they emerged mainly as wage earners occupying positions in the civil, police and teaching services. Some became artisans, skilled workers who built our infrastructure outside of the plantation, either as wage earners or self-employed. Some gravitated to the professions, but as a group, many will agree that they are not very far up the economic ladder. Today, for the wage earners, the jobs they may have considered to be theirs are like 1838, again being threatened and by the same group.

The former East Indian Immigrants while "quarantined" on the plantation, by hard work and painful thrift, together with the culture they preserved, have now become an economic entity. Like the Portuguese of earlier time and the Chinese, the majority of whom had migrated following the advent of working-class governments and the unstable political climate of the 1960's, the East Indians now control the largest part of the Commercial Sector. Further, apart from being wage earners and self employed, they are now Bankers, manufacturers and control a monopoly of a major sector of the economy: The Rice Industry which accounted for 10.5% of GDP in 1997.

It is in the context of the above that we must address Contemporary Labor Relations and the Prospect for National Tripartite social Partnerships.

PART II
PROSPECT FOR TRIPARTITE/SOCIAL PARTNERSHIPS IN GUYANA

It is my view point, that if we are to sensibly discuss the partnership agreements concept as stated in the subject matter of my topic, it is necessary to first establish why we need the partnership agreements, and what we hope to achieve by them.

In the opening remarks, I spoke of the need for capital and labor to plan a strategy that will ensure their "mutual survival" in this age of the global market place. This I said is in view of the challenges the Global market Place will present to both Capital and Labor.

The question that must now be asked, is - What are the challenges of which I speak?

UNION/MANAGEMENT CHALLENGES

The first is making the products we now export competitive. At present, our major exports are sugar, bauxite, gold, rice and timber products. It is now common knowledge that the markets for all of them are in decline, and equally important, our cost of production, in most cases, are at or above world market prices with little prospects for a profitable return on investment. The five products, nonetheless, account for 48% of GDP.

The second challenge is increasing output at reduced cost, so that productivity of both capital and labor is increased.

The third challenge is keeping our existing labor force in gainful employment while ensuring the survival of the enterprises which provide the employment.

The fourth challenge is attracting investment to enhance exports and at the same time, reducing the high level of unemployment.

Yet another challenge is that posed by foreign manufacture to our local fledging manufacturing sector and it consequences.

The final challenge is protecting the environment while we endeavor to achieve the above.

Those are some of the challenges, and which as the topic suggests, solutions must be provided within the I.R.S. If this so, there must be significant changes within the system.

Now, our Industrial Relations System over the years, developed in keeping with the concept of the Rabble Hypothesis of the true nature of man, which advances that it is when each group fights for itself that the best interests of the body politic is served.

It is this concept that no doubt led D. Wight Bakke to advance this view of the job of the manager in his publication already referred to. As he said;

> "The job for which he is immediately rewarded or punished, is promoting the welfare, not of the world, not of the national economy, not of the industry, but of his own company."

It is probably the same hypothesis that caused the I.C.F.T.U. to advance this definition of a trade union which speaks of:

> A continuing permanent and democratic organization voluntarily created by the worker, to protect them at

their work...

The I.C.F.T.U. definition obviously suggests that the workers need a union to protect them from the employer whose sole objective was that of profit, and from his managers, for whom profit was their sole motivation.

Next to be considered is the role of the third party, the specialized Government Agency, in the development process of the I.R.S. As I have advanced in Part I, since 1953, Guyana has been governed by "Working Class Parties" and there is no doubt that between 1953 to 1976 the workers benefited in respect to the rule making function of the I.R.S. However, between the periods 1976 – 1989, during which the Government was the largest employer of labor with 80% of the economy under government control, many will say that Government's motivation was more employer than worker oriented.

However, in our contemporary I.R.S., the role of the Government has been somewhat problematical. It can still be termed Working Class Government. However, the country is still plagued with "racial politics", an offshoot of "political unionism" due to the ethnic polarization of our people.

Consequently, in matters concerned with industrial relations, it is at times difficult for the Government not to be guided by partisan interests. Regrettably, in situations such as exist in Guyana, it is likely to find that the old adage – "he who pays the piper calls the tune" – holding well. In its political context this will read – he who elects the Government calls the tune. This, of course refers to the "spoils system".

It is for this reason that National Tripartite/Social partnership agreements, though necessary will experience difficulties in being workable entities.

What we have here in Guyana is a Labor movement which is predominantly Black. Equally a Business Community predominantly East Indian, and a Government that is yet unable to convince the majority of the black community that it is not solely an "East Indian Political Party," which comprises the Government.

Notwithstanding what I have said above, there is a dire need for the three parties involved in industrial relations to sit down and plan a strategy that can be utilized to ensure our survival as a nation. I say this, for unless we can preserve and strengthen our economy, we will continue to be no more than mendicants and subjected to the dictates of others. The old adage still holds good, unless we swim together we will sink together.

Professor Nettleford has summed up the position quite clearly. In his paper already quoted, he informs us that the World Bank has classified the Caribbean region as a whole, as one of the "wealthiest in the developing world". The Bank, he said, places the territories into the reference group of 'middle-income countries" where Barbados; Belize; Trinidad and Tobago; and St Lucia are termed "upper middle-income countries" where pockets of poverty are to be found. Jamaica and St Vincent and the Grenadines, Professor Nettleford informs us, are designated "lower middle-income countries with large numbers of poor.

In reference to Guyana, Professor Nettleford informs that Guyana falls into the category of "Lower-income countries with widespread and persistent poverty." Interestingly, like his colleague Professor Mc Intyre, Professor Nettleford also bracketed us with Haiti. The table set out below gives a picture of the relativities of Per Capita Income.

PER CAPITA INCOME US$

COUNTRIES	1986	1990	1991	1992	1993	1994	1995
Barbados	6267	6657	6459	6130	6213	6457	6580
Trinidad & Tobago	4918	4259	4347	4236	4127	4267	4369
Jamaica	1352	1633	1629	1639	1646	1641	1637
Suriname	838	824	847	891	806	765	817
Guyana	613	471	515	566	635	686	722
Haiti	360	314	298	249	238	223	229
Source: IDB Report 1996							

I have already advanced that there will be difficulties in having the much needed tripartite/social agreements become workable entities. I have also advanced that if we are to make them viable entities a considerable amount of changes will have to be introduced within the I.R.S.

Here, what Bakke in his CONCEPTS OF SOCIAL ORGANISATION says, becomes important. In speaking of the Actors in the I.R.S., this is what he posited:

> "The individuals who make decisions and undertake action with respect to industrial relations are not completely free agents. The workers, union leaders, managers and government officials are associated in organizations (companies, unions, and government bureaus) whose resources, customary patterns of collective behavior and codes stabilizing that behavior stimulate individuals to decisions and actions of particular types and also restrain them within certain bounds."

Bakke has no doubt identified a major stumbling block to the Tripartite/Social Agreements. If the stumbling block is to be removed, it will call for change and if it is truly our desire to strengthen our economy, as the need is clearly established in the table included above, time is not on our side.

The issue is, what must now be done if we are to make the Tripartite/Social Partnership Agreements not only possible but also workable and effective.

First, must be a commitment that the Agreements are necessary by the three social partners, as I am convinced they are. If this can be acquired, an informative process must be put in place to convince all the stakeholders that the Agreements are necessary, and much more important, and further that they will bring benefits to all the stakeholders. Here all the stakeholders must be targeted, i.e.:

1. Managers and their representatives in supervision.
2. Trade Union leaders and union members.
3. The state through the Ministry of Labor.
4. All of those who can be affected by the interplay between the principal actors.

The major problem as I see it, relative to the informative process, would be at the level of the trade union leaders and union members. I say this, since as Adam Smith argued in his "Wealth of Nations," it is easier for the employers/managers to combine on such issues, due to their smaller numbers, vis-à-vis the trade union leaders and the union members. More importantly, also, is that the employer/manager would have more financial resources at their disposal.

Here, it is important that I mention the disparity in funding being offered for institutional strengthening throughout the Region. The Private Sector has been singled out for special attention, and at this seminar, the Specialized Government Agency seems to have been given special attention.

I am submitting that here in Guyana, there is dire need for institutional strengthening at the level of the Trade Union Movement, and the greatest need is at the level of the National Center – The Guyana Trades Union Congress.

What we have witnessed in Guyana is that due to the changes that have occurred in the power relationships in the I.R.S., individual unions, through the collective bargaining process and its extension, conciliation and arbitration, have made lengthy strides. Although they have not been able to match the skills at the disposal of management across the table, they have gone a long way since the first attempt at collective bargaining in 1916. Unfortunately while many of our unions have made great strides, the same cannot be said of the National Center, hence the urgent need for institutional strengthening at that level.

There is yet another feature of the union problem that must not be overlooked. The advent of the Global market Place will definitely introduce a new approach to collective bargaining and that is – Productivity Bargaining. In productivity bargaining, the amount of profit made by the enterprise will no long be the sole criteria for determining increases in employment costs. The issues at the bargaining table will center on the "productivity of labor" and all its ramifications.

The Global Market Place will demand that if the enterprise is to remain a viable entity, whatsoever it produces, must be competitive. Protectionism will be a thing of the past. The competitors of the Enterprise will no longer be local, or regional but sited in every country of the world. Each striving to be more productive, more efficient.

That is the world toward which we are moving inexorably. We must either face the challenges or be consumed by them.

To conclude, National Tripartite/Social Partnership Agreements are necessary in the Guyana context if we are to bring an end to the widespread and persistent poverty stigma attached to our country and the mendicancy that is becoming a way of life.

ANNEX I
PROVISIONS OF THE ACT OF EMANCIPATION

The Act for the Abolition of Slavery throughout the British Colonies; for promoting the Industry of the Manumitted Slaves; and for compensating the persons hitherto entitled to the Services of such Slaves' was passed by the British Parliament in August, 1833 and brought into effect on 1st August, 1834. Its provisions constituted a guide to colonial legislatures to pass ancillary acts on similar terms.

(i)   From 1st August 1834, slavery was to be 'utterly and forever abolished and declared unlawful throughout the British Colonies.'

(ii)   Slave children under six years of age, and all children born to slave mothers were to be free. Exceptions were children between twelve and twenty-one who were destitute – these might be apprenticed out.

(iii)   All other slaves were to serve a period of apprenticeship to their masters: in the case of praedials (field slaves) until 1st August 1840, and non-praedials (non-field slaves) until 1st August 1838.

(iv)   Apprentices were to work for three-quarters of the working week for their masters; for the remainder of the week they could labor for their own benefit, or if they preferred, for their master but for agreed wages.

(v)   The apprenticeship might be brought to an end before the specified time either by voluntary discharge by the master, or by purchase by the apprentice. Freedom could be purchased even against the wishes of the master. In case of voluntary discharge, the master was to remain responsible for the care of aged and infirm apprentices during the remaining portion of their apprenticeship.

(vi)   The apprentice was to continue to be provided by his master with 'food, clothing, lodging, medicine, medical attendance, and such other Maintenance and Allowance' as he was accustomed to have during slavery. If food was not supplied, then the apprentice should be provided with adequate provision grounds and leisure time to grow his own food.

(vii)   The apprentice was bound to work honestly, to refrain from insolence and insubordination, and to abandon all attempts to escape the fulfillment of his contract.

(viii)   The 'Effectual Superintendence' of the apprentices and jurisdiction over them was entrusted to Stipendiary Magistrates who were to be paid £300 a year from the British Treasury.

(ix)   Slave-owners were to be compensated for the loss of their property in slaves, and the British Government allocated a grant of £20 million for this purpose.

Source: A Pre-Emancipation History Of the West Indies By: Isaac Dookhan

ANNEX II
CONDITIONS OF INDENTURESHIP

(i)   The immigrant was assigned to a particular estate for a five-year period after which the planter had to pay his return passage back to India. In cases where the immigrant chooses to remain in the colony, he could sign on for a further period of indentureship.

(ii)   The planter had to supply free housing and medical facilities to the immigrant.

(iii)   The immigrant had to be paid a fixed sum for his work, which ranged from eight cents to twenty-four cents per day.

(iv)   The immigrant could not leave the estates to which he was assigned without the permission of the estate manager.

The conditions of indentureship were altered from time to time especially that dealing with the return passage and by the end of the nineteenth century the planter was only responsible for half of the return passage.

WITH INDEPENDENCE IN SIGHT - A NEW LOOK FOR THE MOVEMENT
1965

INTRODUCTION

With Independence in sight, the Trade Union Movement in Guyana now stands at the cross-roads and the next few months will decide whether we will be able to maintain the militancy and influence we established over the pasts seven years, or fragment into the weak and near purposeless organizations that existed prior to the election of the Peoples Progressive Party Government in 1957.

It is my view, that by maintaining our individuality and developing our own philosophy, we can more contribute to our Society. For after Independence many problems will arise that will require the collective efforts of all institutions comprising our Society. It follows, that if the working class Movement is to contribute of its best, a free and independent Trade Union Movement is necessary, for in spite of what may be the claims of the political Movement, the Trade Unions are the only true and exclusive advocate of the working class.

For the Independent Government to govern successfully, it will have to represent the interest of all sections of the Society. By ensuring our independence, we can best advise the Government on matters pertaining to the working class interests, instead of just being rubber stamps for governmental policy.

We must, therefore, do everything to ensure our independence and, at the same time, build upon what we have established over the past seven years. Confidence of our members in our leadership must be maintained, for without it, we are doomed to failure. This confidence is not going to be easily maintained, for now that the fight for survival is over, the workers are looking forward to acquiring benefits and the fulfillment of the many promises made. As I see it, some radical changes are needed in the structure of the Movement and the attitude of its leadership. This is a new era, and while many excuses may be accepted for the inefficiencies of the past, we cannot hope to exist for long, if we do not gear ourselves to meet the new demands. My proposal addresses this aspect of our future development.

BACKGROUND

Before presenting my proposal, I would like to give a brief history of the Trade Union Movement in the period leading up to Independence.

The fear generated by the Jagan Regime in the Industrial and Commercial sectors of the community as a result of its socialist policies bordering on the extreme left, forced many an employer to grant sweeping concessions to the Trade Union Movement during the period, 1957-1965.

Shortly after being elected to office in 1957 it became evident that the PPP Government was totally opposed to the existing Trade Union Leadership. They dubbed it a part of the reactionary element in the Society, and it was this attitude of the Jagan Government, which forced the Movement into open conflict with it. So the employers, as a group, in the hope of convincing the Movement of its changing attitude towards labor, and not being able to challenge two forces at the same time, i.e. the Government and the Unions, lent more in favor of the Unions, recognizing them as the lesser of two evils.

The employers were hoping at the same time, that the growing strength of the Movement would prove an even match for the might of the PPP in the ensuring struggle. They were also expecting that its apparent change of attitude and offers of co-operation would be construed as a gesture of friendship by the Unions. This came at the time when the Unions were regaining their full strength after the now historic 1953 elections that brought about a split right down the center of the movement, and the entrance of the International Trade Union Movement on the local scene.

Fear was also generated abroad, more so in the U.S.A. That caused those who were fearful of the spread of International communism in the Western Hemisphere to become interested in the affairs of British Guiana. The Jagan Regime was clearly signifying where its sympathy lie, and its opposition to the recognized Trade Union Movement was viewed with suspicion. It was recognized very early, therefore, that the surest way to stop the spread of communism in British Guiana was to help establish a strong anti-communist block. So, as a result of the existing hostility between the supposed communist Government headed by Jagan and the already organized Trade Union Movement, which had by now aligned itself to the pro-Western Anti-communist block, it was accepted that the movement was ideally suited for the purpose

The Trade Union Movement, as a result of these two developments, made rapid progress. Money was made available from several sympathetic agencies to assist in organizing and educating members, and the local employers were for the first time prepared to co-operate with the Unions. The Movement as a consequence rapidly increased in strength, earning yet greater hostility from the PPP Government. That eventually led to open conflict in 1962 and 1963, to be followed by the unfortunate events of 1964, terminating in the eventual defeat of the

PPP Government in December of that year.

These events are significant, for they are responsible for the present strength and influence of the Trade Union Movement. How ironic it is, that the Movement which the PPP Government termed a "shell organization" and "a beer guzzling set-up" and endeavored to destroy, was that which was eventually responsible for its downfall. Had the PPP Government on its election to office in 1957, or even at the time of its re-election in 1961, attempted to earn the confidence and win the support of the Trade Union Movement, our independence would have been long since won, and no doubt, our history from then on greatly changed.

The policy makers within the party blundered when they under-estimated the strength of the local Movement. They failed to take cognizance of its international affiliations and over-looked the fact that within the Unions were conscientious and hard-working officials who had earned the confidence of the work force and were prepared to fight for the continuing existence of the Movement, as they knew it. It must also be remembered, that there were many of these officials who were prepared to offer full co-operation to the PPP Government had they been approached or had the PPP created an environment in which this would have been possible.

Instead of seeking co-operation, the policy of head rolling was introduced and attempts made to smash the Unions by setting up a series of rival puppets. The PPP also attempt to control the Unions by legislation, thus adding to the hostility already referred to.

The Peoples Progressive Party, without doubt, mainly contributed through its attitude to the Unions, to the present strength of the Movement. In order to fight off the threat, the Unions had to muster all their resources, and the ensuing struggle, developed the qualities of its leadership and banded the membership into a militant body. In the struggle, also, it is important to note that the Movement had to align itself with the several other opposing groups within our society who were themselves, either under attack from the PPP Governmental forces, or were fearful of eventual liquidation. As a result, there was a close association between the then elected political opposition and the Trade Union Movement. That led to many accusations being leveled against the Movement that it was the tool of the political opposition and the instrument being used to bring about the fall of the PPP Government.

The facts are, that the organized strength of the Trade Union Movement made it an effective fighting force. This was recognized by all, including the political opposition, and every use was made of it by all engaged in the struggle for survival, as the vanguard to halt the avalanche of the PPP, bent on destroying all of those who did not share their points of view. This is of importance, for the Movement was never really the tool of any group, but was itself *fighting a battle for survival*. Consequently, its effectiveness as the only organized fighting force capable of stopping the PPP in its quest for dominance, meant that it either had to spearhead and at times fight alongside those who were also engaged in the struggle, or go it alone and face eventual liquidation.

The battle is none-the-less won. The alliance so often described as an unholy one must be dissolved and the form of association that must now exist between the former allies is of importance to the Movement. The political opposition has now become the Government, and they, with many platitudes, have openly sought the co-operation of the Trade Union Movement. Just how far can this co-operation extend without embarrassing the Movement, must be determined, for the policy of the Government, from here on, will be under deep scrutiny and it is known that at some time, its policy would divert from that of the Movement and it is not going to be easy for the Movement to decide on a line of action.

The association over the seven years of PPP rule has developed into a position where the leaders of the Movement are, in the main; sympathetic to the now governing coalition, and many of them may be considered as activists of one of the two parties comprising the coalition. It is here where the difficulty lies, for as a result of this association, it is going to be extremely difficult for the Trade Union Leadership to arrive at decisions uninfluenced by political views and concepts. These are pitfalls that we must avoid if we are to maintain our individuality and militancy, and not become, as claimed by our detractor, the puppet of the new Government. It is for the leadership of the Movement to decide where their loyalty first lies.

PROPOSAL FOR A NEW MOVEMENT

If it is our desire to meet the challenge that confronts the emergent territories in this latter half of the 20th century, and if we are to be treated as a reputable institution making a substantial contribution towards the creation of our new Society, serious thought must be given to the task of raising the efficiency of our Unions by making the Movement self-supporting.

Had it not been for the substantial grants received through our International Affiliations and from other sympathetic agencies, the gains we have accrued over the past seven years would not have been possible. At the moment, there are several Unions that exist as a result of subsidies. The financial statements of the TUC reveal that over 70% of its revenue for 1962 was raised by way of grants from International Affiliates. In the age of Independence, serious thought must be given to this the structure of the Movement to minimize the maintenance cost of the Unions, and raise efficiency.

To address this, I propose the following with two important factors in mind, the thirst for leadership, and for the Unions to have a strong head:

- Make the General Council of the Trade Union Council (TUC) the supreme authority or head of the local Movement and the major policy forming body
- Reduce the number of Unions

THE NATIONAL BODY (THE GENERAL COUNCIL OF THE TUC)

The supreme authority will rest in the General Council of what should now be termed the Guyana Trade Union Congress and this should comprise of an equal number of delegates from each affiliate, regardless of membership size. The responsibility of this body will be to elect an Executive Council and to determine broad National Policy. The Executive Council will administer the day-to-day affairs of the Congress and the General Secretary of this body must be a full time Officer. The following four advisory Councils will be required at the Executive Council Level:

- Economic Advisory Council
- Legal Advisory Council
- Education Board
- Dispute Committee.

The function of the two advisory councils i.e. Economic and Legal, are important. These are services that the individual Unions cannot supply by themselves and they are necessary in modern negotiations, therefore, it is requisite to provide them on a collective basis. The Education Board will plan and execute an education program to meet the requirements of the affiliates. That is why it is necessary to have a representative of each affiliate on this Board, and it is visualized that this Board will eventually manage the Guyana Labor Institute.

Recent events have shown how important it is to have a dispute Committee to assist in settling all inter-Union and internal Union disputes. The recent intervention of the Courts in the affairs of the Unions must be of concern to us all. The International Movement has been resisting such intrusions quite successfully for many years and it is imperative that we, in the emergent Guyana, endeavor at this stage, to ensure that this principle be maintained in our new society in the making.

Next, it is my firm view that it should be binding on all Unions to have entrenched in their constitutions, a system whereby disputes can be settled, and it is for the TUC to ensure that the system functions. I would propose that the constitution of the TUC should include measures whereby fines can be instituted for the failure of such machinery to function and even termination of affiliation. It is also necessary that an appeal body beyond the individual union machinery be established and it is here where the dispute committee of the TUC comes in.

This must be a standing committee comprising a Chairman and four other members with its procedure laid down in the constitution of the TUC. It is recommended that the Chairman of this Committee should be elected from among a panel of names submitted by the Executive Council to the Annual Congress of the National Body and these persons should be of repute and knowledgeable in trade Union matters but not actively engaged in the work of the movement. The other persons to complete this Committee should be agreed on mutually by the parties to the dispute, drawn from among nominees of the affiliated Unions, submitted prior to the said Congress. It may be found necessary for each affiliate to submit two nominees.

I am of the firm view that apart from this machinery being necessary, the Trades Union Council should endeavor to have legislation enacted to restrict the intervention of the Courts of law in a Union dispute until the above suggested procedures have been allowed to function. It would be necessary therefore, that limits be determined to ensure the speedy functioning of the Union Dispute Machinery, and its proper functioning. It is further advocated that legal opinions be sought on this issue, hence our legal Advisory Board.

The above takes care of the proposed structure of the Movement, which to my mind will assist in raising the standard of efficiency of the individual Unions and the National Body. Yet, there is another aspect of the problem that must be considered and this is the dues paid by the members.

It is my view that an exercise must be carried out to determine the minimum contribution that is necessary to supply the basic services necessary to ensure efficient administration of the Movement. Unless this is done, we will be in no position to guarantee an improvement in our administrative system, for everything rests on the money available. After this is determine, it is for the Unions to decide what further services and benefits they would like to offer, and fix their contributions accordingly. We must, nonetheless, ensure that in no instance should the contribution of an affiliate fall below the minimum, for this will eventually lead to inefficient service and the proverbial weak link in the chain.

REDUCING THE NUMBER OF UNIONS

This can be done by a series of mergers and/or federations, thereby setting up not more than five or six National Unions, each with not less than five thousand members which should ensure financial stability.

Six affiliates of the TUC will be created by a series of mergers or close-nit Federations with the power concentrated at the top, and each with a membership of over five thousand. The basis of the grouping would allow for exclusive Public Service Unions and Private Enterprise Unions.

FEDERATIONS

When we consider a federation as in the public Sector, we must have, foremost, a strong executive at the top provided with the necessary funds to supply the services needed to meet the demands of the workers. National planning is essential and we must endeavor to establish a unified wage and salary structure inclusive of working condition throughout the public sector and have the necessary staff to see to it that the contracts are honored and the membership properly serviced.

The income of the Federation should therefore be assured, and should be a percentage of the income of the Unions comprising the Federation payable quarterly in advance. It must also be taken into account that it is from the funds of the Federation that the National Body (TUC) must be maintained.

This type of organization will satisfy the aspiration of the many leaders we are producing, for there would be Offices for all and many forums of expression for the most abled. The one safe-guard we must make, though is that we do not make the cost of maintaining the structure too expensive, since that will defeat the real purpose of the limiting the number of Unions i.e. cutting down on the cost of maintaining the several Unions by the system of "economies of scale".

These federations will have a structure similar to that as set out for the T.U.C. i.e.

- Convention of the Federation
- General Council of the Federation
- Executive Council of the Federation
- Congress of individual affiliates
- Executive Council of Affiliates
- Branches, etc. of Affiliates

MERGERS

The other approach is by way of mergers. This would be the more economical approach as it leads to the unification of the several Unions, but it nonetheless, calls for the sinking of identities and this has always posed a problem since the personality factor is not accounted for. I would advocate that the system of mergers be maintained for the Guyana Labor Union, for this has historical significance. It is the first Union to be registered locally (1921) and it is even argued that it is the first within the British Overseas Territories. This system may also be applicable to the National Union of Teachers and the National Union of Commercial and Industrial Workers where the personality problem is not so acute, but it may be found necessary to have a federation in the agricultural and plantation section where there is rivalry and even political differences.

The suggested administrative structure is as follows:

- National Convention
- National Executive Council
- Sectional Conferences
- Sectional Executive Councils
- Branches etc.

In this structure, the existing Unions will now become Sections of the new Union and by the delegates system; they will meet together as a Convention and elect a National Executive Council that shall administer the Union. Again every care must be taken to see that the power and influence of the Union lie at the top.

PUBLIC AND PRIVATE SECTORS

In the public sector, provisions are made for three Unions, one for the blue collared workers, one for the white collared worker and one for the Teachers. In the private sector, it is not so easy to maintain a similar pattern as a result of the present composition of the Unions, they being mostly General Unions. It is hoped; nonetheless, that a pattern will eventually evolve which would avert any further inter union conflict.

It may nonetheless be found necessary to keep the Clerical and Commercial Workers Union as the National Union for all commercial and Clerical Workers in the private sectors, and have a seventh group of all industrial workers in which case a merger of the Mine Workers Union and the Printers Industrial Union would be necessary and instead of my previous recommendation, transfer the Bank Breweries Branch of the General Workers Union to the new organization together with all the other workers in the several aerated factories, etc. The only problem that may be encountered, is that of membership, for it is doubtful whether it will be possible to meet the five thousand membership in these two new Unions, but it should have no serious affect financially as most of the workers can make up the cash deficit, due to low membership, by higher than average contributions.

AFFILIATES

The proposed six affiliates are as follows:

1. Federated Union of Public Service Employees
2. Public Officers Federated Unions (National Unions of Public Service Officers)
3. National Union of Commercial & Industrial Workers
4. Guyana Labor Union
5. National Union of Agricultural and Plantation Workers
6. National Union of Teachers

1 - Federated Union of Public Service Employees:
This Union will be an enlargement of the now Federated Union of Government Employees to include the wage earners of all Government Boards and Corporations, inclusive of the Municipalities of Georgetown and New Amsterdam together with all present and future local Authorities.

It follows that the Unions, which are at the moment representing employees who fall within this category and are not Public Service Unions, will either have to transfer their members over to one of the affiliates of this federation, or if it is practical from a numerical point of view, set them up as individual affiliates of the new Federation. This refers to the Electricity Corporation members of the MPCA and the New Amsterdam, Kitty, Bartica, and Atkinson Field Branches of the BGLU.

The proposed Union will comprise the following: -

- Transport Workers Union
- Post Office Workers Union
- Government Employees Union
- Medical Employees Union
- National Union of Public Service Employees
- Guyana Air Transport Union
- Electricity Corp. Branch of the M.P.G.A.
- New Amsterdam Town Council, Kitty Village Council, Bartica Village Council and Atkinson Field Branches of the B.G.L.U.

The structure of this Union would be important if a success is to be made of the venture. Personality has been one of the problems that prevented mergers or federations in the past, and this must be taken into consideration when drafting a constitution, for the thirst for leadership, so much prevalent in our society, must be satisfied. The points to be considered in preparing a constitution will be later dealt with as a separate exercise.

2 - Public Officers Federated Unions (National Unions of Public Service Officers)

This Union would cater for the salaried Staff of all Government Boards and Corporations inclusive of the supervisory, salaried Staff of all Municipalities and local Authorities. It would therefore be necessary for all Unions presently engaged in the field, to transfer their membership over to the new Union. This will include the Staff of the Credit Corporation, the Staff of the Electricity Corporation and the Staff of the Bank of Guyana. The Clerical and Supervisory Staff of the Municipalities of New Amsterdam and Georgetown will be covered by this Union.

The proposed Union will comprise the following:

- B.C. Civil Service Association
- B.G. Local Govt. Officers Association
- B.G. Pilots Association
- B.G. Post Masters' Union

3 - National Union of Commercial & Industrial Workers

The new Union would have a wide field in the light of our expected industrial development and the Mine Workers Union association with this merger will tend to restore the Guyanese character, which the Union was losing within recent times.

It would also be necessary for the General Workers Union to transfer its members in the Bank Breweries Branch and D.I.H. Branch to this new Union

The proposed Union will comprise the following:

- Clerical & Commercial Workers Union
- Printers Industrial Union
- B.G. Mine Workers Union

4 - Guyana Labor Union

It is proposed that the identity of the B.G. Labor Union be maintained by the other Unions going into voluntary liquidation and transferring their assets and membership to the Guyana Labor Union. By this measure, it is hoped to maintain the registration number of the B.G. Labor Union, for all that will be necessary is a poll of the members of the Union to change the name from British Guiana to Guyana in the light of our pending constitutional advance.

The proposed Union will comprise the following:

- B.G Labor Union
- General Workers Union
- B.G Amalgamated Building Trade Workers Union
- B.G Sea Fearers Union
- Rice Workers Union

5 - National Union of Agricultural and Plantation Workers

In addition to the unions listed below, it is proposed that this Union would expand its sphere of influence to include rice and other plantation workers who are at the moment, mainly unorganized.

The proposed Union will comprise the following:

- Manpower Citizens Association
- B.G Headmen's Union
- Sugar Estates Clerks Association
- B.G and W.I. Sugar Boilers Union

6 - National Union of Teachers

My proposal anticipates that secondary education would be completely free in a short while and most teachers will be employees of Government with shared issues.

The proposed Union will comprise of a merger of the following:

- B.G. Teachers Association
- Association of Masters & Mistresses

ISSUES TO BE ADDRESSED WITH THE NEW PROPOSAL

It is essential for changes to be instituted, to gear the Unions to meet the challenges of the future and as I have advocated, a change in the structure will assist in this direction. There are, of course, many other measures that must be adopted if we are to achieve our ultimate objective, which is the emancipation of the worker. Foremost are a philosophy and the determining of the program we will adopt in realizing our goal.

A philosophy is important, for it will be the driving force behind us. This must be clearly categorized so that all and sundry will be aware of the things we believe in and are prepared to either achieve or defend. The program is also necessary, for planning is essential if our progress is to be harmonious. As I have said, this must at all times, originate from the top, but, nonetheless, having general acceptance so that the Solidarity we so often speak of, will indeed be a certainty.

There is yet the most important factor, and that is the quality of leadership. No matter what is the structure, or how good is the program we prepare, success can only be achieved if the leadership of the Movement at all level, re-dedicate themselves to the service of the working class movement and forget the petty jealousies of the past, shroud with sectional thinking and confinement of vision. At all times we must think of our ultimate objective in deciding our actions, remembering that we were all elected to serve.

When we consider leadership, we must also take cognizance of those coming behind to take over our leadership positions, for it is important that we ensure that they are equipped to take up the mantle. It is my view that our greatest omission to date is that we have so far failed to establish a youth arm of the Movement, and in this, respect, we are the only reputable institution that has, as yet, failed to do so. This should be a top priority and a post on the Executive of the Trade Union Congress should be created especially for this purpose.

In this regard, the individual affiliates of the TUC should be encouraged and assisted to form Youth arms of their Unions and these Youth Sections must also have a National Assembly where the views of our young workers may be expressed, and this calls for a structure of its own, similar to the parent Movement. The earlier this is done, the quicker we can be assured of the continuance of the Movement as an influential institution.

CONCLUSION

The Trade Union Movement can make a valuable contribution to the New Society in the making, but there are some basic flaws in our structure that must be corrected. Next, the leadership of the Movement must determine what is its objective and for the first time, prepare a concise plan, detailing the measures to be adopted in achieving them. A new approach must be made, for there are new problems confronting us, and with Independence now a certainly, these problems will become more complex and we must be prepared to answer the challenge.

The leadership must rededicate itself to service, conscious of the fact that all engage in the struggle are merely part of a team with the same objectives that lead to the emancipation of the working class. We must at all times endeavor to keep the Unions free of any kind of control, political or otherwise, for it is only when our view- points are independent that they become effective. This, I repeat, is not going to be easy as a result of the close association between the leadership of the Political and Trade Union Movements over the past seven years. It must be achieved, nonetheless, so that the working class points of view are forcibly expressed, unaffected by political affiliations.

Finally, there is a great need for the establishment of a Youth Arm of the Movement in order to establish continuity of leadership and to rally the worker of the future in this struggle that must end in their emancipation. The words emblazoned in the borrowed anthem of the local Movement must be our ultimate objective - "We can bring to birth a new world from the ashes of the old". It is for the Guyana Trade Union Movement to show the way.

THE MODERN SUPERVISOR-THE ANSWER TO INCREASED PRODUCTION
1967

INTRODUCTION

To increase production in our emergent society, a new approach will have to be made to our industrial management system. This is more important in the Public Sector where the major problems really lie, for modern trends, which are slowly being introduced in the private sector, seem to be by-passing the Public Service, for the age old concepts, like the malaria pestilence, continue to stultify our productive efforts.

The Supervisor will have to become a critical player in the new world of Industrial Management. The concept that the supervisor's job is a cushy one where no work is done and is basically a reward for past services must be banished. The supervisor in this new environment will be expected to work with his brain for he will be paid to THINK. This is what will differentiate this role as the true leader instead of a follower.

Too much stress cannot be laid on this, for the time has long since past when we could afford to nurture outmoded concepts and I would strongly recommend that a radical change be introduced in this important aspect of management.

This article first addresses the macro view of human behavior before going into detail on the qualities and responsibilities of the modern supervisor in the new industrial management system. The Macro view addresses the human behavior on the job from the perception of the human's aversion to work, and the cause and effect of frustration on the job. The Supervisors' qualities and responsibilities will focus on their impact to production as they oversee the policy of management and advise on any aspect of policy that is harmful to production.

HUMAN BEHAVIOR ON THE JOB

To the supervisor, production is of importance, but just as production is important, it must be remembered that the labor force, - the principal means of production, is of greater importance, for in the final analysis, it is the labor force that determines our output.

The primary task of the supervisor, therefore, is to ensure that the labor force under his supervision is used in such a manner that it ensures maximum production. This is in itself a complex problem, for he is dealing with human beings who are subjected to many emotional factors each of which assists in determining his attitude towards his occupation. It is then necessary for the supervisor to have some knowledge of human behavior for this will determine the relationship that will exist between the supervisor and the supervised, which also eventually determines production.

THE AVERSION TO WORK

Accepting that human behavior is complex, let us consider some of the factors that influence the worker on the job. We must foremost realize that no one by nature likes "work" and for most of us, it is a compulsion that we must endure if we are to exist. For as the saying goes, we must eat to live and society is as such that if we want the where-with-all to eat, we must work. This is important, for the employer through his supervisor has got to overcome this aversion of the employee to work and this is done by making work appear to be attractive, by compensating the worker for the effort he expends in producing something of value or providing a service.

Let us consider this compensation. It takes the form principally of a salary or wages paid to the employee in return for the effort he expends in producing, and it is this salary or wage that is used by the worker in acquiring the things he needs to live and in providing the comfort which lends some meaning to the existence of himself and family. The incentive to work is therefore the remuneration offered. It follows then, that the effort expended would bear some relation to the salary or wage offered and this is in itself related to what comforts the remuneration provide. En passant, it should be noted that remuneration is meaningless, in a society where comforts are unknown or unobtainable and food easily acquired as in certain primitive societies.

Accepting that remuneration influences production, let us now consider another related factor that is of equal importance, and this is comparative remuneration. By this is meant the remuneration paid one worker for his effort in relation to another. Within recent times, it has been established that whenever, in view of the worker, another employee is being paid a salary or wage in excess of his for a job he considers of a lower job value, his effort automatically restricts itself to correct the imbalance. It is further argued that the worker is best able to determine this imbalance, and as his reaction is a subconscious one, it is of importance to the supervisor, for it accounts for a fall in production, the causes of which is not easily recognized.

There are, of course, the personal factors that also condition the attitude of the worker, and these are external influences and in most cases have nothing to do directly with the job. They are for instance, illness in the family, unfavorable financial commitments and other personal problems that affect the emotions adversely. It has often been argued, that as these factors did not arise out of the job, they should not be the concern of the supervisor or management. But it is now recognized that as they affect production, cognizance should be taken of them, as it is not possible for the worker to leave these problems at home, or at the office or factory gate. It is, of course, debatable whether these personal factors did arise out of the job, for there are those who argue that the remuneration received for the job must take care of every need of the worker and if there are needs which the worker cannot satisfy and they pose emotional problems, then it is the responsibility of the employer to provide the solution to the problems. These may be reasonable arguments but just how far the workers' needs can extend is indeterminable, and at some point it must be established where the responsibility of the employer ceases. This responsibility of the employer has within recent times been extending, and today in many progressive undertakings they include medical facilities, recreation and in some cases family counseling, etc.

FRUSTRATION – CAUSE AND EFFECT

The easiest answer to be found for the failure of the labor force to produce, as it should, is that of frustration. Therefore, the reasons for this frustration and its effects on production should be considered. This is primarily the result of a failure to satisfy the growing needs of the worker in terms of additional comforts. Present wages or salary tend to satisfy immediate needs, but no one likes to remain static or ever does, and any system that fails to satisfy the growing needs is going to be adversely affected. The production system must therefore make provision for periodic increases in the living standards of the labor force in order to satisfy the human desire for progress. We have so often found that there is a failure to recognize why there should be frustration in an undertaking where salaries and wages are comparably favorable. This is so, for no one takes cognizance of this urge for progress and so long as there is no forward movement either in the undertaking of itself, or in society as a whole, there is bound to be frustration.

Frustration is also caused by what can be described as a lack of the correct atmosphere on the job. By this is meant the condition of the work-sites, offices and business places, etc. where no consideration is given to proper lighting, ventilation, placement of machinery or merchandise. This eventually leads to frustration on the job and it becomes all the worst, when bad working conditions such as inadequate leave facilities and undue long working hours are coupled with it. It must also be remembered, that the approach of the supervisor to his job also assists in formulating the job atmosphere.

Let us next consider the job satisfaction as a source of frustration. I have said earlier, that no one by nature likes to work, and while this is true, a better response to work may be had if the employee acquires some satisfaction from the article he produces or service he renders. In industrialized communities the assembly line has tended to remove most of the satisfaction from the job, as work has become mere routine, repetitious. But many measures have been introduced in an endeavor to ease the resulting frustration. Such as shorter working hours, and production incentives that afford the worker the opportunity of acquiring not only comforts, but the opportunity of enjoying them.

In the under-developed communities such as ours where the assembly line has not as yet arrived, more so automation, job satisfaction may still be had, but here we have the problems of standards, for in so many instances, we find that energy is spent in producing something, or providing services from which no satisfaction may be derived as a result of the lack of knowledge or inadequate funds, which may cause the article produced or service rendered to be of inferior quality.

This needs further explanation, and our road building is the typical example. It has always been said that the road workers are the laziest of our labor force, and even if this is so, no one seems, as yet, to have determined the reason. As I see it, the reason can only be the frustration that over a century of defeat in maintaining proper road, have brought about among this section of the work force. Our roads have always been an eyesore and forever a cause for complaint and it should be easy for anyone to see why those who toil, but to no avail, have become victims of frustration. I am convinced that with the modern techniques, better machinery and the present recognition of the need for more and better (asphalt sealed) roads, a better product would result which, in turn, would introduce a change in the demeanor of this part of our labor force.

QUALITIES AND RESPONSIBILITIES OF THE MODERN SUPERVISOR

Qualities:

The supervisor, as I have said, influences production, and is an important wheel in the production mechanism. So it is important that those performing the supervisory function are not only capable but the best qualified. The following are the qualities that must be possessed by a Supervisor:

- Leadership
- Responsible
- Tolerant and Just
- Insightful
- Job Knowledge

Leadership:

This is the most important attribute of the good supervisor; for this is that peculiar characteristic trait which makes others he comes into contract with, willingly agree to follow him. Wherever a body of people is gathered together, whether at work, at play, or just for leisure, there is one thing that stands out and that is, there must be one person who will be the center of attraction. It is accepted that all animals are divided into two basic groups, those who are born to lead and those who are born to follow, and industry, if it is to approach maximum efficiency, must take cognizance of this, for as the saying goes, leaders are born and not made.

It is for management to select their future supervisors from the leadership group, for as I have stated above, this quality is an immeasurable asset and must bear future dividends. Further, overlooking the natural leaders in selecting supervisor trainees can be sowing the seeds for future industrial unrest and this aspect will be dealt with later.

Responsible:

The second most important asset of the supervisor is responsible since they must be prepared to make decisions and bear the consequence. Further, he must have confidence in his judgment if he expects others to have confidence in him. Passing the "buck" should never be contemplated, for this trait, though prevalent within our society, only tends to make those under his control lose respect for him and tarnishes his integrity. The supervisor who can shoulder responsibility is the one who will succeed. It must be remembered that he is always under the scrutiny of the work force, and any character weaknesses are quickly revealed to the detriment of his control of those under him.

Tolerant and Just:

Here it is advanced that the good supervisor must be tolerant and just. This is also important, for tolerance is of inestimable value when dealing with that part of the work force which is under training, for imparting knowledge, which is one of the functions of the supervisor, calls for a considerable amount of tolerance if he is to succeed. In the dispensation of justice, this asset is also a virtue and it must always be remembered that at all times, he must be honest in his dealings with the work force.

Foresight:

This speaks of the ability to look into the future and determine trends, and this is of importance, for success of any venture is dependent on how well we plan for the future. This also calls for a sound knowledge of the job for the ability to assess future requirements must be dependent on a through knowledge of the present.

Job Knowledge:

Knowledge of the job should be the last consideration, for this asset could easily be acquired so long as there is intelligence and to some extent, aptitude. This may be new concept in Guyana, but it has been operating successfully for some time now in the advanced industrialized societies, for there, the importance of the supervisor as the means of increasing production has long been recognized. In Guyana, we still share the view that knowledge of the job obtained through long service is the basis upon which the supervisor should be selected, and this has been responsible for many of our work stoppages in the past. For in most cases, they were influenced by clashes of personality between the knowledgeable supervisor and the natural leader of the work force who in most cases winds up as the trade union representative on the job. This is a natural reaction, for as said before, we are still part of the animal kingdom and no different from the animals of the lower order when it comes to the fight for leadership, so often witnessed.

Further consideration must be given to "the knowledge of the job"; nonetheless, for it stands to reason that without such knowledge, no supervisor can function effectively. The acquisition of this kind of knowledge is therefore both necessary and vital. That I argue is the responsibility of management, for here, knowledge must be general instead of specific, and it follows that the supervisor must be conversant with all aspects of the job and this is only possible by planning, for a laissez-faire approach will be most ineffective.

Management, I have said, should be responsible for the training of the supervisory staff, and for that matter the entire work force, for they are in a better position to determine the needs and, as I have said, nothing should be left to chance. In every industrial undertaking, inclusive of public institutions and corporations, surveys should be regularly conducted to determine staff requirements, and programs conducted to satisfy the needs. Efficiency in the productive mechanism is only possible if we have a competent work force and this calls for a new approach to training, for it must extend from the top, though all layers of management down, to the bottom-most level.

Responsibilities:

Who is the supervisor and what are his functions? These are important questions, for the entire productive machinery of our society is dependent on what the supervisor can get out of the labor force. It is therefore essential that the supervisor possesses a clear under-standing as to what are his functions, and more so, for those within the labor force to know when they are termed Supervisors.

The Supervisor is anyone in charge of a part of the labor force of any undertaking, whether it is private enterprise or a public institution or corporation. He may be a workshop foreman, foreman in charge of a construction project, clerk-in-charge of an office, a storekeeper or anyone who is responsible for a body of men at work. This is extended to include those in charge of workers such as superintendents, overseers, engineers, for so long as your occupation requires you to supervise men at work, you are a supervisor.

The supervisor is expected to see that the policy of management is carried out and he is also expected to advise management on any aspect of policy that is in his opinion, injurious to production. In other words, he should assist in determining policy, for as some people put it – he is an arm of management.

 The following are the functions of the supervisor as I see it:

- Responsibility for maintaining and increasing production.
- Responsibility for maintaining the labor force under his supervision at its maximum efficiency.
- Responsibility for the maintenance of discipline.
- Validate and oversee the enforcement of the collective labor agreement of service between the employer and the labor force
- Consult with the workers' representatives whenever warranted per the Labor Agreement.

Maintaining and Increasing Production:

This is the major function of a supervisor and it must be noted that this primary function is not just maintaining production, but increasing it. This is important, for the progress of society is dependent on how much more we can increase production and it should also be evident, that if the supervisor is to increase production, it is essential that he first makes a success of his endeavors to accomplish the objectives as set out in 2-5 to above. Failing to do so can have adverse effects on production or even bring the entire productive machinery to a standstill. It is therefore necessary that we make a study of the following items.

Maintaining Maximum Efficiency:

By this we mean maintaining a capable and competent labor force. Here it must be understood that it is the responsibility of the supervisor to ensure that every job handled by a worker under his supervision is done with maximum efficiency, and this brings us to training, which is essential to ensure competence on the job. Training is one of the main responsibilities of a good supervisor and when we speak of training, we just do not only mean that which satisfies present need, but also future needs, for the supervisor must be able to look ahead and determine future needs with a fair amount of accuracy. He must consider replacements of both man-power and machinery, for workers fall ill, go on leave, retire or leave the job and accidents do occur and all of these should cause no disruption in the productive process. There is yet another aspect of job efficiency, and that is ensuring that every job is completed, as the supervisor wants it. This is vital to production, for there is nothing more time wasting and causing greater dissatisfaction than spoilt work.

This is solely the responsibility of the supervisor for it is left to him to make certain that all instructions he passes on to the worker is clearly defined and understood and one of the tenets of T.W.I. here holds good, for under "job instructions" it is stated – "If the worker had not learned – the supervisor has not taught". This every supervisor should take cognizance of, for no good supervisor passes the "buck". He must be prepared to assume the responsibility for all failure.

To ensure efficiency, therefore, it is necessary to have a well-trained work force, which is the responsibility of the supervisor, and also it is necessary for the supervisor to ensure that all instructions he passes on are fully understood by those to whom they are addressed.

Maintain Discipline:

Whenever a body of people are assembled for the purpose of achieving a known goal, success could only be achieved when there is discipline and for this to be accomplished someone must be in authority over the group or body.

In Industry, the responsibility for maintaining discipline rests with the supervisor, and to achieve this successfully, proves the good supervisor. The most disciplined force they say is the army, but the measures adopted by the army in instituting discipline if tried in industry would bring about an insurrection and industrial chaos, for as it is said, the worst soldiers are those who think. It was the Physicist Einstein who said; that anyone who professes a love for the army should have been born without a brain, for the spinal cord would have been good enough.

In Industry, we expect more, for the workers must use their brain and at the same time be responsible. Yet, to maintain discipline effectively, the supervisor must posses the quality of leadership, which gives the possessor the ability of commanding respect and obedience from those around him. Notwithstanding that, the supervisor must be tolerant and at the same time firm and convincing, and more than ever, he must be just in the dispensing of discipline.

Discipline must therefore be something responsive instead of demanded and we must always bear in mind that there is no room in modern industry for the tyrants of old.

Honoring the Contract:

This introduces a new aspect of job supervision, for the supervisor does not only deal with the labor force individually but collectively through the workers' representatives (i.e. Shop Stewards, etc.) In honoring the collective labor agreement it is essential for the supervisor to be fully conversant with all its aspect and must at all times have a copy at hand to use as reference. He must always bear in mind that the agreement is important to the worker, for in most cases all of the beneficial clauses were won after bitter struggle with the employer.

Joint Consultation:
This is where the supervisor must prove himself if he is to make a success of his job. The trade union is now recognized as an integral part of the modern industrial environment and its importance must be recognized, for it wields the power to bring the entire industrial machinery to a standstill against all those who fail to realize that the voice of worker, channeled through his representatives, cannot be silenced.

The supervisor's primary function is to ensure that production is maintained and increased and it is beyond question that nothing can have greater ill effect on production than industrial unrest, leading to work stoppages. The only way to avoid this is for the supervisor to accept the fact that joint consultation is necessary, and that cooperation with the Trade Unions is the surest way to ensure industrial peace that creates the climate for better production.

It must be remembered that when we speak of joint consultation, we do not only mean that the supervisor must meet the workers' representatives when he is requested to do so. It is also essential that he consults with them whenever matters involving policy arise or whenever production is being hampered. This should also be done whenever disciplinary measures are being contemplated.

It follows that what is necessary, is union/management cooperation, which dictates that supervisors convince the workers that his response to the Trade Union is genuine, and not the acceptance of a necessary evil that must be endured. For should such an impression be portrayed cooperation is hardly likely, and labor unrest a certainty.

The supervisor must at all times remember that the worker is also interested in production. He knows that his wages depend upon it, and more so, that it determines his standard of living.

CONCLUSION

Supervision is a science which can only be acquired by training, but as said, there are certain inherent qualities to the individual that are necessary if the acquired knowledge is to prove successful when put into execution.

It is for management to take all these points into consideration when they are selecting future supervisors, for the days are long past when supervisors are appointed by just looking around for the most senior employee and saddling him with the responsibility. The search must always be on for those who must man our industries in the future, and the best available must be those that are selected and trained. This is very much needed throughout the Public Service where training is only carried out at the top i.e. the Cadetship System for supplying senior administrative officers, for with the proposed acceleration of our economic development, trained supervisors at all levels will be needed if the hard acquired funds to be spent, are to bring maximum returns.

Management must also realize that it has an important part to play in accelerating our drive for increase production. The supervisor can only give of his best when he knows that he enjoys the confidence of those above him, but this confidence must stem out of the respect of his ability to do a competent job. Enlightened management is what is needed at the present time, for changes have taken place all around us, and science has supplied the answer to many of the industrial problems that plagued us in the past, and use must be made of this knowledge.

In the public sector, a revolution in thinking must be brought about and stages of responsibility clearly defined so as to abolish the habit of passing the buck that is so much prevalent, and honest attempts made to have competent supervisors at all levels, fully aware of their responsibilities.

REASONS FOR LOW PRODUCTION AND MEASURES THAT CAN HELP TOWARDS IMPROVEMENT

1968

INTRODUCTION

It is beyond question that production in Guyana and the West Indies for that matter is way below acceptable standards. What is needed in the Public Sector is a new approach to industrial management, and a close look at us in an endeavor to established standards that are truly Guyanese and not borrowed.

The Guyanese workers must be treated with the dignity they deserve. Any short comings of the workers, some of which I contend are out of their control, must be viewed sympathetically and a realistic attempt be made to change their outlook towards their occupation. It cannot be done by threats, for this will only cause unnecessary industrial unrest, which we can ill afford.

The cost of production must be addressed if we are to be successful. As a result of our fairly high standard of living, reflected from reasonable high wage structure as compared with other under developed territories, our cost of production is way above what it should be, and a problem that must be the concern of any progressive government.

It is essential therefore that a solution be found, if we are to maintain a buoyant economy and make a success of our independence which is new around the corner, and to accomplish this we must first determine what were the reasons for this peculiar situation and then devise the means of correcting it.

This article details my explanation for our low output and recommendation for improvement.

REASONS FOR OUR LOW OUTPUT

The reasons for our low per capita output are, of course, many and varied but foremost among them are the following:

- Our Colonial Heritage
- Climatic Conditions
- Wrong Working Hours
- Bad Supervision
- Lack of Skills

Our Colonial Heritage:

This has been blamed for nearly all the ills affecting our society, and whether it is justified or not, is not of concern here, but what concerns us is that it has bad adverse effects on the approach of the Guyanese to work generally. Within the past three or four decades, the cry of the workers was that of exploitation, but unlike the metropolitan countries of the West, exploitation in Guyana and all the colonies for that matter, carried with it the stigma of imperialism, for in most cases the employer was a foreign or absent capitalist. This, until recently, also occurred in the public service where all the executive staff comprised of European or accepted agents and rules were from Whitehall. This created a feeling of frustration among the colonial workers, which eventually led them to believe that they were not part of the productive machinery, for in most cases, the Guyanese were never consulted in such matters, and treated as mere chattel.

It has always been asked why exploitation affected production to such an extent in the colonies and not the developed countries, and many reasons have been advanced, including the effects of slavery and the abhorrence of the freed slaves to work after emancipation. This has, no doubt, had its effect on production, for it assisted in formulating the present attitude of the Guyanese to work, but is my view that the political aspect of the problem had as great an influence on this peculiar attitude, not prevalent in our society.

The Guyanese politician in an endeavor to gain popular support attuned the mental attitude of the worker to the fact that their unfortunate position was the direct result of imperialism and exploitation. The workforce was constantly reminded by the politician that the fruits of its labor were being used to maintain the high standard of living of their colonial masters. The workers, in an endeavor to hit back at the Colonial employers convinced themselves that by shirking work they were achieving their objective. This attitude of the worker was condoned by both the political and Trade Union Movements, for nothing was ever done to halt or change this attitude. Unfortunately this destructive attitude has transitioned to our post-independence and has now become a way of life for the worker. To solve the problem that it poses, we will have to be realistic in our approach. In my opinion, we will have to decolonize the attitude of the Guyanese Workers to his employment.

Climatic Conditions and Working Hours:

In Guyana the weather has always posed a problem and has always had serious effect on production for in the agricultural sector we have experienced serious wastage as a result of floods and droughts, and again in industry, the changing climate has had its affect on production by way of ill health, absenteeism and undue exhaustion.

The work period has also been a contributory factor for the hours 7.00 and to 11/00 am; 12.00 noon to 4.00 pm is hopelessly out of tune with condition existing in the tropics. It would be of interest to observe the production figures for the second work session, for it will be noted that in most cases, it drops by about 10% to 15% and, also, absenteeism and the accident rate are then at their highest. The reasons are of course mental and physical and exhaustion and it is my firm view that the luncheon hour assist in this direction, for it is difficult to see what purpose it serves in view of the distance of the working-class housing areas from their place of employment. This is in itself a source of further exhaustion for transportation to and from work, in most cases, is done by cycling, as the public bus service is hopelessly inadequate for this purpose.

It should also be noted that there are many offices, workshops, etc., where no consideration was taken of climatic conditions in their designing and this assist in making work more uncomfortable if no laborious with its consequential affect on production.

Bad Supervision:

This, to my thinking, has been the greatest set back to increase production in Guyana, for we still live in an age where we believe that the only requirement of the supervisor is knowledge of the work, and that production could be maintained by the big-stick measure.

Within the past decade, many accusations have been leveled against the leadership of the workers' organizations for the frequent stoppages of work, but, so far, most of those making the charges have failed to see where the blame really lie. They have accurse the Trade Union Leadership of being immature and irresponsible, but the truth of the matter is that the Trade Union leadership, at all levels, have reached a state of maturity far in advance of the agent of the employer supervision labor, and as a result, they are more knowledgeable in matters appertaining to modern industrial practices. This has created a bottle-neck and have brought about an atmosphere of frustration among the workers and their representatives, for the ill-equipped representative of management hides his short-coming in hostility while sheltering under the strong arm of the employer.

There is no doubt that the representatives of management are ill-equipped to deal with the complex problems presented by today's labor force, and it may be of interest to note the amounts spent by the workers' organizations in training their representatives as compared to that of the employer, and this disparity is greatest in the public sector for here no training programmed exists. As I see it, it is time that Management realizes that job supervision is today considered a science, for ultimately production depends on what the supervisor can get out of his work force with the least amount of effort.

Lack of Skills:

This has had its effect on production in the past, for there was never any real planning to satisfy the requirement of our community, but it is expected that from the man-power survey carried out recently, a realistic program will be executed to product the skills needed.

There is, none-the-less, a problem that must be solved and that is the making of the skilled Trade attractive in the endeavor to get the right material channeled in this direction. It is my view that there is a serious imbalance in our wage and salary structure, and it is essential that a job evaluation exercise be carried out commencing in the Public Sector, for every threat to industrial peace should be taken care of.

RECOMMENDATIONS TO INCREASE OUR OUTPUT

It is unfortunate that within recent times, we have observed statements coming from governmental quarters with reference to what they term the "Lackadaisical attitude", of laborers, and it is even more unfortunate that no attempt has yet been made to recognize the problem as it exists. Statements of the intention to take stern measures against those who under-produce, are not answer to the problem for, as I have said, it is not just working more, but a change of attitude that is necessary, and such statement only help to create a further industrial problem.

As I have said, it is the political movement that contributed more than any other in developing this "attitude" and any attempt to use strong arm tactics to correct it by and Government, will never be understood. What must be done is to devise the means of changing the attitude of the Guyanese or as I have said, earlier, prepare a program for decolonizing the attitude of the workers.

This is no easy problem, for the workers really believe that he is being exploited, i.e. overworked and underpaid, and this is so in many cases. The major problem lie in the Public Sector, for her, where profit, the yardstick for measuring production, is absent, there is no real means of determining cost of production.

Any start in correcting the attitude of the labor force must be made with those now entering the labor market, by working out a constructive program for their smooth entry. It is essential that, on the whole, each worker gain employment in the field where he is most suited, and equipped, for there is nothing that causes greater frustration than doing something for eight hours per day, which you detest. The problem of unemployment must also be hurriedly tackled for the young adult not being able to acquire work soon becomes disillusioned and develops anti-social tendencies which make him a social rebel throughout his life. It is needless to say that unemployment has also contributed to the present attitude refer to, for the colonial capitalist thrived on the overabundance of our labor force and this has created the social problems that we to inherit.

The matter of the existing labor force is an entirely different problem, for years of exploitation, unemployment and brutality of the job, has left marks that cannot easily be erased. The greater problem, as I have said, lie in the public sector and as a large part of the labor force is employed in this sector, I will confine my proposals to Governmental enterprises.

It is my view that Government should first expand the functions of the Ministry of Labor by appointing a junior Minister responsible for production. It would then be necessary to acquire the service of a competent production engineer with a competent field staff, equipped to advise the several ministries on matters affecting production, for, in most cases, the methods of production adopted in most of the Ministries of Government, are antiquated and bear scientific investigation.

Having accomplished this, it would then be necessary to expand the services of the present personnel divisions to include all aspects of industrial relation, for a sound employer/employee relation is vital to good production. It would be necessary to appoint a training office in each Ministry whose responsibility it would be to see that all employees who come in direct contact with the labor force is a supervisory capacity are knowledgeable of the modern techniques of industrial management, for the lack of this skill in dealing with people has been responsible for many wild-cat strikes with its serious effect on production.

It would be the responsibility of this division to carry the departmental programs to the labor force, outlining targets etc., so that they would be fully conscious of what is taking place, and develop a feeling of participation, and, in this respect, the workers organization must also be consulted at all levels.

The worker, who was forever treated as chattel, must be made to realize a change in the attitude of his employer, if he is, himself, to change his, and must, at the same time, be made to realize that he is an important part of the productive machinery and different from the tools and machinery he uses at the means of producing. In other words, he must feel that the evils of colonialism so ably put to him by his political leaders, are at an end and that it is not just a change of masters, for national consciousness and pride can never be developed if there is no sense of belonging. The nation must mean something to the individual and not just fanatical utterings.

In discussing the reasons for low production, mention was made to the existing working hours in relation to our climate. The problems of the working hours must be seriously considered for it is important to production in the tropics and, at the moment, there are two schools of thought both advocating the forty hour week, but varying in the following periods:

- Monday through Friday 7.00 a.m. – 11.00 a.m., 12.00 noon – 4.00 p.m.
- Monday through Friday 7.00 a.m. – 2.00 p.m., Saturday 7.00 a.m. - 12.00 noon

The first advocates the principle of the long weekend while maintaining the same work period as exist in most of the metropolitan countries. It is argued that a long weekend offers more time to the employees to pursue matters appertaining to his welfare.

The second advocates the principles of the shorter workday, as it offers the employee greater opportunity to pursue the matter on an intellectual nature, and more leisure to direct toward recreation. It is also argued that the shorter workday shortens the period of fatigue and as such, has lesser effect on production, lower the accident rate, and extend the work life of the employee.

Both has its advantages but I strongly support the latter for it is my view that it is more suitable to conditions existing in the tropics. The maintenance of the one hour lunch break serves the purpose, for it is time wasting and creates more fatigue, for it puts the worker out of the rhythm at a time when he is at his peak. The maintenance of the workday extending to 4.00 p.m. also would have its affect of sport and other intellectual pursuits.

There are of course, many other measures that can be adopted to improve the attitude of the Guyanese workers and the most important among them is that of providing proper facilities whereby the leisure hours of the worker can be used. I feel that government, like the more progressive industrial employers, should interest itself in this field, and make provision whereby healthy forms of recreation are provided, together with other intellectual pursuits, for today it is accepted that association between supervisors and those supervised, off the job, in an atmosphere of equality goes a far way to ensure industrial peace, which is so vital to production.

CONCLUSION

In conclusion, our primary concern must be the worker. The Guyanese workers must be treated with the dignity they deserve. A realistic attempt must be made to change their outlook towards their occupation. It cannot be done by threats, for this will only cause unnecessary industrial unrest, which we can ill afford.

TOWARDS GREATER PRODUCTION

INTRODUCTION

This article is separated into two parts; Part I deals with the Government as an employer and Part II deals with the Government, the Economy and the Trade union. Part 1, outlines measures which, if adopted, can assist in increasing production and better efficiency. Part II discusses the existing industrial unrest and proposes measures to improve the industrial climate.

There is yet another cry of a shortfall in production and, yet again, the blame is being placed on the frequency of strikes and workers not giving a full day's work for a full day's pay.

It is beyond question that the above are some of the reasons for the shortfall in our production, as no doubt there is, but what must be the concern of those whose responsibility it is to see that maximum production is attained, is what are the reasons for the spate of strikes we have been experiencing and, also, the reasons why the average worker does not supply, for his efforts, "full day's work for full day's pay" as is the claim of the employer class.

So far, it seems as if no one has, as yet, endeavored to determine the reasons, much less tackle the problem, and, as I have already mentioned in an earlier paper, the attitude of our work-force is not conducive to the productive standard now necessary if our new nation is to maintain and improve the standard of living of its peoples.

None can deny that it is the responsibility of Government to create the atmosphere whereby this would be possible and, it is my intention, to outline measures, which, if adopted, will go a long way to bring about a change of attitude, thereby limiting the man-hours lost as a result of the many wildcat strikes and the time-wasting habits of our work-force.

Before proceeding however, I must mention that the problem is to-fold. The attitude of our work force can only be changed by recognition of the problem, and the adoption of realistic measures designed to supply a solution. This, I submit, is solely the responsibility of the employer. On the other hand, the curtailment of the indiscriminate use of the strike-weapon is the joint responsibility of the employer and the agent of the employee, the Trade Union.

PART 1 - GOVERNMENT AS AN EMPLOYER

Production is primarily the responsibility of the employer, and the standard of production to be acquired is directly dependent on the supervisor. This statement is the basis of my contention and in a previous paper, "The Modern Supervisor"; I have outlined the functions and responsibilities of the supervisor. I will not deal with the responsibility of Government as an employer, which is important to us as this time, in view of the vast sums so money to be spent on developmental works, money acquired mostly by loans, at interest that must place a strain on the national purse.

It is the responsibility of the Government, The Employer, to see that production targets are met, and to accomplish this, they must provide the supervisor with the tools or skills with which he can use to extract the best out of the workforce, and any such tool, must provide the following, which are now none-existent or inadequate:

1. Communication: The Spoken Word

The absence of a proper system of communication has been the cause of nearly all of the industrial problems in the Government Services, for it has resulted in many minor grievances, growing into=to complex problems, and at the same tie, shutting out a flow of ideas, up and down, and throughout the workforce. It is vital to the national interest that this be corrected, for many man-hours are lost or wasted through stoppages of work, and the none-flow of ideas has brought about frustration and a steep drop in morale, which, in itself, seriously hampers production.

As effective communication medium is the staff-conference, if properly organized, and I would advocate that it be made compulsory that such conferences be held in all Ministries and Divisions of Ministries. To be effective though, these conferences must be on the Employer/Employee basis and not the Industrial Relation kind of meeting between Management and the union. This is important, for what we hope to achieve, is better relations between employer and employee, so as to better efficiency and raise production. I must mention that it often happens that good relations may existed between the employer and the union, while, at the same time, relations between employer and employee remain bad.

This, we find today, is so often the case, for the trend, within recent times, has been for contact to exist solely between the employer and the trade union with the exclusion of the employee. This has created a gap between the employer and the employee a gap filled with suspicion and distrust, which has resulted in many wildcat strikes and the ever-present atmosphere of hospitality.

Wildcat strikes as I see it, is really a rebellion of the employee against both the employer and the union. It is not my intention to suggest a limitation of the Trade union activity, for there is still a great need in the field of bargaining and representations for trade union action, but I am convinced that if a better contract is maintained between the employer and employee it will lead to a more healthy industrial climate.

In the same vein, work councils should be set up on all projects and production sites, and here every aspect of the job should be represented, i.e. clerical, technical, and manual. These councils should meet regularly and once per week is suggested. The function of these councils would be to review targets, outline future programs and resolve all problems that tend to hamper production.

It is of great importance to state that the employee representation on the several occupational groups of staff conferences and work-councils is done by way of ballot, wherever possible.

2. Communication: The written word

So far we have spoken of communication by the spoken work which is of great importance, but this has its limitations, and in every endeavor, communication by the written word, which is as important if not more so, is the wider used.

It must be borne in mind that in passing on decisions or even information, the system must make provision to ensure that all decisions or information reaches the source where it is intended to reach. The rank and file also of importance that the language used is easily understands it.

The final aspect of communication is that of feedback. This ensures that what is passed on is received by those for whom it is intended, and further, just how it is received, which is the most important. It must be remembered that any decision for introducing new ideas or change that tend to produce contrary reaction to that which is intended, or which meets with resistance for the workforce, must be reviewed. The reason can either be that the communication system is faulty, as it omitted the preparation for introducing change which is all so necessary, and it need not be that the ideas or change is bad.

3. Propaganda

Very little use has been made of the use of our propaganda drive, which can be very effective if used correctly. Here, the services of the government printer can be of immense benefit, for printed slogans have been found to be most effective when tacked up on the walls of offices, workshops and production sites.

It is also advocated that departmental booklets or leaflets be issued which can carry departmental tid-bits and other propaganda designed to assist the production drive. I would further suggest that greater publicity be given to yearly, monthly, or weekly targets, so that all participating are made aware of the progress being made and, more so, what is expected of them.

Within each ministry should be a division whose main responsibility soul deb to disseminate information, thereby keeping the workforce alive as to what is taking place. This division must be the nerve center where information is received, processed, and passed on, and what is of importance, passed on in the manner that can be most effective.

4. Education

There is dire need for a crash program to be conducted to train all supervisors presently employed in the technique of modern supervision and I would recommend that courses in "Training Within Industry" be run in all ministries. It is my view that training within industry was found to be of invaluable assistance to the American war effort (1941-1945) when the nation was confronted with a drain of supervisors to the armed forces, it could play an equal role in equipping our supervisor to meet the greatest challenge confronting our young nation.

GENERAL

In a previous paper submitted to you, I expressed the view that employees should develop a sense of belonging, for without this, there is no morale. It must be remembered that every worker spends on average, six to eight of their working hours daily on the worksite and it is here that he partners with many of his friends. It follows, therefore that the worksite is meaningful to him, and the job atmosphere goes a long way in determining his attitude towards his employment.

This job atmosphere is important, and it is the responsibility of the employer to ensure that it is treated as such so that the employee develops a pride in belonging. They must be made to realize that he is part of the team, and not just a sideliner.

The question is, just how can the elected government assist in this direction?

First, I would recommend that the Prime Minister as head of the government, donate a trophy to be awarded annually to the Ministry that achieved the highest standard of efficiency. This will no doubt stimulate interest and offer a morale booster to the workforce.

In the same manner, I strongly recommend that the personnel divisions, which, by the way, have been termed "Frustration Centers", be expanded to include matters of intra-ministries relations, which is all so necessary at this time. In so doing, it should then ne the responsibility of these divisions to fuse the several units of the workforce in the respective ministries into efficient teams.

To achieve this fusion, I would recommend that ministerial trophies be awarded for competitive games between divisions and sub-divisions of a ministry, and such activities as debates and similar pursuits be encouraged for the less robust.

Every individual strives after recognition from those with whom he is associated, and for many of us, this recognition may not he found on the job itself, but if it is made possible for the supervision and the supervised to meet off the job under circumstances where the supervised can show his mastery and with ins acclaim, a better employee must necessarily evolve.

CONCLUSION

If we are to increase production this must be coupled with a war on waste of materials and man-hours. To achieve this a new kind of supervisor is needed, and a re-adjusted and better-equipped employee. We also need a better industrial climate and in this regard, the onus rests on the elected government.

I have outlined above the faults in our productive machinery and these have been itemized as follows:

1. Bad Supervision
2. Lack of effective propaganda
3. No training program for supervisors
4. Absence of morale boosting measures

To correct these faults I have advocated the implementation of the following:

1. The introduction of staff conferences and works councils in all ministries
2. Planning of a propaganda campaign to restore and maintain interest and circulate information
3. The introduction of a training program for supervisors, designed to equip them with the techniques of modern supervision, and training within industry is recommended
4. The use of radio time to educate and assist supervisors in solving problems confronting them
5. Positive action by elected government in and endeavor to raise morale.

It is my firm view that if these proposals are implemented it would go a long way in raising production by a possible 10 – 15% and minimize waste which has been consuming so much of our hard earned money, materials and man-hours.

PART II - GOVERNMENT, THE ECONOMY AND THE TRADE UNIONS

"The trade unions are not eternal, they will exist for as long as they are compatible to the society within which they seek to exist."

The above quotation are the words of Ray Gunther, Minister of Labor in Mr. Wilson's Cabinet of 1965 and himself a trade unionist, therefore, notice must be taken of them. The view expressed Mr. Wilson are factual, and the present labor situation in Guyana forces all of those interested in labor to take a serious look at our trade unions in the light of Mr. Gunther's statement.

The question is obviously whether our unions are compatible to our society, and I am aware that there are those who are of the view that our unions are not functioning in our best interests and have expressed the view that legislation should be enacted to curtail the frequency of the strike action taken by the unions.

I do not share the above view point entirely for while I am convinced that frequent strikes have hampered production, hence the national economy, I an not convinced that curtailing strike action, through legislation will necessarily increase production, thereby bettering the economy. It is my view that increased production or production for that matter, is dependent on many factors over which the legislature has no control.

The real problem confronting the nation is what must be done to ensure that our unions function in the best interest of our society. While I am in full agreement with the views, as expressed by Mr. Gunther, like, him, I am also convinced that the unions can still contribute immensely to the furtherance of our society, but, Mr. Gunhter went on to say that the unions were capable of correcting their short-comings and it is here where we differ.

It is possible that the unions in the United Kingdom may be able to adjust their own shortcomings and it is here where we differ.

It is possible that the unions in the UK may be able to adjust their own shortcomings, but I am doubtful whether the unions in Guyana, if left to themselves, can do likewise. I am of the view that within the unions, there exists, in the main, an absence of those with the necessary vision and courage to adjust them to tackle so sizeable a problem, for indeed it is.

The problem affecting the local unions is basically one of finance, for we have a multiplicity of unions, most under three thousand members, each existing on the borderline of bankruptcy, with very little room for expansion. This existence, on the borderline of bankruptcy, has resulted in a situation where there are few unions capable of offering the services expected of a trade union today, and as a result they hide their inefficiency in vote catching statements, which are most often irresponsible, in the endeavor to hide their incapacities, while protecting their continuance and the controllers of power and enjoyers of privileges. It must also be noted that their unfavorable financial position has forced many unions to transcend their spheres of influence in piratical ventures that has let to inter-union warfare, thus adding to the existing labor unrest.

The question confronting the nation is what must be done to ensure that inept trade union leadership does not jeopardize the national interest. The economic growth of the nation is threatened; what must government do?

It is my view that the time has come for government as the trustees of the people to take positive action, and any action taken, must result in or has as it its intention, the strengthening of the financial position of the unions, for upon this, is dependent, responsible leadership and effective trade union representation. The efficiency of the unions must be improved if we are to better industrial climate.

To accomplish this, a drastic reduction in the number of unions is desired for this will eventually lead to better financed organizations offering better services and capable of facing the realities of the day.

The problem is just how far can government go without being accused of interference and as an initial step, I will propose that government seek to set up a committee under chairmanship of the Minister of Labor, comprising of a representative of each affiliate of the T.U.C>, with the sole objective of determining the number of unions necessary to provide adequate trade union representation to the workforce of Guyana, and also, determining or laying out clear cut spheres of influence.

This is a problem that must be solved, and I am convinced that if left to the unions themselves, nothing worthwhile will be done, for this is an age old problem, which the trade unions have recognized and have been considering, from as far back as 1952. Government, as I have said, must take the initiative for they owe a responsibility to the people.

There are of course other measure which can be instituted to ensure the future stability of our unions, and foremost, is a revision of the trade union ordinance to introduce such clauses that will give greater protection to the membership of the unions, and powers to the Registrar to investigate complaints of members. It is my view that most of all, the Trade Union Ordinance should include provision that guarantee the fair and proper election of office bearers. This, as I see it, must be a priority.

Some thought must now be given to the unions and government as an employer. I must firs establish that collective bargaining, the basic tenet of the free trade union movement, is at it worst at governmental level, for no proper machinery exists for the effective processing of grievances; the Whitley Council being but a mere mockery.

There is a complete absence of a collective bargaining agreement as general orders are antiquated and an absurdity, having been arrived at almost unilaterally by the establishment.

The general orders must be withdrawn, and immediate steps taken to determine a new contract of service by the process of collective bargaining. I would further suggest that the life of an y such contract be no more that two years and also, that a contract arrived at be printed in pocket-book form and sold to employees at a cost well within their means.

Every measure, which we may feel, can help in mobilizing our workforce into an efficient productive mechanism must be pursued. It is only by achieving this that we can hope to produce more and at cheaper costs, so as to make our goods and our services competitive.

The trade unions can play an important part in achieving these objectives, but before this can be done they must be transformed into efficient organizations fully conscious of the vital role they have to play in the economic development of a nation. It is left to the Government to ensure this.

A CASE FOR MERGERS
1972

In a paper prepared in 1965 entitled "A New Look for the Movement" I advocated a reduction in the number of unions expressing the view that there was no need for more than six unions. I further advocated that trade union operation on a national basis reaches average efficiency when its membership approached the 5,000-membership mark.

The situation since 1965 has changed somewhat, not to the extent that there is need for more than six unions.

What has changed may be the power structure within the movement, which will cause different groupings but sill based on the principle that a trade union operating on a national basis reaches average efficiency when its membership approaches the 5,000 level.

The obvious question to be answered is how can a reduction in the number of unions improve their efficiency, and at the same time strengthen the movement at the national level? I will now deal with this aspect.

I am contending that to improve the efficiency of the unions, we must first consider what are the services that trade unions should be providing of its members at this point in time, and also, at what level. Knowing this we should endeavor to determine if they are being provided and at what level of efficiency. Having assessed the situation, it is for us to consider how we can improve upon, or introduce these services efficiently and as I see it, the services that every trade union should be providing at this point in time are as follows:

1. Maximum Job Protection
2. Periodic Improvement in living standards
3. Medical Services
4. Recreational Facilities
5. Educational and Cultural Development
6. Opportunity to participate in community or environmental improvement projects

Above I am contending should be provided by all unions and I will proceed to deal with them in sequence, but grouping1 and 2, dealing with them in greater detail as they are the primary purpose of the trade union action.

JOB PROTECTION AND IMPROVING LIVING STANDARDS

Job security is dependent on the strength of the union and strength is a reflection of the condition won in the collective bargaining agreement together with the ability of the leadership to police the agreement or contract.

The same can be said for improvement in living standards, for I have always contended that we are compelled to live at today's level because our unions are incapable of acquiring more, and further the level at which we will live tem years hence will depend on the strength of our unions at that time. In other words, we are at this time, by the way we run our unions, determining the standard at which our members will live in the future. In previous paper, "Measures for Evaluations", I expressed the view that the strength of a union is a function of its membership and the competence of its leadership, and this, in my mind, in indisputable.

In considering membership, however, we are of course referring to percentage of membership and this introduce that function of trade union leadership organizing, which can he most costly but without which, few unions can hope to survive for any length of time and we must consider this relative to our exercise.

ORGANIZING

In most unions, organizing is left primarily to the shop stewards when the industry or service is already unionized, and in the context of our situation at most times little or no propaganda material is available for use by the shop stewards to execute this vital function. It often happens, also, that the shop steward is also untrained and ill equipped for this sizable task.

In the case of the industries or services which are unorganized, the situation is all the worse, for few unions possess the skilled personnel or money to mount a proper organizing drive.

The problem as stated is money to finance the program and money to remunerate those who will man the program. The reason for the shortfall of funds is of course lower membership, and at times even lower dues, which account for over 95% of the revenue of most local unions.

We must however remember that organizing it not something we can afford to do without, for every new member means more revenue of the union. Two hundred more members may well determine whether we can afford to employ another grievance officer to speedily process or grievances and end the many frustrations we experience, or whether we can afford to mount those seminars to educate our second tier and grassroots leadership to raise their level of competence. It can also mean whether the union or the movement can survive the pressure being exerted by those who believe that the trade unions have served their time and purpose.

Every union operation on a national level needs a competent officer to be in charge of its organizing program, so as to ensure optimum membership. Coupled with this, the union must be able to afford the money necessary to finance a continuous membership drive, especially in those industries or services where there is a high labor turnover.

If protection and improved living standards are accepted as being dependent on the strength of the unions, we must build our strength and this means building our membership, for from this will come the money to effectively service the membership and provide the insurance that every worker so much needs.

The financial aspect of this function will be later dealt with but I must mention that no union with a membership of under 5,000 can raise the necessary funds to efficiently execute the type of organizing program needed a this time.

Job protection and improved living standards are however not only dependent on high membership. Security is also dependent on the ability of the leadership to negotiate proper conditions of work and wages, and also to competently advocate the rights of their members.

It is therefore necessary for us to consider another functional aspect of trade unions leadership – negotiation.

NEGOTIATION

In the context of our exercise, we must ask the question – How many unions are capable of efficiently processing a grievance from the shop steward level through the other stages of the process, e.g. conciliation and arbitration? The answer is of course, very few, if any.

The ability I submit to process a grievance successfully calls for competent officers at all levels fully trained and also many of them on full time service. There is also the problem of arbitration, for how many unions can afford its cost.

Negotiation is a skill that can only be acquired by training and practice, and training for this nature can be very costly. It is in the interest of the union to ensure that the highest degree of competence is attained this skill.

Many charges have been leveled against the unions for generating industrial unrest, by the frequent and unnecessary use of the strike weapon. The blame is of course, not only to be laid at the doorstep of the unions, for the employers are equally and very often more blameful, but it is disputable that the situation could be much more improved if at the second tier and grass root leadership, there is greater skill in the art of advocacy.

It is my contention that there is greater need for improved efficiency in our negotiation techniques for this in itself will assist in ensuring greater job protection and improved living standards by the effective use of the collective bargaining mechanism. The problem is, of course, money to be spent on training, and money again is a function of membership.

Next to be considered is our ability to sit around the table and negotiate a collective agreement that will offer the type of job security expected by our members, and one that periodically provides improvement in their living standards.

While optimum membership and negotiating skill can be of great assistance, in the final analysis it is the facts at our disposal that will determine the results, and the facts will be dependent on our homework.

The successes gained in a collective agreement is dependent on the amount of research done and once again we introduce another function of trade union leadership, research, which is a field long neglected and which more than anything else is responsible for the meager gains we have made over the years.

RESEARCH

To appreciate the importance of research in collective bargaining, we must first understand what is the data that should be at the disposal of those who negotiate on our behalf when they sit around the table.

As a consequence of the above, I will now deal with this aspect of the function of the trade union leadership in some detail, for it is most important and as I have said a field sadly neglected, but, a function that must be efficiently executed, if we are to make appreciative gains in our collective agreements. The data to consider are: -

1. Wage Data – Every negotiator (Union) when sitting around the table must know everything about the wages paid in the industry or service. The question may be asked, why is this knowledge necessary. The answer is that management will have, and will make use of these figures, and the unions must be in a position to verify their accuracy, failing which they will be forced to rely exclusively on those presented by management, accepting them unquestionably. Therefore, the following must be known to the union:
    a. The internal pay structure i.e. the various jobs in terms of importance from the highest to the lowest. This includes every job in the industry
    b. The external job structures. The union must be in a position to compare every job in the industry with those out of the industry, so as to compare trends
    c. Salary for men vs. women for we are living in an age where women are entering every field of occupation and the temptation is always there for employers to employ women in jobs normally performed by men at lower rates
    d. The average hourly rate for every job in the industry and also how it compares with those out of the industry.

e. The average hourly rate for the entire industry, for these figures are vital when working our production costs

f. The average weekly earnings of every category of work and this must differentiate between straight pay and overtime pay.

2. Hour Data – It is important that the negotiators possess all information in respect to hours of work. It is very important since the rate per day is only meaningful if we know how many hours must be worked to earn that rate. Further to that, what is paid per day must be related to what the worker earns per week and also per year, including shift work, for what we earn is that which we must utilize to maintain ourselves and families for every day of the year. Here again we are considering our standard of living, which is determined to a large extent on what we earn and also influenced by the ability of the union negotiators to effectively make use of the collective bargaining machinery.

3. Employee Data – The union's negotiating team must know everything in respect to the manpower employed in the industry. Below is the research required:

    a. Number of employees - we can arrive at the weekly labor cost, if we know the average weekly rate, and similarly we can determine the yearly labor cost

    b. Composition of men and women– by knowing the number of men vs. women, the negotiators can spot or observe trends in the labor composition. This is especially important if there are differentials between the rates for men and women. There is also, the negotiating of conditions or fringe benefits for women, the cost of which can only be determined if we first know the number of women to be affected by conditions.

    c. Age distribution of employees – this is most important in determining where the union demand will be heavily concentrated. The average age will determine whether the union will press for high wages as opposed to greater security. The younger employees will support higher wages as opposed to the older, who will tend toward greater security

d. Period of employment – This is vital when considering such things as vacation as this benefit is at time related to length of service

e. History of wages – research in this area looks at the trend to determine if there is a need for change. Researcher will look to see if there has been a change in the composition of the workforce etc.

4. Productivity Data – It is imperative that the union's negotiation team knows as much of the productivity information as the industry's management team. The following are critical knowledge areas:

a. Total production, including production per man-hour. If they know this, they can assess such things as the cost of work stoppages and also compare the productivity of the industry as against others

b. Labor cost per unit of production? This is necessary in industries where more than one union enjoy bargaining rights. The information is also useful in spotting areas where production costs are rising, for at times they are due to mismanagement and such information is always needed to nail the lie that rises in cost of production is due solely to rising labor cost

c. Capital investment of the company, for from this percentage profit can be determined. A $100,000 profit is meaningless unless we know what was the capital invested

d. Percentage of labor cost to total cost of production. This information is useful in determining shifting trends and also to counter the so often leveled accusations

that it is the labor factor that affects production
adversely.

5. Fringe Data – it is useful for the negotiators to have at their
    disposal all of the information relevant to following fringe
    benefits especially in respect to cost to the industry:
    a. Cost of the pension plan
    b. Vacation policy
    c. Maternity benefits
    d. Sickness benefits

All of the information listed above must be at the disposal of the union
team. Everything about the benefits must be known and it is of great
importance also that the union team even knows of the conditions,
customs and practices enjoyed by the employees, which are not
embodied in the agreement.

In considering research, I have attempted to focus attention on its
importance, for the trade union movement has identified collective
bargaining as the instrument to be used in achieving its objective and if
we are to successfully improve the living standard of the members we
represent, it is imperative that we make very efficient use of the
collective bargaining machinery. To do this successfully we must pay
detailed attention to research and it is my contention that this can only
be done if your unions can employ competent officers fulltime to handle
this vital function. Again this calls for money.

I have so far in considering job protection and improved living standards
looked at three functions of trade union leadership, organizing,
negotiating, and research, these field that have been undeveloped or
overlooked for some time now, and I have contended that the reason
for the present position is that our unions, as a result of insufficient
funds due to low membership and low dues could not find it possible to
employ the kind of skilled persons necessary to execute these functions
efficiently and effectively.

Operating at their present low level of efficiency the unions are incapable of providing the kind of protection demanded by their members and also have only been able to make meager gains in respect of improved living standards.

In considering protection also it is a fact that while individually the unions cannot offer the kind of protection demanded, collectively, the situation is not better, for if the unions are poor, the T.U.C. is even poorer, and the paucity of funds at the disposal of this body has blunted the edge of this rapier that should be used by the working class in wining battle after battle in this our war for emancipation.

The question is however, what can be done to improve the position? My contention is reducing the number of unions to no more than six with each having a membership of not less than five thousand members. As I see it, to employ the personnel to effectively execute the functions mentioned, will cost about $87,180 annually and how many of our unions can carry this overhead and at the same time execute the functions efficiently.

MEDICAL FACILITIES

People group together for purposes of protection and by grouping together, they find that there are many services that could be provided by the group that individually will be beyond their means. One such service is medical benefits.

It is not beyond the means of a trade union with 5,000 and a proper dues structure to provide for their members sickness and death benefits beyond that which is presently provided by N.I.S.

It may well be argued why should the unions duplicate the services already offered by the N.I.S. but the obvious answer is "Can the benefit offered by N.I.S. take care of survival, optical, and dental treatment when industrial injury is not involved?'

To appreciate this need, we should endeavor to determine what happens to a family when serious illness befalls the breadwinner, especially if surgical treatment is involved. There is of course the problem of death, and the meager benefit offered by the N.I.S.

There is no doubt that this kind of service is greatly needed by our members but how many unions can possible afford this. As I pointed out above, by group or collective action, it will be possible to offer this service if we can ensure a minimum membership of 5,000 and a proper dues structure.

To appreciate this let us consider what could be done with the income earned by a union having 5,000 members with an average contribution of $3.00 per member, $15,000 per month, $180,000 per year. It will be possible for such a union to offer medical benefits to the extent of $400.00 per member within any three-year period and a guaranteed death benefit of at least $800 after a period of two years, provided that the scheme is well funded.

It is in our interest to consider structuring our unions to make provision for such a scheme, as I am sure that this will assist in improving membership participation and at the same time offer the kind of security that our members cannot afford to do without. The possibility of what can be done with funds to be accrued definitely needs investigating. A membership of $5,000 paying $3 per member per month, of which 75c is allocated towards a benefit fund can accrue to $45,000 per year, earning an interest of $3,000 for the first year and $15,000 at the end of five years provided that the capital subscribed is not touched.

The possibilities of such a scheme is enormous for benefits can be met of out the interest alone and the proper investment of such a fund can mean so many additional benefits for the membership.

RECREATIONAL FACILITIES

What the worker should do with his leisure time must be the concern of the union. It is useless bargaining for increased leisure hours and increased pay if at the same time we do not concern ourselves with what must be done with the additional hours and in what avenues the additional earnings are spent.

The unions must therefore become involved in promoting recreational facilities that are beneficial to the worker and thus avoid the additional leisure hours being used to engage in pursuits that can lower his potential production level. We must at all times endeavor to ensure that advances in living standards do not adversely affect national production.

A union headquarters can assist in providing some form of recreation but does this embrace all members? We must go further, we must engage ourselves in promoting outdoor games and indoor. What of weekend tours to places of interest? Can the unions not get involved in this especially in view of the expected five-day week?

The above are questions we must consider for they apply to the needs of our members and we must endeavor to satisfy them, but to do this successfully, stronger and better-financed unions are needed.

EDUCATIONAL CULTURAL DEVELOPMENT
In considering education, we must look at both trade union education and education that assists in improving the earning capacity of the worker. It is beyond question that there is a great need for these services.

In respect of trade union education there are just a few unions that can find it possible to finance their owned internal education program and at the same time meet the charge as approved by the T.U.C. Congress in 1970, of one dollar per member per year to subsidize the Critchlow Labor College.

The reason is, of course, limited funds and this is seriously affecting education within the unions and to a greater extent the functioning of the Critchlow Labor College. The college is at moment financed almost entirely by a government grant and it would be tragic if this source of revenue were to be cut off.

The problem of the college is a serious one and if it is to remain the property of the trade union congress, some deep thought should be given to its financing. One thing is certain, however, and that is the movement will never be able to properly finance the college unless something is quickly done to reduce the number of unions and at the same time improve on the dues structure of the amalgamated unions as I have proposed.

There is also the other aspect of grassroots education presently supplied by the T.U.C. It is hoped that as a result of the extended program now being run, it will be possible to increase union membership to the extent that affiliation fees to the T.U.C. will improve so that it will be possible for the congress to continue the program on its own by the employment of a person on full time service responsible for education.

Whether this can be achieved is doubtful for I am convinced that any increase in membership will not reflect a proportionate increase in affiliation fees to the T.U.C. as the additional revenue will be used up by the unions in meeting their current shortfall in income.

Here again, the problem is insufficient funds and the answer is as pointed out before improving the finances of the affiliates by increased membership and an improved dues structure following upon a reduction in the number of unions.

What now of education to improve the earning capacity of our members. It is my belief that this is something that must be seriously considered by the movement if we are to make a contribution to the improvement of national productivity.

There is great need for more and improved skills among our workforce for this can mean better wages, which is a prerequisite to an improved dues structure. The unions must seriously consider this, but should the situation remain as it is, nothing worthwhile can be achieved for any such program will call for money.

CULTURAL DEVELOPMENT

Our young nation is still in its formative stage and seeking a cultural identify. It follows therefore, that if the struggles and way of life of the labor force of Guyana is to be embodied in the culture that must evolve, the trade union movement must play its part in the molding of this culture.

Plays and other works of art depicting the struggles and achievements of the labor movement must be written and enacted. From within the movement these artists must arise and opportunity for this type of expression must be afforded the membership of the movement.

The question that must be asked is whether our unions as they are presently constituted can afford this kind of service. The answer is definitely in the negative for the money is just not there for any form of cultural pursuits.

At the disposal of the movement is the multi-purpose hall of the Critchlow Labor College, hopelessly under utilized and ideally suited for the purposes I am advocating, and this poses a challenge to the movement. Here again we must see why it is important for this building, an institution in the making, to remain the property of the trade union movement for if it can be fully utilized by the movement it can thereby make an invaluable contribution to the cultural development of our young nation.

This is something that must be seriously considered by our unions for we should no longer be solely concerned with bread and butter issues but venture out into satisfying the new needs of our members and the question that again confronts us is "where is the money for such a venture to come from?"

Increased membership and a better dues structure is of course the answer and this will again call for a reduction in the number of unions and the economies that can be affected due to the theory of economies of scale which will definitely make it possible for the introduction of these new pursuits in our trade union program.

Finally, we must consider the involvement of the movement in the community development programs of the nation, for there is a great need outside of our major townships for many of the basic social amenities that assist in making life meaningful.

It is without doubt, that the central government will find itself hard-pressed to satisfy these needs in the traditional manner and as such, community development must be the concern of the entire nation, and, as an important institution within the society the trade union movement must make community development a part of its program.

OPPORTUNITY TO PARTICIPATE IN COMMUNITY OR ENVIRONMENTAL DEVELOPMENT PROJECTS

Our young nation has declared itself a cooperative republic and has identified self-help as the way of developing our less developed communities. The trade union movement must be identified with this development for it must be remembered that our members form part of these communities and it must mean so much more to them if they know that their union is also concerned with this aspect of their daily lives.

The problem of involvement is again that of manpower and money and I am still contending that the only way to ensure union involvement is community work is by a reduction in the number of unions in the manner I am advocating as this will make it possible for setting up a kind of administration capable of operating the kind of program I am visualizing.

There is one important point to be also considered and that is such a program will give more of our members an opportunity of becoming involved in union activities and also it would be a good training ground for leadership, so much needed in our unions.

The movement must be identified with the changes within the society especially with those that involve the improvement of the working class for it is imperative that our functions remain compatible with the trend within the society.

To become involved calls for money and the setting up of the kind of machinery that is capable of meeting the new challenges, but what is of greater importance, it is imperative that we apply ourselves to these ventures if we are to motivate our membership in the right direction.

CONCLUSION

In preparing my case for a reduction in the number of unions, I have identified the needs of our membership at this point in time and have endeavored to stress their importance. In this exercise I was forever mindful of the words of Ray Gunther, Minister of Labor, in the last labor government, who in an address to trade union leaders said "The trade unions are not eternal…they will continue to exist for as long as they remain compatible to the society within which they seek to exist".

Gunther's words must be seriously considered for as time changes so do the needs of the people and it is imperative for institutions such as the trade union movement to take repeated looks at themselves to ensure that they are in step with the times.

My conviction is that our movement, as it is presently constituted is incapable of satisfying the current needs of its members and the attempts to bring it in line are moving much too slow a pace.

The problem is of course leadership, for when on considers what is leadership and we take a look at what is taking place or is not taking place within the movement, we must definitely come to the conclusion that at this point in time, there is paucity of leadership within the movement.

My definition of leadership or leaders is "Change Initiators". "A leader seeks to change an organization's structure, rules or regulations and at times even objectives, so as to achieve the goals or objectives of the organization or group".

How many of our leaders do measure up to this definition? Where are the change initiators? As I see it, we must all take a serious look at ourselves as time is passing too swiftly by and our young nation is on the move. So if we do not want to be left behind, a decision must be taken now as to what the future of the movement must be.

We have to resurrect the revolutionary fervor of the fathers of our movement and reshape our unions to meet the challenges of our time. This can only be done by reducing the number of unions to no more than six and the introduction of a proper dues structure that will for the first time offer financial stability to our unions.

ESTABLISHING NEW RELATIONSHIPS BETWEEN THE TRADES UNION YOUTH MOVEMENT (TUYM) AND THE TRADE UNION CONGRESS (TUC)

Audience: The TUYM Annual Conference Attendees at Den Amstel

Date: July 1975

PART 1: WHY A TRADE UNION YOUTH MOVEMENT (TUYM)

In a paper submitted to the then Trades Union Council in 1965, I stated that the Trades Union Movement in Guyana was the only organization of repute that did not have a youth arm. I strongly recommended that urgent steps should be taken to correct that most obvious shortcoming.

This great need was recognized due to the situation that existed in the Ruimveldt/La Penitence area where thousands of children – sons and daughters of workers who are members of our unions, loitered on the streets with nothing to do between the ours of 4:00 pm and 6:30 pm each day; and then the countless others who were unemployed – some already social problems, others on the verge of becoming delinquents. The situation today is hardly any different.

Whose responsibility is it to correct these social problems? Is it a matter of concern for the individual unions only or the TUC? I strongly felt then that the problem was the concern of the TUC and I still do.

There were of course, other factors that contributed to my viewpoint on the need for a youth arm for the Trades Union Movement, for even at that time the unions were experiencing great difficulty in getting the young members of their unions involved in union activity and even greater difficulty in getting them organized.

The reason was not difficult to determine, for the movement had somehow seemed old. It was more of an institution than a Movement. It was no longer dynamic. It had lost its revolutionary fervor and many more were of the view that its leadership had become reactionary.

The movement held no attraction for the young and somehow it appeared that a sizeable part of the leadership was even afraid to welcome the youth within their ranks.

The Trades Union Youth Movement (TUYM) was, however, established after great persuasive efforts, but over the ten years of its existence apart from its first two years, it has never lived up to what I expected of it.

The reasons for the TUYM's failures to make the impact I expected are many and varied, but if I were asked to venture the most important reason for the lack of dynamism within the organization over the ten year period, I will answer – leadership or lack of it.

As I see it, the leadership was much too conservative and failed to attract within its ranks dynamic young men and women, capable of charting new courses and earning new experience.

I know that it will be said that little encouragement was given to the TUYM by the existing trade union leadership and while this may be so, it is not a justifiable excuse for the lack of positive leadership.

It may also be said that in order to exist, the TUYM had to be conservative, for it was the arm of a conservative movement. This is all well and good, but is youth by nature conservative? I think not.

In spite of the above, however, the organization has remained alive and has made some contributions, mostly in the field of education, and its effort in that direction over the past two years is commendable.

The question posed in the introduction of this part of my paper was "Why a Trade Union Youth Movement?" If it has not been answered, it is best for you to now ask yourself this question: What is it that you expect to get out of life. Must it be an endless struggle for existence, or just living so as to die?

Picture the kind of life you would like to live and reflect on this: The only assurance you have that your dreams of a full life can be realized, is if you have a strong militant and dynamic Trade Union Movement working in your interest and towards your well-being.

To most of you, the importance of these words may not be realized. Yours is still a sheltered existence, your meager income coupled with what your mother and/or father may be able to provide, can afford you the kind of life that you now enjoy. But for how long will it continue? Very shortly, most of you will venture out, to go it on your own, to paddle along life's uncertain streams. Somewhere and sometime along the way you won't be alone, you'll acquire additional responsibilities – passengers – a husband or a wife – children. The going can be rough – very rough.

Some of you, I know will say that such a life is not for you; you'll carry no burdens along the way. This may be true, but what of that home, that shiny new motorcycle, that car. That trip to the U.S.A, or even the West Indies? Even the life of a single male or female can be expensive. And remember, it is inevitable that we get old.

We are living in uncertain times. Ours, they say, is the age of sacrifice. We must sacrifice to build the future. This is good. It is inevitable and it is the fact of history. The question is however, "How much sacrifice must you make?" And remember, the amount of sacrifice you make determines your standard of living.

My contention, therefore, is that if youth or the young worker is interested in his welfare or well-being, he or she must be interested in the trade union movement; for in the final analysis, it is the trade union movement that determines the amount of sacrifice the workers in the country will be called upon to make, through the process of collective bargaining.

Becoming interested in the movement is however not enough. The problems of the young worker are peculiar to their age grouping. Your needs are different from those of your mothers or fathers. The leadership of the movement, chronologically, can speak with certain amount of authority for those within the 35 – 60 age group, and while they may be sympathetic to the young, youth needs a mouth-piece of its own, and what better mouth-piece that a Trade Union Youth Movement.

SCOPE FOR ESTABLISHING NEW RELATIONSHIPS

The needs of the membership of the Trade Union Movement have undoubtedly changed over the past ten years, and all recognize that the role and concept of the movement have also changed; more so, with the new national thrust.

In considering, therefore, the scope for new relationships between the TUYM and the TUC one must consider this in the context of the new needs and new role.

Before proceeding however, there are some sore points that first should be clarified and understood.

The TUYM has always been complaining of not having a voice at the decision-making bodies of the movement. This may be so to some extent, but at least they have the right to speak at the level of the Annual Delegates conference of the Congress, even if not to vote.

I am sympathetic to their claim that they should have a voice at the Executive Council level of the Congress, for no doubt this is the chief decision making forum, but what I disagree with is the means by which the TUYM wants to have that voice.

It is their claim that they should have observer status on the Executive Council, but I wonder just how meaningful this would be. It must be remembered that there are some unions unrepresented on the Council that subscribe towards the financing of the Congress – a claim which the TUYM cannot make; so any such request will be subject to question.

I however agree, that the matter should not be left at that, and the first point that should be considered is – "For whom does the TUYM speak?" This as I see it is the problem, and until such time that they convince others that they truly speak for youth and the young worker, or that they have a mandate to do so, no one will pay heed to their claim.

The TUYM if it is indeed to have a say in the decision making process of the Movement, must first organize youths and young workers within its ranks and there is tremendous scope for this. Relationships must he set up with affiliates of the Congress and there are two areas that I can see them becoming immediately involved, education and recreation.

EDUCATION

In the field of education the TUYM has made some progress but there is much more to be done. I would recommend that the program be expanded to the point where it can be accepted that the TUYM is the agency for carrying trade union education to youth and young workers.

This kind of education can eventually be institutionalized using the facilities of the CLC, for, as I have said, there is need, great need, for this kind of service. My experience has been that the majority of young workers who are members of trade unions, receive no training whatsoever, unless, by good fortune they become involved in the second tier leadership of their unions at an early age.

What of the youth of the society? Those in the senior forms of our secondary and technical schools, and those unemployed. A start was once made in this direction and the TUYM established some kind of relationship with a few secondary schools, but my information is that this no longer exists. Those programs must be resuscitated, for it is one of our greatest needs.

It is imperative that those about to enter the job market, have some idea or knowledge of the Trade Union Movement and its achievements. Let us face facts, these young people are being organized into other groups and organizations and not all of the may be interested or sympathetic to the Movement, and unless something positive is done, the demise or weakening of the Movement can subtly be achieved.

Education must however not be confined to trade unions, for one of the principal objectives of the Movement is improving the economic welfare of the worker, and I will submit that the economic welfare of the worker is greatly dependent on how much goods and services his pay packet can purchase.

It is in this area that the TUYM can be of service. Programs can be organized to improve the skills of the young worker, and also to make those who are now unemployed, employable. It is by doing this that we can improve the earning capacity of the young worker and make the unemployed productive.

RECREATION

What must the young worker do with his time away from the job? There are those who advocate that this time can best be spent in other forms of economic pursuits.

I agree that some of the free time of the young worker must be spent on things productive, but recreation is also vital for the full development of the individual. There is also the other aspect, and that is productive pursuits can be coupled with recreation.

Youth and the young worker need to congregate and recreation is the means of doing this. Why can't the TUYM become involved in things like holiday camps for youth and the young workers? Why can't six or seven days of the two-week annual leave period, be spent camping out in areas such as the Rupunini, Upper and Lower Mazaruni, and North West District, etc.?

As I have said, for education, these must not be sporadic ventures, but things planned, and if need be, institutionalized.

Three days will be spent here at Den Amstel by you the participants in an educational exercise, but you will also be engaged in other pursuits. What I do know is that you will learn as much and even more out of the classroom as you will gain within.

It is ventures like this that the TUYM must become more involved. I would like to see a program for the next year embodying no less that twelve ventures. I know the question will be asked about the funding, but let us not worry about this too much. If the Movement is assured that the real objectives of the seminars are being attained, I can see no reason why the financial assistance will not be forthcoming.

It has already been mentioned that the needs of the membership of our unions have changed and it can also be said that their lifestyles (especially the young) have changed. Fifteen to twenty years ago, a seminar such as this would have been unheard of. The Movement would have been accused of planning an orgy – your parents would have been up in arms, and, there, obviously, would have been no seminar.

Times have changed. This is the new lifestyles of the young and it no doubt appeals to you. In speaking therefore of scope for the new relationships, there is tremendous scope for the TUYM to exploit this area of recreation using it as a means of carrying education to the young, for and on behalf of the TUC.

Let us face facts. The young worker is not enamored over sitting in a classroom, reminiscent of his days in school. So if we want to educate we must use the measures that have the greatest appeal. We must however, ensure that we keep in mind the purpose of the exercises, and that we do not move too far away from the norms established by society.

A lot has been said about the scope for education and recreation but these are just two areas of need. Youth needs the opportunity also for self-expression; an opportunity to express your views on how you see the society; what you expect of the society and even an opportunity to be critical. This is your right.

A FORUM OF EXPRESSION

The TUYM can afford youth and the young worker the opportunity for self-expression. I know that there are many who claim to speak for the youth, but they only seem to be uttering the mouthing of others. Mere acolytes serving before the altars of the status quo. This is not my concept of youth or youth leadership.

Youth must be fully conscious of the role they have to play in shaping the new society. By numbers, you comprise the largest age grouping, and it is a fact of life, that it is youth who always inherits – mistakes and all.

What is the scope for this kind of expression? The constitution of the TUYM, no doubt, makes provision for this, but is it being used to its fullest advantage? I think not.

The first thing that I would like to see done is a reverting to the original constitution of the TUYM in respect to the date of your Annual

Delegates Conference. I cannot see what impact your conference can have when held in November, after the Annual Delegates Conference of the TUC, which as you know, is held in late September

Originally, your conferences were held in the months of August/September, before the annual Delegates Conference of the TUC so that you could discuss issues and arrive at decisions, then, following upon the results of your conference, you had the opportunity of forwarding resolutions and other matters you wanted discussed to the Congress for including in the agenda. This, as I see it, is much more meaningful and a better arrangement.

The point I am making is that youth needs a forum of expression, which must be at a time that would give them the opportunity of coming through both loud and clear, and equally, at a time when attention can be focused on what they are saying. Why compete with Santa Claus. November is not the time for your Conference.

What also of your other meetings; what of the attendance and participation? Are you affording youth and the young worker the full scope for self-expression?

CONCLUSION

My subject is – scope for establishing new relationships between the TUYM and the TUC – and, by now, you are asking how relevant what I have said is to the subject on which I was asked to speak.

I have spoken about the need for a TUYM and the scope for satisfying the new needs of youth and the young worker. Is this relevant to the subject? I think it is. If any new relationships are to be set up between the TUYM and the TUC, the TUYM must convince us of the following:

- It truly speaks for youth and the young worker
- It is satisfying or possesses the potential to satisfy those needs of the members of our unions which they themselves, cannot satisfy

- It has a mandate to speak for youth and the young worker

I once had a dream of a TUYM being the foremost, or one of the foremost youth organizations in our country, offering youth and the young worker for the first time the opportunity to make a contribution towards the building of a strong, militant and dynamic Trade Union Movement, conscious of the fact that this cannot be achieved without the full support and involvement of the youth and the young worker.

The new relationship that must be established between the TUYM and the TUC must be hinged upon what I have said above. But how can this be achieved? The TUYM needs the assistance of the youth and the young worker and the youth and the young worker need a TUYM, and you had better believe it.

Those of you who are representatives of affiliates, must see to it that you and others like yourselves get involved in the activities of the TUYM ensuring that its leadership achieve the things you expect of it. There is room for you in the TUYM, lots of room, and tremendous scope for you to use your energy, skills and talent in building the kind of organization that can help shape your tomorrow.

The new relationship therefore, would depend on what the TUYM can achieve, and what the TUYM can achieve, depends on you – all of you. Let us remember that we all need a strong Trade Union Movement and a strong TUYM, must mean a stronger Trade Union Congress.

YOUTH AND THE CHANGING SOCIETY

<u>Audience: The TUYM Annual Conference Attendees</u>

<u>1975</u>

OPENING REMARKS

Today I open with the following questions:

- Are the young people of Guyana really youthful?
- Can they contribute positively towards the nation-building process now taking place?

PART 1 – YOUTH AND SOCIETY

There is a tremendous challenge confronting the young people of Guyana and how well they answer the challenge would be dependent on whether our young people are truly imbued with the qualities of youth.

Since Independence, we have seen the need to institute many changes within our society and if the changes to be instituted are to be meaningful, youth must play its part in determining and implementing these changes, for all change have but one objective, and this is to make society, or the world for that matter a better place in which to live, and it must always be remembered, that it is youth who, in the final analysis, will inherit the product resulting from change.

The question that follows is whether our young people are competent to determine what changes are needed, and equipped to implement the changes, once they are determined. There are many who are of the view that Guyana's young people are ill-equipped for undertaking such an exercise, and I must admit that the attitude of our young people, as a whole, leads one to believe that this is rightly so, but it must be remembered that our young people are a product of the society, and the Guyanese society is noted for its complacency, lack of originality and sacrificial rituals on youth.

We are good followers. In the field of music, our artists can sing any song as good as the original product released in the USA, Great Britain, or even Jamaica. We can dance the latest steps as good as the originators. The American and British Pop stars grow their hair long, so must the Guyanese, despite its discomfort. Down with the tie they say, yet up with the turtlenecks. Woolens are popular, so we wear banlons and other jerseys. Our women are adorned with the latest styles and make-up preparation popular in New York, London and Paris, all unsuited for the tropics. Not to be left out, the Trade Union Movement adopts for its anthem – Solidarity Forever – set to the tune of the Battle Hymn of the Republic, but not the Cooperative Republic of Guyana. An inspiring tune, but not Guyanese.

It is in this context that we must judge our young people. We live in a society that developed out of colonialism, with the permeating concepts being 1) "Nothing good can come out of Guyana", 2) "Eventually others will solve our problems." A change in attitude is needed and youth must show the way. This introduces the question – What constitutes youth?

Youth I once described as "that zest for living with a low premium placed on life of itself. The ability to seek and fight for change, while still not certain what is to replace that which they seek to change.

Those who profess to teach offer the quest after knowledge, yet challenging and at times rejecting all that. The spirit of revolution, always on the go, possesses tremendous confidence in them and in their ability to solve all problems! Youth, never understood, but always in the forefront of progress."

It is only by possessing these attributes that our young people can answer the challenge that confronts the nation and makes our hard won independence meaningful, and it will be noted that I have all along spoken of young people as separated from youth, for my view is that youth does not necessarily appertain to the young in age, for many are born old.

THE CHALLENGE

What is needed of youth is creative thinking. We need to build a new society in which it is fit for youth to live, not a replica of the old and aged societies, but a new society with new concepts of life and living. A society that must take cognizance of the fact that the independence of Guyana was won by the working class at tremendous sacrifice, and if is to be meaningful, it must bring further economic benefit to the working man and woman with the ultimate objective of hastening the just society.

Towards this objective we must work. We must cut ourselves adrift from the tragedies of the past and undertake the serious task of nation building. Youth must visualize the society they want, and work towards its achievement, bearing in mind the words of Gandhi – "A classless society is an ideal not merely to be aimed at, but to be worked for".

It is for youth to take a close look at the institutions comprising our society put them under your scrutiny and approach your task with the outlook of the scientist, then, knowing the type of society you consider as fit for youth, ask yourselves whether the institution as they are presently constituted are capable of molding the society you have visualized. If the answer is in the negative, they must either be changed or replaced.

This introduces an important question. What methods must be used in instituting change? A pattern is evolving in metropolitan societies, whereby destruction is the answer to the resistance to change. In Guyana we have had our biter experiences, but let it be known that aping the trends in developed societies can do us no good, for we can ill afford the luxuries of destruction.

Youth must campaign for change, for change is both inevitable and needed, but we must convince others of the need for change. Youth Leadership must be competent advocates of the cause of youth and change. Let me pause here to quote the views of the co-directors of the Toastmasters International Youth Leadership Program – "Young men and women who will be the leaders of tomorrow must learn to listen analytically; to think clearly; and to speak effectively. This comes easy to some, but with great difficulty to others, and society bears the impact of those whose inability to communicate, drives them to strike back in physical anger.

Mastering the art of effective communication must be the primary object of Youth Leadership. Youth must put an end to the axiom that children should be seen and not heard, for this has handicapped so many of our Youth Leaders.

PART II – THE CHANGING SOCIETY

Independence has brought with it new problems. Apart from that of creating a just society, the nation is confronted with rapacious neighbors who possess evil designs on the territory we wrested from the British after long and bitter struggles. For two centuries we were herded on the seacoast producing wealth for absentee owners under conditions that bred frustration and dissatisfaction. Our education system was geared to meet the demands of those who exploited our labor; our institutions, groomed to pay homage to a white and foreign master; our vast interior left untouched, was tabooed to the native coast landers by white missionaries.

A new society must evolve. On the seacoast we must make good the damage and scars left by colonialism and use the slim resources it produces as the springboard for a leap forward into the hinterland that we must occupy to prove our right of ownership.

The problems of the seacoast are to say the least, tremendous but not insoluble. It requires foremost recognition of the weaknesses in the structure of our society. Our efforts from here on should be dedicated to unity and to use the words of the Prime Minister, "make the small man a real man," and society owes this to the small man. All our institutions must be geared towards the common cause of nation building, conscious of the fact that how much more we can produce here on the seacoast, means so much more to be spent on interior development, and the more we occupy our interior, the more the problems of the seacoast will fade into insignificance.

For the small man to be made a real man, the workers institution must be alive to the small man's interest, and restructure itself to meet the sizable tasks that lie ahead. The Trade Union Movement it is argued, is a change agent, and so if it is to function effectively it must realize that it must also be subjected to change. Since independence, the functional aspects of the movement has changed, the major role is no longer agitation for its purpose as the vanguard of the freedom movement has been realized. The major function of the Movement in this early post independence era, as I can see it, is to equip the working class for the sizeable part it has to play in nation-building and ensuring that the society that must evolve, affords the working man both dignity and a just reward for his labor.

How can this be done? First to come under the scrutiny of youth must be the worker's institution – the TUC, and this should be primary function of the TUYM. The TUYM must realize, and very early, that its function is not to defend the age-old concepts; you must never be acolytes serving before the altars of the status quo. Yours is the responsibility to develop new concepts and chart new courses.

What of the strike weapon? How important is it to the Movement in Guyana? Investigate its advantages and disadvantages and arrive at decisions uninfluenced by custom. Take a look at the structure of the Movement and determine if it is equipped to meet the challenges of the seventies. What of the workers education programs? How effective are they? What are the deficiencies? These are some of the questions for which immediate answers must be provided.

Next to be considered, is the means by which the economic independence of the working man and woman can be assured, and this introduces the Economic Arm of the Working Class Movement – The Cooperatives.

THE COOPERATIVE REPUBLIC

On the 23rd February 1970, Guyana became a Republic, severing all connections with the British Crown and making, for the first time, a reality of our independence.

The Prime Minister on Thursday 28th August last, informed Parliament that ours would be a Cooperative Republic and that the Cooperative Department had already been reorganized to meet the change and the challenges that lie ahead. He also said that it was the intention of his Government, to use the Cooperative way of life as the second thrust of our economic development program.

I have stated above that the Cooperative Movement is the economic arm of the Trade Unions, for it sprang out of the Trade Unions to become a part of the Working class Movement, as a result of sheer necessity. It is most unfortunate however that the Movement in Guyana has never thought of capitalizing on the benefits that the Cooperatives have to offer.

This was no doubt due to the type of society in which we lived for being capitalist oriented and colonialist in outlook, it was not in the interest of the leaders of the society to have a workforce economically viable and not solely dependent on the meager wage they had to offer. This however, does not remove the blame from the leaders of the working class movement for their short-sightedness in not using the facilitates that existed as no doubt they were.

There is of course the other aspect, and that is the attitude of the worker to the Cooperative Movement. The worker is suspicious as to its stability, distrustful as to its benefits, and is most cases, ignorant as to its intent. There are many who are openly antagonistic to the Movement, no doubt as a result of distrust; and for many, the only form of cooperatives of which they are aware, is the burial societies, no doubt, giving the impression that the Movement was more concerned with the dead than the living. This is unfortunate, for the cooperative way of life, is the workers' means of strengthening their economic position and chartering the route to their emancipation.

The major problem of most cooperatives is that of management, and this has been responsible for most of the many failures that has assisted in bringing about, the general skepticism that exists. What is now needed is a new look for the Movement. First, there must be closer association between the Trade Unions and the Cooperative Union, for the organized strength of labor is the sure platform to preach the doctrine of Cooperativism, and already the call has been made by the Cooperative Union to the Trade Unions in its September issue of the

"Co-op News".

The challenge of the Cooperative Republic must be answered, and Youth must investigate its potential. On the seacoast, cooperatives must be introduced into every possible means of our existence. We must start by saving cooperatively to amass the capital for investment in ventures that will improve the economic status of the small man. In the interior, the Burnham "Doctrine of Repossession" is our only answer, if we are to occupy and develop our interior.

The basis has already been established on the coast, and all that is now needed is to build upon the existing foundation. This calls for the motivation of the small man and of youth, and it is here where the organized Trade Union Movement, together with its Youth Arm can assist. First to be tackled must be that of education since the doctrine of Cooperativism can easily be introduced through our education programs.

Where does youth fit into this overall picture of changing society? The major coastal problem is that of unemployment and underemployment. We must accept that by clinging to the old customs, we will never be able for quite some time to provide the number of jobs necessary to keep pace with those entering the job market. This is the stark reality, but on the other hand, the vast landmass of Guyana possesses the potential of providing a living, and a decent living at that, for anyone with the guts to grasp the opportunities it offers.

The problem of unemployment and under-employment is a problem of Youth. It is they who are mostly affected and it follows that if youth is to be beneficially occupied, they must look to the land. There is the other significance; settlement of Guyanese in our hinterland is a political necessity if we are to prove our right of ownership.

We struggled over many long and bitter years to gain possession of what we had always considered to be rightfully ours, but now our western neighbor who once had similar struggles, and who had spearheaded the freedom movement on this South American continent, has today, like the imperial powers of old, developed the disease of land mania. A Chinese novelist once said, "one of the tragedies of life is that men get old", and how right is she? This is applicable to societies for no doubt the Venezuelan society has gotten old, she has become rich and she has become reactionary. Your birthright is threatened, the inheritance of youth is threatened, the least the nation can expect of Youth, is to defend that inheritance. We must occupy our hinterland.

CONCLUSION

The answers to these questions will determine the structure of the new society that will evolve, and no doubt, the size and shape of our country. It will also determine whether we have progressed towards the achievement of the just society and this is of most importance. Finally, the leadership of our country is under trial. The leadership you will term as old, and the old at times tend towards stability. They will need impetus, and that impetus must come from youth, fully conscious of their objectives and untiring in the pursuit of the just society. Today you are walking with history

THE ROLE OF BRANCH OFFICER AND SHOP STEWARDS IN THE CHANGING SOCIETY

INTRODUCTION

The role of the Branch, Branch Officer and the Shop Steward in the changing society, could only be understood or explained if we first establish or determine if the changes are consciously planned to achieve a stated or known goal, and if so, what is the goal or objective of the conscious effort.

Next to be considered, is whether the goal coincides with that of the Trade Union, and also, if it is opportune for the trade union to play a part in the achievement of the goal.

If the goal or end product of the change conflicts with that of the trade union, it is difficult to visualize the Branch or those who manage the branch, playing a positive role towards the achievement of the objective. It could possibly be that by so doing, they could be contributing towards their own destruction and at the same time, hampering the well-being of the Union's membership.

The role of the branch, the branch officers and the shop steward in the changing society could, therefore, be only explained within the context of the objective of the change. This being so, the role could either be positive or negative, depending on how the branch, the branch officers and the shop stewards see themselves being affected by the change.

To discuss the "Role of the Branch, the Branch Officers and Shop Stewards in the Changing Society," it is therefore necessary for us to analyze the objective of the change to see whether it coincides or conflicts with that of the trade union. If there is no conflict, and if the trade union considers the change in the interest of the union and its members, and also, if it is opportune that they contribute towards the achievement of the objective, the role they must play could only be positive. This, however, should be arrived at after an analysis of the objective.

THE SOCIALIST STATE

In the context of the Guyana situation, it has been accepted that the changes now taking place in the society are directed towards the creation of a socialist state. The ruling party, the People's National Congress, has openly and unapologetically expressed its commitment to the restructuring of the economic and political systems of the society along socialist lines. It is also proceeding with great haste towards the restructuring of the education system to prepare it for the tremendous job it must undertake to sell the new ideology to the masses.

The creation of a socialist society must, however, take some time, and could only be achieved with great effort and sacrifice by the working class. We are now in what is described as the "transition period." This speaks of the period of reconstructions and vigilance, when efforts must be expended towards changing the several institutions within the society to equip them for their new role in the present period, and, also, that which they must play in the future. It is also the period during which greater effort and sacrifice would be demanded of the workers, all, of which, would hopefully be rewarded with a better life in the future.

The question to be asked is – What is Socialism?   Marx, Lenin and others have written volumes on the socialist philosophy and ideology. All very useful, but as a practical trade unionist I would endeavor to deal with that aspect which is concerned with what socialism has to offer the working-class, especially the wage and salary earners.

Socialism, in this context, is described as a system in which there is:

1. Individual freedom.
2. Conscious social production for use.
3. Conscious Social Exchange of surplus.
4. Conscious social control of distribution.
5. Conscious social apportioning of duties, and
6. Conscious social development of the full potential of the citizen.

Conscious in the context of the above, speaks of a planned economy, objectively pursuing the achievement of the six determinants stated above.

It must be mentioned, however, that basic to the system is the complete destruction of capitalism. Socialism implies a society in which private profit would be replaced by service, and the surplus resulting or accruing from the services, consciously used for the benefit of the whole society.

This means that capitalist enterprises, operating on the profit-for-private-gain motive, would be replaced in the initial stage by what could be termed state capitalism or state capitalist monopoly. Following this, worker participation in the industry or service must be introduced, moving on finally to worker control of industry and services.

An understanding of the implications of socialism is necessary; therefore, if we are to meaningfully discuss the role of the branch, etc., in the changing society. It is also necessary for us at this time, to counter one of the charges leveled against state capitalism by some advocates of socialisms that it is not in keeping with the socialist ideology.

Lenin described this stage in socialist development in his work "Towards the Seizure of Power" as follows: -

> "Socialism is nothing but the next step
> Forward from state capitalist monopoly.
> In other words, socialism is nothing but
> State capitalist monopoly made to benefit
> The whole people; by this token it ceases
> To be capitalist monopoly."

It follows that in the transition period, we must expect to see the acceleration of the nationalization of industries and services. A start has been made with Demba, Sandbach and the Demerara Company, Reynolds, Sprostons, and now Bookers. This is only the beginning and must continue until all industries and services, both foreign and local, including the banks, are owned and managed by the state as custodians of the people.

Nationalization and an extension of the function of the state are important and necessary in the context of the six determinants of the socialist society, as above set out.

It must be pointed out, however, that nationalization is not the end but the means by which state capitalist monopoly can be made to benefit the whole people. It is in the context of the implications of socialism that we must discuss the determinants of the socialist society. This is necessary, since what we must endeavor to do, is not only discuss the determinants, but also their implications for, and effect on those of the working-class as represented by trade unions.

INDIVIDUAL FREEDOM:

Individual freedom implies that every citizen "must have the right to freely express his views as to the attitude, conduct, and efficiency of those entrusted with government and administration. It also implies that the citizen must possess the right to dispense with any government that does not satisfy him and his fellows."

Many arguments have been advanced that socialism is just another word for despotism. It is said that it connotes a one party system of government and thus a dictatorship by the party comprising the government.

How right is this? Is it necessarily so? Marxist ideology speaks of the dictatorship of the proletariat, this implies that the workers in an effort to bring an end to the class system and exploitative capitalism must seize political power and then take control of the means of production. Having done so, they must seek to ensure that the power they now possess is not wrested from their hands. It is advocated that the capitalist, through their agents, would make every effort to regain the power that was once theirs, and that this must be resisted by the workers to the extent of establishing a dictatorship to crush capitalism. Capitalism once defeated must never be permitted to raise its head again.

Marx stated that the working-class led by the urban industrial proletariat has been destined by history to end capitalism and exploitation of man by man. This, he said, would lead to the destruction of the class system and the creation of a new system – socialism.

The workers, however, to ensure that power remain in their hands, must create a political party into whose hands they must entrust the responsibility of Government. This party, acting on behalf of the workers, is charged with the responsibility of ensuring that exploitative capitalism is crushed and destroyed forever.

The party, termed the vanguard party, as to be expected, draws its membership from the working-class i.e. the industrial and service workers plus the rural peasantry. In most socialist parties, the leadership is elected from the membership, by the membership. It is also from the party leadership that the government is elected.

It follows, therefore, that the worker, provided that he is politically militant and realizes the importance of freedom, could ensure his individual freedom by acting in consort with his fellow workers, to ensure that those elected to party leadership are firm believers in democracy and of the highest possible integrity and morality. It is also important that the worker becomes politically involved to the extent that he studies the party's program and policies to determine whether they are in the interest of the whole society. It is also necessary that he uses the available political machinery to influence the party's program and policies. This must be done, by acting together with his fellows.

Freedom is of course relative. In socialist societies there is usually a one party system as there is no compromise on ideology. The individual is free to criticize the attitude, conduct, and efficiency of those entrusted with government and administration but not the system or ideology.

In the context of Guyana, a worker should be free to criticize the performance of the Government, or administration in respect of, say; its policy on worker participation in management in a nationalized industry, but his criticism of the principle of nationalization which is one of ideology would not be countenanced.

The same could be said of co-operatives. Individual citizens should be free to criticize the functioning of co-operatives and their contribution to the society. They may, however, not be permitted to criticize the underlying principle of co-operatives as a counter to private or individual enterprises for personal gain.

A lot has been said of the lack of freedom of speech in socialist states, and this has been advanced as arguments as to why socialism should be rejected by the workers. Those who propagate these arguments are mostly agents of the capitalist exploiters bent on perpetuating a system from which only they, and those who they represent, benefit.

Of what use is freedom of speech to the exploited workers and the thousands of unemployed? Could freedom of speech bring to their tables the much needed food that is denied them? The medical services that is beyond their means? The opportunity for education that is set aside for the privileged few?

In accepting socialism or the socialist ideology, one automatically accepts the destruction of capitalism. It follows that in the transition period when workers are most vulnerable to anti-socialist propaganda, the government and administration cannot permit the type of criticism that has as it underlying motive the defeat of the "revolution."

The question is, why are today's workers vulnerable? The fact is they were part of the exploitative capitalist system. Their education was geared towards equipping them to function within such a system. They were conditioned into accepting that the Creator ordained their lot in life and a penalty for the sins committed, most probably, by their fore-parents. To confiscate private property is stealing; which is sinful. If we do not covet our neighbor's goods, we would enter paradise when we die and enjoy forever the thing we must now do without.

What the socialists seek to do during the transition period, therefore, is to preserve the revolution by protecting the workers against themselves. Criticism must be constructive and not destructive. The ideology is therefore sacrosanct.

To conclude this aspect, freedom in socialist states is relative to the conditions set out above. The individual is free to speak and act provided that what is said and done does not jeopardize the system. This must be considered in the context of the ideological war now being waged, and it is known that in all countries in times of war, no one is permitted to do or say anything directed to cause disruption. Such offences are treasonable.

CONSCIOUS SOCIAL PRODUCTION FOR USE:

In developing societies such as ours, there is always a scarcity of capital. It follows, therefore, that if the use of this limited resource is to benefit the whole people, this could only be done by a centralized agency planning and monitoring its use.

Let us discuss the investment of capital in the much talked about television. The question to be considered here, must be how much needed is television in the society. This will include both transmitting and broadcasting equipment together with receiving sets. Should scarce capital be invested in the production or importation of such equipment, or say, in the expansion of the timber industry so as to make more lumber available for the building industry?

The decision on this issue during the transition period would be made by a centralized agency after determining which investment would benefit the whole society more. Which is more socially useful? Television or houses?

The other question to be asked is, what should be the centralized agency charged with the responsibility of determining what is socially useful? The answer can only be the Cabinet acting on behalf of a Government democratically elected by the people from amongst the people. It cannot be otherwise.

To conclude, therefore, by conscious social production for use, it is meant that the state as represented by the Cabinet, which must be well informed and through the use of the machinery at its disposal, determine the priorities in respect of what is to be produced within the society and how much. Its decision must obviously be based on how useful the commodity would be to the society and who would benefit. Should it be a privileged few or the mass of the people.

Finally, while the state, via the Cabinet would determine the priorities, it must be accepted that their decision should be subjected to criticism by the people. Unless this is so, there would be no democracy.

CONSCIOUS SOCIAL EXCHANGE OF SURPLUS:

It was Karl Marx who first pointed out that profit or surplus value was created solely by the working-class. As he explained, it was in applying labor to the means of production that an additional value, in excess of the cost of production, was created. This excess value was what he termed profit or surplus. He further explained that exploitation takes place when capitalists or the owners of the means of production, appropriate or seize this surplus as further compensation in excess of that for which they were already rewarded or socially entitled.

Marx further argued, that as it was the working-class who created surplus value, it should be utilized in improving the lot of the working-class. He further advocated, that as it was those who owned the means of production to whom the surplus value went, it followed that the workers in an effort to end exploitation should seize control of the means of production and, ipso facto, the state machinery.

By the process of nationalization as witnessed in Guyana, the state takes control of the means of production, thereby appropriating the surplus value from the nationalized industries and used it for the benefit of the whole society. In this instance, it is the state, on behalf of the people, which acquires the means of production.

We have so far been speaking of the surplus value resulting from the exchange of commodities in the market. What is implied here is that the state consciously sets out to exchange the products of the industry or industries, to acquire surpluses, which it could use in improving the lot of the working-class. It must, however, be remembered that in doing so, the state must be, at all times, conscious that to a large extent, the commodities to be exchanged are in most cases, purchased by the workers, and so, the acquiring of a surplus must not be the sole consideration of the administration or managers of the industry.

Surplus, however, also includes that of the agriculture sector. In the context of the Guyana situation the question to be considered is how must the surplus of this sector be treated.

Let us consider the rice industry. What should be done with the resulting surplus after the farmers have extracted that to which they are entitled for their use? Should the surplus be exchanged in the market for the highest price it can fetch, irrespective of whether the majority of the people could afford the price?

Socialism entails that the surplus of every endeavor, must be consciously exchanged so that the society as a whole might benefit. In Guyana the surplus rice is collected by the state with the producers being adequately compensated for their effort. The product is then exchanged in the market at a price that would benefit the whole people. That portion of the surplus not required for local use, is exchanged in the external markets at the most favorable price so that the accruing surplus value could be used to benefit all of the people.

Under this system, the state becomes responsible for the exchange of the surplus and this is to ensure that the resulting surplus value could be used by the state for the benefit of the majority of the people.

The view has been expressed, however, that the surplus value of each industry should be used for the benefit of the workers in that industry. Unless this is done, then exploitation takes place.

How right is this? Let us consider the sugar industry.

If we accept that the surplus value of the sugar industry should be used for the benefit of the worker in the sugar industry alone, it must also follow that the industry would have to finance all of the services it now enjoys. This would include such services as schools, hospitals, roads, water supply, electricity, telephone, security, sea defenses, etc.

No doubt, the industry had been providing some of these services but what of the others. It must be remembered also that no industry can exist in complete isolation of others, for it must maintain links with other industries and service and even communities. Who must pay for the maintenance of these links?

Socialism, therefore, implies that the society must be considered as a whole, and the development of the total society must be centrally planned. Unless this is done, it could well happen that all that would develop is the creation of additional classes within the society and this would defeat one of the primary objectives of socialism. That is, the abolition of the class system.

To conclude this aspect, it is only by pooling the surplus value created by each economic activity, that we would best be able to efficiently plan and spend the surplus value so as to benefit the whole society.

Again, only the state could efficiently perform this function.

CONSCIOUS SOCIAL CONTROL OF DISTRIBUTION:

What should be the yardstick for determining how the product of society should be distributed? Must it be regulated by the concept of the market economy i.e. primarily on the ability of the person to purchase same, at the price to be determined by supply and demand?

The question, to be considered, is how are we to ensure that some within the society would not live at starvation level while others have much more than they need.

The answer is obviously a conscious social control of distribution. This would ensure that all who contribute to the creation of the national product enjoy a share in proportion to their contribution.

In socialist countries, the distribution of the national product is the responsibility of the state. It is the state's responsibility to ensure that all within the society benefit from what is produced within the society, and that those who are responsible for the distribution, are answerable to the society.

In discussing conscious social production for use, it was pointed out that it was the state's responsibility to ensure that what was needed by the whole society was produced in sufficient numbers to satisfy the whole society. It therefore follows, that it is obligatory that the state ensures that what is produced reaches all the people and at a price that is constant throughout the society.

There must be times, however, when what is produced cannot satisfy the total need of the whole society. It is at times like these when the state must ensure that what is produced is equitably distributed. Equitable must be relative, of course, to both need and contribution.

In capitalist or free enterprise societies, distribution is primarily the responsibility of what is termed the middleman. It is the middleman who receives the product of the producers, and distributes it to the consumers. For this, the middleman is compensated since he performs a service.

This system has resulted in many deficiencies as it encourages manipulation of the market by the distributors. This manipulation creates such things as artificial shortages designed to raise prices so as to gain maximum profit. It has also been responsible for such things as hoarding and black-marketing.

Distribution in socialist societies is, however, not solely confined to consumer goods, but includes such services as education, health, transportation, security, etc.

Let us consider education. What should be the yardstick for determining who should benefit from, or enjoy the scarce facility of higher education?

In socialist societies, who should benefit from higher learning is determined by those who can best benefit from the higher learning. The decision would be unlike that in capitalist societies where opportunity is dependent on one's ability to pay for the service and, further, where the choice of the discipline to be pursued is left to one's choosing.

In most societies, facilities do not exist, nor is it necessary, for all persons to enjoy the benefit of higher learning and this includes all socialist societies. It follows, therefore, that if efficient use is to be made of the service, this can only be done if those who enjoy the facility are those who can best benefit from the service. The proviso must exist, however, that those who enjoy the facility should be those who would later be best abled to contribute back to the society at acceptable levels in keeping with their acquired discipline.

This is how services such as education is distributed in a socialist state. It must also be mentioned that in order to avoid wastage, the discipline to be pursued would depend on NEED, both present and future. If there were greater need, say, for surgeons than engineers, more concentration would be made in the field of surgery than engineering.

In the context of the Guyana situation, it should be expected that the state would endeavor to ensure that the consumer goods produced within the society or imported from without, are distributed within the society at a price, and in such numbers, that the needs of the whole society could be satisfied. However, it should also be expected that the state would ensure that in times of shortages, equity exists in the distribution of consumer goods.

It is also to be expected that in the distribution of services, the state would ensure that it is done, not only in a manner to benefit the whole society, but also in such a manner that the highest possible level of efficiency is maintained.

In the distribution of goods and services, it must be expected, that the basic tenets of socialism – "each according to his ability, each according to his contribution," would be adhered to. This should be the responsibility of the state and for this, the government and the administration must be answerable to the people.

CONSCIOUS SOCIAL APPORTIONING OF DUTIES:

One of the claims of the advocates of socialism is that it is more efficient than capitalism or the free enterprise system. They claim that this greater efficiency is achieved by the most efficient use of human resources.

In socialist states, planning is executed to ensure that all of the needs for human resources within the society are satisfied. It follows that if planning is done to secure an adequate supply of skills and other expertise, it is in the interest of the state to ensue that efficient use is made of the available skills, etc.

In socialist states, therefore, there is conscious social apportioning of duties to ensure that there are no "square pegs in round holes," or that skilled labor is not lying idle while there is need for the relevant skills elsewhere In the society. It is also the state's responsibility to ensure that in those areas where there are shortages of skills, this limited resource is utilized in those occupations where they can best contribute to the society.

The above must be considered in the light that all education and training in socialist states are free to the individual, so when we speak of apportioning of duties, it means that society would demand, of the individual, that he or she contributes back to the society in such fields as he or she is qualified, and at levels in keeping with their abilities and the accepted norms.

What is implied by the above, is that the skills possessed by the individual were made possible or supplied by the society, and as such, the society must have first claim upon the skills.

The critics of socialism in discussing these aspects, advance the view that the individual is owned by the state, for it is the state that demands that the potential worker does work; that he works where the state demands that he works; and at what pace. This they say is nothing short of slavery.

How right is this? It must be remembered that the state is only the agent of the society of which the worker is a part. It follows therefore, that if the worker is a slave, he is in truth a slave of the society, so that all within the society are slaves of the society, i.e. slaves of themselves. It must also be remembered, that the work performed by the individual, benefits no one person or group of persons more than others. It benefits the society and the society is the employer.

It can only be accepted, therefore, that any suggestion that workers are slaves within socialist societies is fictitious and designed as propaganda directed to cause confusion and destroy what is termed the revolution. Such must be rejected.

Discussion, however, on the apportioning of duties would be incomplete unless we also discuss how the worker would be rewarded for the duties he performs at a level in keeping with his ability.

As was already said, one of the basic tenets of socialism is – "each according to his contribution." The question to be answered, therefore, is - how do we price the level of contribution? In other words, how could we ensure that the total national wage package is equitably distributed?

In socialist states, there is usually a fixed differential between the highest and the lowest wage or salary paid within the society. This ensures that great disparity does not exist to the extent that one person, as a result of his high wage or salary, has excessive claim on the goods produced by the society.

In the Soviet Union the wage differential is as low as 1: 2.5 or 3 while in Cuba it is said to be as low as 1: 3.2. This means that in Cuba, if a worker in the lowest paid job were in receipt of a remuneration of $100.00 per month, the highest paid job would be remunerated at $320.00 per month.

The next question to be discussed is how are the several jobs rated one to the other? This is usually done by a job evaluation exercise similar to that conducted in the Public Service. With the low spread between the highest and the lowest wage, it follows that unlike the public service, it is then possible to have fewer pay bands, and in Cuba it is reported to be just eight.

Each job is therefore evaluated in respect of job content and rated one to the other, and dependent on the rated value, which is usually determined on a points system, the job is placed in the appropriate pay band.

It must be pointed out, however, that additional premiums are at times added to the job rate, to compensate for unfavorable job conditions such as dirt, heat and locality. By locality is meant, areas far removed from the economic and cultural centers, and also, as in the Soviet Union, areas far north and subjected to long winter seasons.

It has already been stated that jobs are rewarded on the basis of the level of contribution. This means that the actual pay for the job is dependent on ones production, as most jobs are on the piece-rate system. By this method it is common to find skilled craftsmen working for more wages/salaries than graduates.

Coupled with the system as explained above, is the opportunity afforded the individual for vertical mobility? Training is an integral part of the system, so the individual by personal application can qualify for a better paying job in keeping with any additional skill acquired. It must also be noted, that in all socialist, societies unemployment has long since been abolished.

Reward in socialist societies is therefore dependent on contribution and what is of equal importance, the value of the job to society. All of this is done with the underlying principle of ensuring that wage income is equitably distributed between members of the society.

To conclude this aspect, it is in the context of the above that duties are apportioned within the society. It should be easy to see that the system endeavors to control the drift after higher wages, which, as in capitalist societies means greater privileges at the expense of greater efficiency. Socialist societies seek to ensure that every citizen contributes to the society in keeping with his ability and in the areas where he can best contribute. It is only by doing this that maximum efficiency could be guaranteed.

CONSCIOUS SOCIAL DEVELOPMENT OF THE FULL POTENTIAL OF THE CITIZEN:

Man is a social animal possessing many social attributes. No consideration could be extended to the full development of the citizen, unless some consideration is given to the culture of the society and the part the citizen must play in its preservation and development.

In the context of the working class, especially in the context of Guyana, the worker was a mere tool to be used in the production of goods and services, and as such, no conscious effort was made to preserve his culture much less his development. Any effort made in this direction, was to serve the interests of the exploiters, by using culture as a means of dividing the people, since it was part and parcel of the class system.

In all socialist societies, the development of art and culture moves hand in hand with economic development, since the society is people oriented. Every factory or economic grouping has its cultural program and the funds of the industry or service is used to finance the program.

Coupled with cultural pursuits, is a program for recreation and sport. Great emphasis is placed in these areas and again the facilities and programs are financed entirely by industry and service organizations.

All socialist societies are proud of their achievement in the fields of art, culture, and sports, and rightly so. Guyana has been fortunate in witnessing the achievements of the Cubans and the Chinese in those areas, and their undoubted high standards were only achieved because culture and sport is an integral part of the development in their respective countries.

The full development of the potential of the citizen therefore is one of the primary objectives of socialist development. To achieve this, funds must be provided for pursuits in the field of culture and sport, and this is the responsibility of the state out of the national income.

In many socialist states, funds are made available for these activities to the trade union. It is the responsibility of the trade union, therefore, to plan and execute the program for the cultural development of the worker.

GENERAL CONCLUSION:

In accepting socialism, we seek to bring an end to the exploitation of man by man. No one person or group of persons should compel another person or group of persons to submit to exploitation for personal gain. "Only society as a whole should have the right to impose compulsory duties on anyone and this must be done by the accredited agent of society – the state. The relationship of man to man within the state should be one of free contract based on respect for the dignity of man, with no irresistible pressure on either side, except the laws of society itself."

Guyana is now in the transition period towards socialism, and changes unprecedented in our history would be taking place. Trade Unions which were in the fore-front of those waging the war against imperialism, must realize that they have only just achieved a mere victory here at home, for the war is far from won. On many fronts without the country, the war continues.

Again, trade unions were, also, once considered instruments of conflict and abuse – fighting the boss. If the changes in society are directed towards the achievement of the socialist objectives as spelt out in the determinants earlier discussed, a decision must be made as to where the trade union movement stands in the thrust.

As I see it, the role of the Trade Union can be nothing other than positive, for the achievement of the objectives, as stated, are all in the interest of the working class. Further, it is only a militant trade union movement that can guarantee for the worker, that the sacrifices he makes, is not met with failure.

In other words, the trade union movement has a stake in the success of the revolution, and it is in this context that we will discuss the role of the Branch, the Branch Officer and the Shop Steward in the changing society.

TRADE UNIONS AND LIVING STANDARDS
July 1983

INTRODUCTION

The definition of a trade union offered by the International Confederation of free Trade Unions reads as follows:

"A trade union is a continuing, permanent and democratic organization voluntarily by the workers to protect them at their work, to improve the conditions of their work through collective bargaining, to seek to better the conditions of their lives, and to provide a means of expression for the workers' views on problems of society."

It is important for us to carefully observe this definition, for it is necessary that we look at our union and see whether it is measuring up to what this international organization of which we are a part, due to our affiliation to the Guyana Trade Union Congress, considers to be a Trade Union.

It is my contention that our Union – The Guyana Public Service Union, conforms generally to the definition, but I am sure you will all agree with me that while we measure up in some extent to the definition, there is much more we can do as a Union to satisfy that part of the definition that speaks of improving the conditions of work of our members and also bettering the conditions of their lives.

Here, we are speaking of the living standards of our members, and again, I am sure you will agree with me that the living standards of our members are far from satisfactory, for as we all know, our living standards are falling.

Another definition that I sometimes use in classrooms such as this, lists the objectives of Trade Unions, and among them are:

1. "Maintaining and improving the salary, wages and conditions of service of its members by the process of collective bargaining."
2. "Seeking to satisfy the social needs of its members…………."
3. "Contributing to the satisfaction of the needs of the society as a whole and the achievement of the objectives of the nation…………………."

Again the objectives embrace the living standards of workers, and in relation to our Union, the living standards of the members of the Guyana Public Service Union.

It follows, therefore, that living standards must be the concern of Unions, and as I have already said, living standards are falling. What, however, do we mean by this?

WHAT WE MEAN BY LIVING STANDARDS

Let us look at the position of the Public Servant since 1973, when by a job evaluation exercise, a salary and wage structure was established.

An officer in January of 1973 on the A9 Salary Scale would have been in receipt of $184.00 per month, (minimum of scale). The minimum of the said scale at January 1983 was $316.30 representing an increase of $132.30 or 72% (approx.)

This shows a significant increase over the ten-year period, but if we are to determine what is the real position of the workers, we must take into consideration what was happening to consumer prices over the said period. Consumer prices, being the prices that workers must pay for the things they must buy so as to live. These include food, clothing, housing, household goods, recreation, transportation, etc.

The figures published by the Bank of Guyana, show that between 1973 and June 1982, the Consumer Price Index increased by approximately 237% and it is safe to say that by January 1983 the increase was about 250%. (The actual increase was 278%).

It therefore follows, that while salaries increased by 72%, the cost of living had increased by 250%, so that the worker was worse off than he was in 1973. This is by comparing an officer at the minimum of the A9 Salary Scale in 1973 with an officer at the minimum of the same A9 Salary Scale in 1983. It is of interest to note that if an officer on the minimum of the A9 Salary Scale were to live at the same level as his counterpart in 1973, he would require a salary of $644.00 per month.

But what is the position of an officer who had received his/her increments for 1974, 1975 and 1976. That is prior to the Minimum Wage Agreement at 1977. Such an officer in 1983 would be earning $322.19 if he were not promoted to a higher pay band during the ten-year period. For such an officer, his salary would have increased by 75% over the period. It follows therefore, that he or she would have been no better off; at least significantly, due to his increments.

The above example shows one of the major problems in the public service today, for there are many officers in employment prior to 1973 who are today earning just a few dollars more than those employed after January 1982.

To express what we have been discussing in the language of the economists and statisticians, the real value of the $184.00 in 1973 was $161.64 while the real value of the $316.30 (1983) is now approximately $83.41. What this means is that the living standard of the worker on the

A9 salary scale has deteriorated seriously, and this must be the concern of every trade union, and I can assure you that it is the concern of your Union, the Guyana Public Service Union.

A word, however, of what we mean by real wages. Real wages refer to what the money we earn can now purchase, relative to what it could have purchased at some fixed time in the past. Let us look at the example discussed above. When we say that the real value of the $184.00 in 1973 was $161.64, what we mean is that relative to 1970 when a new consumer price index was introduced, $184.00 would have purchased in goods and services, no more than what $161.64 could have purchased in 1970. It mean that while we had more money in 1973 ($184.00), we would not have been able to purchase more goods than what we would have been able to purchase in 1970 with $161.64. This means that our wages have been inflated. Think of a balloon. We can inflate it to any size but it is the same balloon.

Continuing with our example, when we say that the real value of $184.41 in 1973 was $161.64 and the real value of $316.30 in 1983 was only $83.41, it means that with $184.00 in 1973 we could have purchased a certain quantity of goods, say groceries in a supermarket, but in 1983 with $316.00 in our packets, we would only be able to purchase half the amount of goods we purchased in 1973. As it is said, the dollar had shrunk.

Trade Union Leaders, like myself, are, therefore, not interested in the amount of paper money our members receive every month, but more with what that paper money can buy. This is why we monitor the Consumer Price Index (CPI) and also take a check on the movement of prices in our markets, stores and shops.

There is no doubt that living standards are falling, and our Unions are seriously concerned over the problems with which our members are confronted. We are, however, much more concerned over what is responsible for the decline in living standards and what the Unions can do to halt the decline or bring it to manageable proportions.

WHY A DECLINE IN LIVING SRANDARDS

It is said in Governmental circles, that the decline in real wages is the result of the World Economic Situation that is slowly passing the crisis state. Inflation in the Western democracies, and a slackening of World Trade, have forced many countries to institute measures that have had serious repercussions in the developing countries, which for some time now have ceased developing. Leaders of the developing countries, i.e. countries of the Third World, are all in agreement that what is needed is a new world economic order.

There is no doubt that there is a crisis and that there is need for a new economic order, which would assist in lessening the gap between the haves and the have-nots of this world. World poverty is on the increase, especially in the developing countries and the developed world must realize that they have a moral responsibility to the millions who are starving. A senseless arms race among the super powers consumes billions of dollars that could be used to bring an end to poverty throughout the world.

Here in Guyana, the effects of the economic crisis is witnessed by our inability to get our Bauxite sold in a World Market that is both competitive and discriminatory, as witnessed by the concession granted the Jamaican Bauxite industry as opposed to ours due to the change in administration of the leftist Manley Administration to that of the rightist Seaga Administration. This argument is further supported by the purchase of the Jamaican bauxite by the United States government for its stockpile.

Our sugar is also sold in a very competitive market, and added to this, subsidies offered by the European Community to beet sugar producers in their countries, have brought down the world price of sugar below our cost of production, due to overproduction in the European Community.

Further to this, our rice industry is plagued with many problems that restrict our output. Spare parts for mechanical equipment are difficult to acquire, resulting in sizeable acreages being left unploughed, and coupled with this, it is the view of the farmers that they are not getting adequate returns on their investment. This has resulted in 16,000 families leaving the industry between 1965 – 1980 as claimed by the Rice Producers Association.

Sugar, bauxite and rice are our major foreign exchange earners, and shortfalls in these industries must affect our ability to earn the foreign exchange to import the things needed within the country, and which we do not produce ourselves.

It must be understood, that the things we purchase overseas must be paid for in currency (money) acceptable to the country in which the purchases are made, and more often than not, that is the American or Canadian dollar, the British pound, the Japanese yen or the German mark. It is by selling to those countries that we acquire the currency (foreign exchange) needed to purchase the things that we need from overseas.

This is easily understood when we look at what is taking place in our own country, in respect of the American dollar. Traders are buying the currency on the black market at six to one and at times more, since the American dollar is accepted in all of the countries in which they make their purchases. Those countries will not accept our Guyana currency. So the demand for the American dollar has pushed up its value in the parallel market, presenting serious problems for the economy. (In 1983, the official exchange rate was US$ 1.00 to G$3.00.)

The question is, what can our trade unions do to provide solutions to these problems. As I see it, the problem of a new economic order is something that our political leaders will have to battle for in the many world forums at which they are represented. The Third World, as a group, must let its voice be heard, and trading within the group must be encouraged and developed. Exchange of Technology within the group is also vitally necessary, but it must be understood that we must convince the developed world, that if world peace is to be assured, a more equitable distribution of the wealth of the world is necessary, and further, they must make a contribution to the improvement of living standards of the countries of the Third and Fourth Worlds. This is in their own self-interest.

This does not mean that our Unions must remain silent and leave everything to the political leaders. The voice of our Trade Union Leaders must resound in the several international forums at which they are also represented, articulating the views of the Third World of which they are a part. We must use every opportunity to convince our trade union brothers in the developed world, of the justness of our cause and get them to lobby support in their countries on our behalf.

It is not going to be very easy, for the workers of the developed world have their own problems. Unemployment and inflation are causing many Unions to give up negotiated benefits and, as is said, charity begins at home. It is for us, however, to convince them that their future development is dependent on an economically strong and stable developing Third World.

The question that must be answered, however, is whether falling living standards are due entirely to the world economic crisis. It is my opinion that while the world economic crisis has contributed to the problem, there are other local factors that also contributed.

Let us look again at the consumer price index. As was said, the C.P.I. rose by about 250% between 1973 and 1983, but what is of interest, is the comparison of the movement in the C.P.I. of Guyana with that of other Caribbean countries between March 1981 – June 1982.

Country	Movement in Index	% Increase
Guyana	205 – 264	28.8
Jamaica	209 – 323	8.8
Trinidad	202 – 232	14.9
Barbados	184 – 212	15.2

Source: Bank of Guyana

The above shows the movement in the C.P.I. for the countries listed between March 1981 – June 1982 and it would be observed that Guyana had the highest percentage increase of all the countries (28.8%).

The above must be the concern of Trade Unions, for Guyana's increase is almost double that of the next highest which is Barbados with an increase of 15.2%.

The problem does not end there, for if we look at the comparative figures for 1973 to 1980 a different picture emerges and set out below are the movements in the indices of the said countries for 1973 – 1980.

Country	Movement in Index	% Increase
Guyana	79 – 183	131.6
Jamaica	69 –270	291.3
Trinidad	71 –184	159.2
Barbados	60 – 167	178.3

Source: Bank of Guyana

As can be seen, Guyana had the lowest percentage increase over the period shown. Of interest, though, is the movement in the Jamaica index, for while it recorded the highest percent increase between 1973 – 1980, it had the lowest increase for the period March 1981 – June 1982.

It is obvious that something has gone wrong in Guyana since 1980, for prices, as we all know, have skyrocketed to the level that the pay packet of the worker is under siege.

It is obvious that our problem is not solely imported inflation, which would mean that the astronomical rise between 1981 March to 1982 June was due to increased prices of things we import, for it is widely known that Guyana does not import at the levels to the other countries mentioned.

The answer must be that consumer goods sold in our local supermarkets, shops and stores carry excessive mark-ups, and coupled with this, services that we must pay for, such as electricity and transportation, are all exorbitant in price.

It is my contention that trade Unions have a responsibility to vigorously represent these issues to the Government, to either bring down the costs of consumer goods to reasonable levels, or militantly pursue their demands for a living wage for their members.

The cry of the political directorate is one for sacrifice. It is said that we must make sacrifices now for better living standards in the future. This is as it should be, but as a Trade Unionist, I contend that sacrifices must be reasonable, for as I always advocate – Everyone is entitled to the best possible living standard in his or her lifetime.

This does not say that sacrifice must not be made, but as I said, it must be reasonable. As a Trade Unionist, I reject the view of those Third World politicians who advocate the concept of the sacrifice generation.

Here in Guyana, we have failed in our efforts to unleash the full productive capacity of our workforce, for we have frustrated them by placing burden after burden on their backs in our call for greater and yet greater sacrifice. To add to the frustration, we have also failed in convincing our workforce that the sacrifices they are being called upon to make, will lead to a better life in the future. Our problem is that our work force when they look into the future, they see nothing.

This is our problem – our major problem. Our workforce lacks motivation, and nothing is being done to induce the motivation, for it would appear that the managers of our economy are of the view that they can achieve their objective by use of the whip.

Dismissals and the treats of dismissal, they seem to believe, are the means by which we can get our workforce to produce at the level desired. This has failed, as it has only added to the frustration. It is time that we take a serious assessment of our performance and work out new strategies aimed at getting our people to really get down to the job of producing and producing more efficiently.

It is accepted that living standards depend on the production levels of a society, and Trade Unions must therefore show a keen interest in the growth of our society. By this we mean that Trade Unions, apart from monitoring the consumer Price Index, must also monitor the performance of the economy as shown in the national income accounts published by Government.

What does our national income reveal? For a total investment of 2733.7 million dollars between1970 –1980 our gross domestic product increased by 856.8 million dollars, a multiplier of 0.3. This must be considered a most unfavorable performance and the managers of our economy should spend some time explaining to the people why this was so. Is it that our developmental strategy was badly conceived?

It may be argued, however, that a period of adjustment is necessary, so it may be a bit too early to assess our performance, for should we look at the performance between 1965 – 1975 the picture is somewhat better, for an investment of 1399 million dollars (1965 – 1975) only resulted in an increase in G.D.P. of 1011 million dollars by 1980 a multiplier of 0.7.

Economists speak of the multiplying effect of developmental investment, and I am sure that no one will claim that, here in Guyana, our efforts could be commended. There has obviously been bad strategy or serious leaks in our economy.

This must be the concern of our Trade Unions, including our Union, the Guyana Public Service Union, for as I have said, living standards depend on production and if our economy is not expanding, salaries and wages cannot expand unless inflation is encouraged, as seems to have been the case. What has happened, is that our workers have been given more and more paper money which can buy less and less goods.

SOME SOLUTIONS

So far, we have been looking at the problem, it is now time that we look at possible solutions.

The World economic crisis is not going to end as early as we would like to expect, although signs are appearing in the developed Western economies that offer some hope of an upturn. What we also know is that a new economic order is a far way from being realized.

It is in the context of this that we must plan our strategy, and the Government's program or policy-thrust for survival, is not something that can be faulted. We must produce more.

The question is – How are we to get our people to increase output in all areas of activity. This calls for a united effort of all the people, which, can only be achieved when we have removed the things that tend to divide us as a people. Our number one obstacle is politics and the time has come when within our Unions, we must downplay things political.

It is for our Union Leaders to recognize that their first consideration must be their members and their well-being. Further, they must recognize that the Trade Union Movement has a vital role to play in the development of our society, but for the movement to effectively enact its role, trade Union unity must be assured and pursued. However, not at the expense of the living standards of our members, I must add.

It is for us, the Leaders at every level, to convince ourselves that we have a country with great potential and capable of providing for its people a decent standard of living. It is also for us to convince our members, that our dreams for this country can be made a reality within the lifetime of most of them. But what is of greatest importance, they must have the conviction that they have a Trade Union movement capable of guaranteeing for them, that they will reap the benefits of their labor.

I have said that we must downplay things political, and this needs some development.

I earlier spoke of the context in which we must pursue our policy thrust for survival, and I mentioned that:

1. The world economic crisis in not going to end as early as we would like.
2. The new world economic order is a far way from being realized.
3. The Peoples' National Congress, as a Government, will be there for long time to come and there in nothing that can be done to change that fact, and further, the PNC has no intention of sharing political power with any other group regardless of the consequences.

The above are "givens" to the Economic, Political and Industrial Relations Systems, and it is within these three contexts that the Trade Union Movement must operate.

What does this mean for the Movement? First we must pursue our own goals and leave politicking to those whose business it is, conscious at all times that our primary responsibility is to our members.

Now to get back to the subject of increased production. As I have said, the Trade Unions have a vital role to play. Ours is the task of mobilizing our members toward this effort, but it must be realized that the Trade Union by itself cannot create the motivations needed, and management must contribute towards the creation of an industrial climate that lends itself toward greater production and productivity.

This speaks of the participative approach to management, and I must early make the point, that if we are to bring about an upturn in our economy, concerted effort by management, union and government is needed. No one group can do it alone, and any effort by management and government alone, with the exclusion of the unions, must necessarily meet with failure.

There is a strange twist to our situation. It is my view that the political directorate has done everything to curtail the influence of the Unions and weaken their militancy, somehow sharing the view, that fewer strikes and lesser militancy will create a better productive climate.

Trade Union influence among its members has no doubt waned over the past ten years, for militancy, except from among a few die-hards, is practically non-existent, and a look at the records of industrial action, will no doubt reveal that apart from the sugar industry, strikes are on the decline.

The twist, however, is that while we have been having fewer man-days lost as a result of strikes, productivity has been on the decline over the past ten years. Workers seem to have lost the will to work and, as has already been said, there is acute frustration among the workers of our country, and the public service is no exception.

The fact is that while the workers are disenchanted with their unions and their leadership, they still expect the Unions to take them safely through this crisis, and until such time that Trade Union members can see their Unions, as organizations capable of protecting them at their work, improving the conditions of their work, and bettering the conditions of their lives, the frustration will never end and we will continue to wonder why we cannot raise the levels of production and productivity in our country.

Given the condition as exists, it must be realized that productivity is a function of worker-satisfaction and that satisfaction embodies satisfaction with his Union. So long as we overlook this, increased production and productivity will continue to be an illusive dream.

What we need here in Guyana, as I have mentioned, is the participative approach to management to deal with the problem of falling levels of productivity. In every area of activity within the work enterprise, we must endeavor to become innovators. Our workers must at all times be looking at their jobs to see what they can do in increase output or performance, conscious of the fact that their additional effort will bring, not only greater remuneration, but better social benefits, such as housing, education, health and recreation. They must have this belief, and the belief can only be shared, if they know they have a trade union looking after their interests.

It is not my intention to offer a model of worker participation, but to stress the point, that if we are to tackle the problem of increased production and productivity, it must be a tripartite effort.

The point has been made that improved living standards can only come out of greater production and productivity, so it must be the concern of Trade Unions to ensure that there is growth in the economy, capable of affording the higher living standards, or if not, capable of maintaining existing standards.

As leaders within the movement, ours is the task of mobilizing our members towards this effort. We must take the initiative as management seems unwilling to act and the political directorate has misguidedly adopted the attitude of coercion. As I have said before, dismissals and threats of dismissals seem to be their solution to the problem.

There is a problem, nonetheless, but it is for us to motivate our members and this can only be by strengthening the Unions and here in the Guyana Public Service Union, this must be our goal.

There is need to increase the productivity of workers in the public service. It is my view that with a little effort we can raise productivity by al least 5% and a planned approach by Managers and Union Leaders can carry this to at least 10%.

Union leaders must let their voices be heard. Our members are crying out for a better life. We must convince management and Government that there is need for action.

To conclude, what we must now do at this stage, is to "provide a means of expression for the workers' views on problems of society," and the problem of falling living standards is our greatest challenge. I can only hope that you, the second tier leadership will seriously get down to the task for which you were elected, and again I refer to that definition of the Trade Union advanced by the I.C.F.T.U. Read it , study it and act upon it.

THE SCOPE OF COLLECTIVE BARGAINING IN CENTRAL PLANNING
1985

INTRODUCTION

Every society is concerned with the creation of wealth, and how the wealth that is created, is distributed.

The major differences between societies, however, centers on how the wealth is created and by whom; and also, who benefits from the created wealth.

Under capitalism, the creation of wealth that results from investment is the result of entrepreneurship. Men and women with ideas about how investing money in new enterprises, can earn them wealth. The capitalist theory advances that when each entrepreneur strives to create wealth, the best interest of the whole society is served. This is what Adam Smith termed the invisible hand in his book, *The Wealth of Nations*.

As Adam Smith said:

"By preferring the support of domestic to that of foreign

industry, he intends only his own security; and by directing that industry in such a manner as its produce may be of greatest value, he intends his own gain, and he is in this, as in many other cases, led by an invisible hand to promote an end which was no part of his intention. By pursuing his own interest, he frequently promotes that of the society more effectually than when he really intends to promote it."

In supporting Smith's theory, J.A.C. Brown in his Social Psychology of Industry spoke of - "the rabble hypothesis of the true nature of man – i.e., it is assumed that competition leads to maximum efficiency, that when each man fights for himself the best interests of the group are served ...."

Socialism, on the other hand, advocates that capitalism is exploitive, and as a natural consequence, encourages poverty. Unemployment, says the socialists, is an offshoot of capitalism, as the strong exploits the weak. Labor, they say, is treated as no more than another commodity used in the production process.

Socialism and central planning of the economy, it is advocated, eradicates unemployment and exploitation, and so man becomes glorified, as he is now the focal point of the developmental process. Central planning of the economy, to my mind, calls for the determination of:

1. The economic goals to be achieved by the society
2. The establishing of the goals in order of priority
3. The allocation of the goal achievement and
4. The setting up of the co-operating agencies, and the review or evaluation mechanisms.

Central planning also implies that the planned efforts must result in predetermined achievements (wealth creation), and finally, what is of greatest importance, how the created wealth is to be distributed; that is – what must be diverted towards investments to create future wealth, then who gets what, and in what proportion, from what remains.

For the purpose of this paper, I am assuming that it is Guyana's intention to create a socialist state, and that the structures already exist for the implementation of a planned economy. It is not the objective of my presentation, however, to discuss which of the two social systems mentioned, would be more advantageous to the workers we represent, but to state, en passant, that I have always considered Arthur Lewis's comment, in his *"Theory of Economic Growth"*, that what is important, is not who owns the means of production, but more so, how efficient they are utilized, and who benefits from the product produced. This I will later develop.

It is necessary, none-the-less, for me to mention what are the things that I will expect to find in a socialist state, as this will determine the environment in which bargaining will take place, and which is so vital to the bargaining process. They are:

1. Individual freedom
2. Conscious social production for use
3. Conscious social exchange of surplus
4. Conscious social control of distribution
5. Conscious social apportioning of duties, and
6. Conscious social development of the full potential of the citizen

It is not my intention to discuss what I have termed the six determinants of the socialist state as set out above, as this was done in a previous paper titled – **"The role of the Branch, Branch Officers and Shop Stewards in the Changing Society"**. The paper was presented to a two-week seminar sponsored by the Critchlow Labor College in 1976 and copies are available in the College's library as reference.

What is important, however, is that it is recognized that Guyana is supposedly in the transition stage of its movement from one social order to another, and what takes place during this period must eventually influence the kind of society that will result, and no doubt, the mechanisms that may be developed for determining the salary, wages, hours and the other terms and conditions of service of our members.

TRADITIONAL COLLECTIVE BARGAINING

Collective Bargaining is the system fought for and won by trade unions as a mechanism for determining the salary, wages, hours and other terms and conditions of service of the workers, they represent.

It is to be noted, that the mechanism was not foisted on the workers. The workers in an effort to democratize industry demanded that they have a say in the rule making process of the enterprises in which they worked. The workers of England won the initial victory in 1859 when by the legislative process, collective bargaining was deemed to be legal.

Here in Guyana, it was in 1917 when the Chamber of Commerce as the representative of employers, first agreed to meet with representatives of the workers to discuss wages and hours of work. This was the first effort at Collective Bargaining, and though primitive, resulted in some gains to the workers at that time. Over the years, the process has developed into what we know of today.

The question is – What is Collective Bargaining? This I have described as the process whereby management meets with representatives of the workers (trade unions), to negotiate an agreement which will set out the salary, wages, hours, and the other terms and conditions of service which will be operable in the particular enterprise. The process also includes the negotiation of another agreement that will define the procedures to be used in settling disputes that may arise over violations of the agreement by either party or the interpretation of the intent of any clause or clauses that may be in dispute between the two parties.

The above definition seeks to capture, not only what some people describe as the mechanism for establishing the substantive rules as applied to industrial relations i.e. salary, wages, hours, etc., but also some of the procedural rules. That is, those that outline the procedures for not only making the rules, but establishing a kind of judicial system for ensuring that once the rules are made, the mechanism exists for enforcing them. An important set of the procedural rules are those embodied in the Grievance Procedure or what is also termed, The Agreement for the Avoidance and Settlement of Disputes.

It is important, that we look at two other definitions of Collective Bargaining since the ideology of our industrial relations system seems to be shifting from one of voluntarism, as exists in Britain, to that of legalism, as exists in the United States of America.

Voluntarism is characterized by a system in which there is little or no intervention by the courts of Law in the relationship between the two principal parties to industrial relations i.e. the Management of the Enterprise on the one hand, and the workers as represented by their trade unions on the other.

Under the voluntary kind of relationship, the two parties see the relationship between them as private, and the trade unions have always endeavored to keep it that way, as they had little confidence in the Courts of Law in matters of an industrial relations nature.

This was borne out in a thought provoking admission by Lord Justice Scrutton of th British High Courts in 1920 when he said:

"The habits you are trained in, the people with whom you mix, lead to your having a certain class of ideas, you do not give as sound and accurate judgments as you would wish. This is one of the great difficulties at present with labor. Labor says "Where are your impartial Judges? They all move in the same circle as the employers, and they are all educated and nursed in the same ideas as the employers. How can a labor man or trade unionist get impartial justice? It is very difficult sometimes to be sure that you have put yourself into a thoroughly impartial position between two disputants, one of your own class and one not of your class."

Lord Justice Scrutton's admission is important to our trade union movement at this time when the main employer is the state. The question we must ask as trade unionists, is with whom do our Judges associate? Is it with those who administer the state apparatus, or with the laboring man? We can also extend the question to include the managers of our Public Corporations and Companies.

These answers are important, for the Labor Amendment Act No. 9 of 1984 has changed the entire Collective Bargaining scenario, and as our I.R.S. becomes more legalistic, the more we may have to use the courts to settle our disputes.

Before concluding this aspect, the words of Winston Churchill directed to the House of Commons become so relevant to our situation.

As Churchill said –

"It is not good for trade unions that they should be brought in contact with the courts, and it is not good for the courts. The courts hold justly a high and, I think, unequalled prominence in the respect of the world in criminal cases, and civil cases between man and man, no doubt, they deserve and command the respect and admiration of all classes in the community, but where class issues are involved, it is impossible to pretend that the courts command the same degree of general confidence. On the contrary, they do not, and a very considerable number of our population has been led to the opinion that they are, unconsciously no doubt biased".

The other definitions of Collective Bargaining that I mentioned earlier, is one advanced by the Taft-Hartley Act of the U.S.A. and this states that Collective Bargaining is:

"The performance of the mutual obligation of the employer and representatives of the employees to meet at reasonable times and confer in good faith with respect to wages, hours, and other terms and conditions of employment, or the negotiation of an agreement, or any question arising there-under, and the execution of a written contract incorporating any agreement reached if requested by either party, but such obligation does not compel either party to agree to a proposal or require the making of any concession."

The last clause of the above definition is important, for somehow, I got the impression at the last Government/TUC negotiations, that some of our leaders thought that we had an obligation to reach agreement with Government, regardless of its implications for those whom we represent. What was my impression also, was that it seemed to have been the view of some of the TUC negotiators, that limits could be placed on the negotiating time span and further, once the time limits expired, the Union was obliged to accept the offer of the employer.

As I see it, so long as both parties are acting in good faith while in pursuit of their objective, there should be no cause for concern over the time span, as it is dangerous for any union to reach an agreement that may result in disillusionment among its membership, since it tends to weaken the union and threatens its continuance as the bargaining agent for the workers. It is recognized, nonetheless, that in the Guyana context at this time, it can be very difficult for some workers to change bargaining agents, but whenever such a situation exists, morale is affected and it impacts negatively on productivity.

The other definition to which I would like to direct attention, does not deal with collective bargaining, but collective agreements and this is set out In the Labor (Amendment) Act of 1984. It is this Act that gives the TUC the legal authority to bargain on behalf of public sector workers, and which legalizes central bargaining which is the subject matter of this discourse.

I have thought it necessary, none-the-less, to give an over-view of Collective Bargaining generally, as I consider it relevant to the subject we will discuss. This is so, as the term Collective Bargaining implies certain things, and unless as a movement, we have some common ideas as to what we mean by Collective Bargaining, there is bound to be confusion and this could seriously impair the unity that we need within the movement, and which I understand is the purpose of this three-day exercise.

To conclude this aspect, it is now necessary that we consider what is accepted by trade unionists, as industrial relations practitioners, to be the objectives of the union in Collective Bargaining. This is important, for I consider it vital that as a movement, we reach agreement on whether the objectives I will outline are relevant to today's situation. This is so necessary, as my subject speaks of "The Scope of Collective Bargaining" and it is my intention to advance what, as a movement, we should strive to achieve by way of collective bargaining, and whether in the context of the legal framework and the existing structures we have established as a movement, that there is scope for us to achieve those objectives.

In setting out the objectives of the union in Collective Bargaining, I will offer an excerpt from a lesson I use in the classroom when dealing with this subject, and it reads: -

OBJECTIVES OF UNION IN COLLECTIVE BARGAINING
The objectives of the union Collective Bargaining are as follows: -

(a)   Trade union members are always perplexed when told that the union would sacrifice their economic gains so as to strengthen the union. In negotiating a collective agreement, the leadership of the union is always conscious that there is a long-term objective that can only be achieved if the union remains strong and grows stronger. Coming from the bargaining table, therefore, the union must be stronger than when it went in.

(b)   Therefore, union security (the check-off, closed shop, union shop, agency shop, etc.) is always a primary issue for the union.

It takes precedence over most of the other issues including economic gains for the members. Yet, it must be stated that no union would forego the acquisition of economic gains for it members for trivial union gain, for this can cause membership problem that would in turn weaken the union. Consequently, balance is always sought. The economic welfare of members, of course, includes better salary, wages and fringes that improve the quality of life.

(c)   The union also tries to get greater control over jobs. Trade unions today are challenging the right of management to hire and fire: who to promote and who to demote. This is a non-cost issue and embodies the seniority clauses in the agreement. The union therefore seeks to offer the greatest possible protection to its members, as a satisfied membership leads to a stronger union.

(d)   Trade unions, through collecting bargaining, also seek to achieve broad social and economic objectives. Housing for workers is an issue across the bargaining table. Similarly, medical schemes, pension plans, recreation facilities, and cultural pursuits. Trade unions are even bargaining for managements' contribution to the running of crèches for the working mothers in their employ. (See Trade Unions: What They Are and What They Do.).

(e)   The final objective of trade unions, is promoting the personal ambitions of the union leader. The union leader like every one else is a person with needs to be satisfied. It is therefore within the union that he seeks to have his needs satisfied, and personal ambitions realized. Collective bargaining offers the union leader the opportunity for fulfilling his ambition to be a successful bargainer and outstanding trade unionist. It affords him the opportunity of satisfying his need for recognition (esteem needs) from both his colleagues and those with whom he bargains across the table. It therefore follows, that much more is involved in collective bargaining than just salaries, wages and conditions of work."

As I have said, it is for us to decide whether the objectives I have outlined and briefly commented upon, are today relevant to the movement, which, as workers, we have created to protect us at our work, to improve our conditions of work through collective bargaining; to seek to better the conditions of our lives, and to provide a means of expression for our views on problems of the society.

It was and still is my conviction that the movement we created is as relevant today as it has ever been. Collective Bargaining is still our only mechanism, for not only guaranteeing that we can improve our welfare, but also improving it in proportion to others in our society. Ours is a class interest as even Churchill recognized, and it would be dangerous for us to leave the future of our well-being in the hands of others who may be well intentioned, but over whose actions we have little or no control. So it is in the light of the foregoing that I will deal with the subject matter of my assignment – "THE SCOPE FOR COLLECTIVE BARGAINING IN CENTRAL PLANNING"

THE STRUCTURAL PROBLEM

As I have mentioned, I have accepted that it is our intention to create a socialist state here in Guyana and that the structures exist for the introduction of central planning. I have also assumed that the TUC, as the representative of organized labor, has consciously decided to participate in the planning process.

Now, the State Planning Commission as I understand it, comprises a number of councils which embraces a number of issues concerned with planning (see attachment II) and on these councils the Trade Union Movement is represented. The obvious question is whether we are satisfied that the movement's representation is sufficient to adequately advocate the views of organized labor? But more important, is whether those who represent the movement are knowledgeable of the movement's policy and views on the several issues that must necessarily come before the councils. This, of course, presupposes that the TUC will have a position on the issues raised, as I think it should.

The above is important, for unless there is adequate representation and the co-ordination of ideas between those who bargain and those who participate in the Central Planning Process, the movement's contribution at both levels can be contradictory, confusing and a waste of time.

In my introduction, I outlined my concept of central planning and there I mentioned inter alia –"Central planning also implies that the planned effort must result in predetermined achievements (wealth creation) and finally what is of great, if not greatest importance, how the created wealth is to be distributed….."

As I see it, collective bargaining in a system where the economy is centrally planned, is mainly concerned with the distribution of the wealth created by the society, and towards which, the workers we represent had contributed significantly.

There are, therefore, some important questions that we must consider.

The first question is – If we are to bargain over the distribution of wealth, how as a Movement, concerned over the improved living standards of our members, can we ensure that the planned effort to which we contributed, results in the creation of wealth?

The second question is – If our efforts result in created wealth, in what proportion must it be distributed? i.e.

1. What percentage must be set aside for re-investment for future wealth creation?
2. What must be utilized in maintaining and expanding social services such as education, health, public transport, security, culture, recreation, public welfare, housing, etc.?
3. What must go towards wages, salaries and the other cost issue in collective bargaining with which we are all familiar?

Yet another question, and an important one, is – Must there be rewards for goal achievement, and vice versa, penalties for poor performance? As a follow up to this question, it is also important that we determine whether the collective bargaining mechanism must make provision for rewards and sanctions.

In considering the first question, I will advocate that the only way that the movement can positively contribute to wealth creation with some degree of certainty, is by ensuring that the movement is first represented on the several councils by sufficient, knowledgeable and competent persons, familiar with union policy and positions on the issues that would come up before the councils for consideration. It is also vital that those we appoint to the councils be competent advocates of the union's cause.

This would necessitate a complete restructuring of the movement along regional lines; the reconstitution of the many standing committees of the TUC, and the expansion of the role and programs of the Critchlow Labor College.

The restructuring of the movement, as I see it, is long overdue, as the tightly centralized administration has stifled the growth of the branch system in the individual affiliates of the Congress and aborted the development of the area (regional) councils and other arms of the TUC, as called for in its rules.

The Critchlow Labor College on the other hand, while it has made a significant contribution to the advancement of worker education, has made little contribution to the furthering of the efficiency of our unions, that is by expanding the knowledge of our union leadership so that they can function effectively in the complex society we are in the process of creating. My understanding of Critchlow, is that it should have been geared to meet the need for advanced trade union education that is still today only available outside of Guyana. The fault may not be with Critchlow but with our leadership who seems reluctant to avail themselves for training locally.

The second question, i.e. wealth distribution, obviously poses serious challenges for our leadership. Centralized bargaining calls for new knowledge. A passing knowledge of balance sheets and trading statement, coupled with the ability to, calculate percentages is not enough. The economic issues that must surface across or around the table cannot be brushed aside. Negotiators in centralized bargaining must possess much more than the passing knowledge I have referred to. A detailed knowledge of the working of the several enterprises within the society is vital, and this knowledge will necessitate active branches at each enterprise level with their leadership conscious of the important role they have to play in both the planning and the bargaining processes. The Branch must become a vital link in the communication process of the movement.

It is to be noted, however, that when I speak of enterprises, I speak of both private and public, as they all contribute to the national economy that has become the focus of centralized bargaining.

It follows, therefore, that knowledge of public finance has become a necessity, and also, that of national income accounts. Not to be excluded is knowledge of statistics, necessary to interpret the data that will be presented at both the planning and bargaining forums.

The ball game has changed. If we are to seriously contribute to planning, and bargain effectively on behalf of our membership, our leadership must equip themselves for the new game. The supportive institutions must be set up and/or restructured to meet our new responsibilities.

The second question, however, directs attention to the proportions in which the created wealth is to be distributed i.e. - what must go towards savings, what must go towards social services, and what must go towards salary, wages, etc.

As I said earlier, the supportive institutions must be set up to provide us with the information about the needs of the society and the economy. We, of course, would or should know the needs of our members.

It must be recognized, however, that there are limitations to what the Movement can achieve at both the planning and the bargaining stages, as the final responsibility for the managing of the economy rests with the elected government. Notwithstanding that, it must be noted that what we will have to distribute, would depend on the success of both the planning effort and its implementation. It must be noted, also, that to a large extent, it is our members who must execute the plan, and will share some of the responsibility for the goal achievements. It is for this reason that I have advocated that the branch must be seen as vital to the creation of the wealth that we must amass, if, through the bargaining process, we are to advance the welfare of our members.

As a movement, however, the major problem we will encounter across the table, at bargaining time, will center on savings. The Minister of Finance in his recent budget speech has stressed on this, and also on the great need to lower the deficit of the central government.

This must be a bargainable issue and while the measures to achieve increased savings and lowering the deficit were not outlined in any detail, the movement must get across to the Government side that further savings by the workers we represent can only result in greater hardships, as wages and salaries are already below the subsistence level, and as a result, it impacts negatively on their productive efforts. Table I sets out the problem.

TABLE I

UNIT COST OF SELETED ITEMS AND HOURS TO BE WORKED TO PURCHASE WITH
MEDIAN WAGE OF $577.50 PER MONTH

FOOD		Unit Cost	Hours worked
Beef	one pound	$12.50	4
Chicken	" "	17.00	6
Fish (Wet)	" "	3.50	1
Eggs	" "	9.60	3
Salted Fish	" "	8.50	3
Rice	" "	6.54	2
Black Eye peas	" "	9.00	3
Cooking Oil	" "	88.48	29
Cassava	" "	1.50	½
Plantains	" "	1.75	½
Eschallote	" "	5.00	1 ½
Curry Power	" "	24.00	8
Tomatoes	" "	5.50	1
HOUSING			
Rent	per month	120.00	40
Electricity	" "	80.00	27
Bed & Mattress	Complete	140.00	464
Cooking Gas – 20 lb	Twenty pounds	30.00	10
Kerosene	One gallon	5.29	1 ¾
CLOTHING			
Gents Pants	One Pair	140.00	46
" Shirt Jac	Short Sleeve	70.00	23
" Sandals	One pair	100.00	33
" Shoes	" "	175.00	60
Ladies Dress (Causal)		125.00	41
" Shoes	" "	150.00	50
" Pantie	" "	21.95	7
" Brassiere	" "	35.00	12
MISCELLANEOUS			
Spectacles	" "	400.00	133
Newspapers		5.50	3
Transportation		90.00	30

It follows, therefore, that savings can only come out of increased production, which is in our interest to advance. Then by the bargaining process we can determine what portion must go towards savings and what must go towards improving the quality of life of our people, by way of better social services and adequate salary, wages, etc.

There is one important comment that I must make, since it is important to the success of the planning effort and hence the bargaining process.

I have already advocated the setting up of the structures necessary to achieve our objectives. But the setting up of the structures by themselves is not enough; it must be matched by the placing of competent persons to man the structures. The major problem of third world countries, in this respect, is the square pegs we are prone to place in the round holes we create to achieve efficient performance. So often, we keep changing the pegs from one round hole for another, failing to recognize that the problem lies not in the holes but in the pegs we use.

Our unions and the movement must be so structured that we are able to recognize the square pegs that are mal-functioning, and so preventing the goal achievements that should have created the wealth from which the living standards of our people could have been improved through the bargaining process.

THE LEGAL FRAMEWORK

The Labor Amendment Act No. 9 of 1984, while it gives the right to the TUC to bargain on behalf of public sector workers, and make agreements or arrangements which may or may not be enforceable by the courts of law, it none-the-less has some serious flaws which can effect the right to bargain or limit its scope.

The Act, unlike the Taft Hartley Act of the USA, does not make it mandatory that the employer and/or the union bargain and bargain in good faith. The failure to include this provision leaves it open to the discretionary factor, which can lead to conflict, which is in our national interest to avoid. Yet I do not see the Government, as employer, refusing to bargain, seeing that this has been the case since 1977, but I must admit that events since1984 have raised some fears in respect of the good faith aspect.

There is yet another dimension to the problem, and that is in a circular dated 1982-02-02, issued under the signature of Hugh Desmond Hoyte then Vice President responsible for Economic Planning and Finance, re Salary/Wage Agreement and Employment costs in the Public Sector. The circular precludes public sector employers from negotiating with recognized unions all cost issues that affect employment costs. These cost issues have been and still are the responsibility of the TUC, yet it would appear as if the TUC is either unwilling or afraid to include them in the issues for central bargaining.

There is yet another aspect of our legal framework that needs some comment. It is another omission in the Labor Amendment Act 1984, and that is protection against interference by the employer in the collective bargaining process.

In speaking of Collective Bargaining, Edwin E. Witte in a book titled – "Collective Bargaining and the Democratic Process", had this to say –

> "...In the Wagner Act it was made an unfair labor practice for employers to have any dealings with unions which they helped to organize, which they had aided financially or otherwise, or which they had dominated or interfered with in any manner….."

The above I see as important, due to our peculiar political party/union relationship, and with whom we bargain as a TUC. We cannot speak of the scope to bargain and overlook that the TUC does not bargain with managers of the Public Sector Enterprises but with Ministers of Government to whose party the majority of the affiliates of the TUC are either affiliated or have some close relationship. I refer here to the seventeen-union group.

This must be considered in the context of the express paramountcy of the party over the Government and the expressed view, that the unions affiliated to the party (PNC) must take their policy and ideological direction from the party.

The question that I will pose is −"What effect the party/union relationship can have on collective bargaining?" I have not, overlooked the affiliation, however, or a very close relationship of at least one other affiliate of the TUC, to the major opposition party, the PPP. I speak here of the G.A.W.U.

I know that it may be argued that the party/union relationship I referred to is the norm in socialist countries but to this I will reply that if the union must take its policy and ideological direction from the party that comprises the government, the union should not collect dues from its membership, for if it does, the dues become no more than another government at tax on the pay packet of those workers. As I see it, if a union collects dues from it members, it has an obligation to first consider its obligation to those members. In other words the membership is paramount.

To consider this aspect, I will advance that centralized bargaining should be between the TUC and representatives of Guystac and the Public Service Ministry, as this would at least remove the direct influence the Ministers of Government may have over those unions that are affiliated to the PNC. This will give some semblance of good faith in the process.

THE SCOPE

It is my contention, from all that I have said, that planning and bargaining in the context of the society that we are attempting to create here in Guyana, are inter-related. It is from careful planning and efficient execution of the plan that we will create, the wealth that we must amass and distribute through the bargaining process.

Participating in the planning exercise by itself, I advance, cannot limit the scope of the movement to bargain successfully for its member. As I have said, ours is a class interest and it would be dangerous for us to leave the distribution of the wealth we create, to those who may be well intentioned, but may not share our sympathies.

There is no alternative to collective bargaining, but it is recognized that in the context of central planning, in which we will participate, additional responsibilities will be placed upon the union leadership. The bargainers must not be only knowledgeable, but as I said, must fully understand the environment in which bargaining will take place, and in order to achieve this, a restructuring of the movement is necessary. If this is done, there will be enough scope for us to use the collective bargaining process to advance the welfare of our members, and at the same time, achieve the other objectives of the union in collective bargaining, which I have already outlined at page 6 and which I consider as important.

To continue, I will briefly outline the environment in which we now bargaining, and advance that the scope for bargaining collectively for our members in the context of a centrally planned economy, can be greatly enhanced, if as a movement, we endeavor to influence that environment.

The environmental factors that I consider being those that affect collective bargaining could be placed into four groups – i.e.

1. The Industrial Environment
2. The Political Environment
3. The Community Environment and
4. The Cultural Environment.

It is important, that as trade unionists, we understand, not only the four facets of the environment, but the implications they have, both for us, and those with whom we bargain, for if we must consider the scope that exists for collective bargaining in the context of Central Planning, we must consider the environment that we are planning to change. As I see it, if the environment remains unfavorable, there can be little scope for success across the bargaining table.

The environmental factors, therefore, that I will advance, as those that affect or influence collective bargaining, I will list in summary, as follows:

A.   THE INDUSTRIAL ENVIRONMENT

   I.   The markets or budgetary constraints that, as Dunlop says, operates in the first instance on the management hierarchy and
then inevitably on the hierarchy of workers and their leaders.

   II.   The business cycle as it affects our two major industries Bauxite and Sugar. Historically these industries were of the boom and bust nature, i.e. periods of good time, then periods of bad time.

   III.   The changing technology that may be necessary to maintain competitiveness as seems to be the case with Bauxite and Sugar.

   IV.   The already high production costs that negates increases in
employment costs.

   V.   Balance of payments and public debt problems that strangulate the economy.

B.   POLITICAL ENVIRONMENT

    I.   Inter-union rivalry that affects solidarity at the national level

    II.   Internal union rivalry that divides the membership and destroys moral and militancy.

    III.   Political party affiliations that divide the movement due to the Government/Opposition Syndrome it fosters.

C.   THE COMMUNITY ENVIRONMENT

    I.   The size of the public sector
    II.   An unemployment ratio of 1: 20
    III.   Lack of facilities for influencing Union/Public Relations
    IV.   Greater access by the managerial hierarchy to those who walk the corridors of power
    V.   The company town relationships as applied to the Bauxite Industry.
    VI.   The historical Massa/serf relationship of the Sugar Industry.

D.   THE CULTURAL ENVIRONMENT

    I.   Religious dogmas and intolerance that divided us as a people

    II.   Attitudinal negativism that presents barriers to change

    III.   Information repressionalism that negatived our self-image and self-confidence.

The summary of the environmental factors that impinges on collective bargaining and which I have listed above, have been advanced as a thought provoking exercise and obviously not for consideration in this paper, as they can well be the subject matter of another seminar such as this.

I have advanced them, however, as I feel that the movement should consider them, since if we are to preserve the bargaining process, it is necessary that we understand both the environment and the people it has fashioned.

It is my conclusion that our task at this stage of our development, is to create the scope for us to bargain as a movement for the advancement of the wellbeing of our people, and that there is an interrelationship between the central planning process which seeks to fashion the environment, the people whom it supports, and the Collective Bargaining process which must assist in the distribution of the wealth resulting from the planning process.

As I have said, there is no alternative to Collective Bargaining. Our forefathers fought and died for it. Ours is the task to preserve and extend it.

ATTACHMENT

28B.   (1)   In this Act "collective agreement" means any agreement or arrangement which for the time being is subsisting and –

(a)   Is an agreement or arrangement made (in whatever way and in whatever form) by or on half of one or more organizations of employees and either one or more employers, one or more organizations of employers, or a combination of one or more employers and one or more organizations of employers; and

(b)   Is either an agreement or arrangement prescribing (wholly or in part) the terms and conditions of employment of employees of one or more descriptions, or an agreement or arrangement relating to one or more of the procedural matters specified in subsection

(2), or both?

(2)   The procedural matters referred to in subsection (1) (b)
        are -

(a)   Machinery for consultation with regard to, or for the
        settlement by negotiation or arbitration of, terms and
        conditions of employment:

(b)   Machinery for consultation with regard to, or for the
        settlement by negotiation or arbitration of, other
        questions arising between an employer or group of
        employers and one or more employees or organizations
        of employees;

(c)   Negotiating rights;

(d)   Facilities for officials of trade unions or other
        organizations of employees;

(e)   Procedures relating to dismissal;

(f)   Procedures relating to matters of discipline other than
        dismissal;

(g)   Procedures relating to grievances of individual
        employees.

THE TRADE UNION MOVEMENT A WAY FORWARD

INTRODUCTION

There is a serious challenge confronting the Labor Movement, for it is advocated that there are two roads by which it could travel to achieve its end objective which I have often termed the Economic Emancipation of the Working Man and Woman. The choice is not an easy one, for in choosing, it could well lead to a division of the movement along political or racial lines.

One road takes the direction where the movement aligns itself to the People's National Congress as some of our affiliates have done, and take its ideological and policy directions from that party. Or secondly, remain independent, garner its strength, and use it to influence the decision making of any party that should comprise the government. That is, getting them to do the things the movement would like them to do in the interest of its members.

The first course, it is said, is the norm in socialist countries, and many have cited the relationship that exists between the All Union Central Council of Trade Unions and the Communist Party of the Soviet Union in support of this relationship.

Under the relationship, it is my understanding that it is the Communist Party that determines policy and the union the executing agent. It is said that the relationship works well. However, it cannot be overlooked that the historical development of trade unions in the USSR and Guyana is somewhat dissimilar, for in the USSR, the Communist Party preceded the trade unions. Further, it is my understanding that the Communist party was instrumental in establishing the trade unions of the USSR after the abortive 1905 uprising. In Guyana, it is somewhat different, for political parties came at least thirty years after our trade unions, and in most cases, the trade unions were the springboards for those who sought to launch their political careers. Our first trade union, it must be remembered, was established in 1919 (B.G.L.U.), and our first political party in 1950 (PPP). Not to be overlooked also, is the early struggle of Critchlow to prevent the politicians from taking control of the Labor Union that he founded.

It is my contention that the historical development of our unions negates acceptance of the first concept, more so, as ours is still a multi-party state with racial overtones influencing party policy decisions.

It follows, therefore, that at this period of our development, I am a supporter or advocate of what we call THE FREE TRADE UNION MOVEMENT, but at the same time, I am not an advocate of the conflict approach to industrial relations. I believe that the Movement can more quickly achieve its objective if there can be cooperation between the Government and the trade Union Movement towards the achievement of those common objectives that are in the interest of both the union members and the nation.

All of the major parties (political) in our country claim to be working-class oriented, therefore, co-operation should not be difficult so long as the relationship between the Government and the Movement is one of equals or near equals. Or at least, one in which each party recognizes the right of the other to exist independently of it.

I accept, however, that any government should have the right to govern. I also accept that all governments must govern, conscious of the fact that it is the wishes of the people, and not that of the party, that are paramount, for they need not be one and the same, especially in the Guyana context.

The subject of this paper is - THE TRADE UNION MOVEMENT A WAY FORWARD. Most of my views are those that I expressed to a gathering of young workers in December 1984 with certain inclusions and exclusions, for I consider what I said then of importance to the Trade Union Movement and workers generally. Not to be excluded, of course, are the other actors in our Industrial Relations System, and all of those generally interested in the real development of our country.

The way forward for the trade union movement, I advocate, must be the concern of all Guyanese, for the events we are now witnessing as we endeavor to restructure our society and our relationships, would determine whether we succeed as a nation in avoiding the misfortunes that plague so many of the developing countries.

We have a nation to build, and a trade union movement well organized with the leadership enjoying the confidence of the membership, can contribute more positively to the nation-building process. I posit, therefore, that a movement without influence among its membership is of no use to either the membership, or a government bent on accelerating the developmental process. This, I advance, must not be overlooked.

In this exercise, I would be discussing the trade union, as it now exists, looking at its effectiveness and the pros and cons of the conflict/participative approach to industrial relations. Finally, I would be advocating what I consider to be the way forward for the trade union movement at this period of its development.

WORKERS AND THEIR UNIONS

It is one of our foremost poets, the late A.J. Seymour, who in one of his memorable poems made the profound observation that - "tomorrow belongs to the people," and it is in the context of this statement that I would like to discuss the subject matter of this paper.

In speaking of the people, however, it is important that we identify those about whom Seymour speaks. Martin Carter, another of our poets whom I so often describe as the People's Poet, identifies them as:

> "Those who rose early in the morning
> Watching the Moon die with the dawn.
> Those who heard the shell blow and the iron clang.
> Those who had no voice in the emptiness
> In the unbelievable, in the shadowless.

Let us think a while about those of whom Carter speaks. And more importantly, let us never forget that for many of them, the Trade union Movement is their only hope. It is through their trade unions that they seek to protect themselves at the workplace, improve their condition of work through collective bargaining and seek to better the conditions of their lives. It is through their unions also that they seek to provide a means of expression for their views on problems of society.

Further, let us remember that it is in seeking to ensure the above, that workers created their unions and the movement. So, if we are to assess our movement, we must determine whether our unions, individually, and our Trades Union Congress, collectively, can effectively enact the role that I have outlined, or is capable of performing the functions I have listed. Let me say, here, that the functions I have outlined, are taken from a definition of a trade union advanced by the International Confederation of Free Trade Unions, to which our Trades Union Congress is affiliated.

Yet, the trade union function should go beyond that as listed above, for the trade union could only enact its role as outlined by the International Confederation of Free Trade Unions, if it strives to ensure that the society in which it exists, is one that makes it possible for the Movement to perform its functions unhindered by bureaucratic obstructions or legal encumbrances. This means that the very nature and structure of the society is important to the Movement.

I am aware that there are conflicting views about the effectiveness and capability of our unions and the movement, but it is my opinion that our unions and the movement are a far way from doing the things we are supposed to do, as effectively as we should. Further, I am convinced that we lack the ability, or should I say capability, of doing the things we did between the periods 1905 - 1970, when most of the benefits we now enjoy were won by trade union action.

There are, however, two questions that must be answered. The first is, that if I am right, and I believe I am - Why are our unions ineffective? The second, is it now necessary for our unions to do the things they had to do between 1905-1970?

It is these questions that I would like to address and I consider it important that the leadership of our Movement also addresses their minds to them. As I have said, tomorrow belongs to the people, and if they identify with the people, it is important that they consider the issues now confronting the trade union movement, for the movement is the movement of the people, and the issues confronting our movement would have serious consequences for our young nation.

Here, I consider it important, that I refer to a paper I presented to a Conference of our Trade Union Youth Movement in 1970, for the views I expressed then are to my mind more important today than they were then, and should be of concern to all the people of Guyana, especially the workers.

THE CHALLENGE

What is needed of youths is creative thinking, we need to build a new society, a society that befits our youths.

Not a replica of the old and aged societies, but a new society that must take cognizance of the fact that the independence of Guyana was won by the working class at tremendous sacrifice, and if it is to be meaningful, it must bring further economic benefit to the working man, with the ultimate objective of hastening the just society.

Towards this objective we must work. We must cut ourselves adrift from the tragedies of the past, and undertake the serious task of nation building. Youths must visualize the society they want, and work towards its achievement, keeping in mind the words of Gandhi -"A classless society is an ideal not merely to be aimed at, but to be worked for".

It is for youth to take a close look at the institutions comprising our society, put them under your scrutiny and approach your task with the outlook of the scientist, then knowing the type of society you consider as befitting the youths of our country, ask yourselves whether the institutions as they are presently constituted, are capable of molding the society you have visualized. If the answer is in the negative, they must either be changed or replaced.

This introduces an important question. What methods must be used in instituting change? A pattern is evolving in many societies, whereby destruction is the answer to the resistance to change. In Guyana, we have had our bitter experiences, but let it be known that aping the trends in the those societies, can do us no good, for we can ill afford the luxuries of destruction."

That is the challenge confronting not only youths, but also the work force of our nation, so it is apt that I ask:

1. Must the Trade Union Movement be concerned with the society we are in the process of building?
2. Must the Movement be concerned with rights and freedom?
3. Must the Movement be concerned with the lot of the workingman and woman?

The answers to the three questions are important, for if we are concerned, then we must be concerned with the future of our unions and the movement. I say this, for without them; there can be no guarantee that the evolving society would be the kind of society we desire. Without our unions also, there is no guarantee that the rights and freedoms we cherish would be ours: especially the freedoms of expression and association without which no trade union could function. Next, there is no guarantee that the working man and woman of tomorrow would enjoy the right to leisure and the enjoyment of the fruits of their labor. There is even no guarantee, that their labor would bear fruit.

These are the issues with which I am concerned, and they should also be the concern of workers and their trade unions. All I can advise, is that these issues be the concern of our Trade union Movement, and for that matter, all Trade Union Movements, the world over.

THE EFFECTIVENESS OF OUR UNIONS

The effectiveness of a union could only be determined by its ability to protect its members against the injustices that can be, and are meted out to them by the management of enterprises, both private and public with which they work. Also, its ability to negotiate agreements with management that afford its members wages and conditions of work that are just and fair.

Job protection is vital to the workers, and it is for this reason that workers create or join trade unions, and any union that cannot, or fails to provide the protection its members need, must be considered as ineffective.

There is yet another dimension to the issue, for it could be argued that effectiveness should not be considered only in the short term. By this I mean that a trade union may today be getting for its membership what many may consider to be just and fair wages. But the just and fair wage may be the result of the benevolence of management and not the effectiveness of the union. This must not be overlooked.

Here lies a problem, for it leads to complacency and even non-recognition of the need for the union by the membership. Then, should the need ever arise for what I term "trade union action", we may well find that the union is found wanting. It lacks the ability to offer the membership the protection they need at their work-place, and also, the capacity to negotiate for them the just and fair wages that they need or desire, and to which they are entitled.

A trade union, it is said, is a continuing organization, and some have said that it is also permanent. It is also said that it is a democratic organization, voluntarily created by the workers.

I accept this viewpoint, for trade unionists must not only be concerned with the short term, but the long term. While for some, there may be no problems confronting the union and its members today, we must ask ourselves this fundamental question: Are we sure that what we are now doing, is guaranteeing that in ten or twenty years hence, the movement would be capable of offering its members the protection they would need at their work, and, also, negotiate for them wages and conditions of work that would be just and fair? This I advance, must be of concern, for we owe it to those workers yet to come, that we preserve and pass on to them the only vehicle that is capable of giving them protection at their work while negotiating the salary and wage that would be considered just and fair as it takes them into the new society. Further, our unions are the only guarantee that the new society that we all aspire to, is achieved without unnecessary pain.

This is the real issue confronting the Trade Union Movement. I would argue, therefore, that we must do nothing, or permit no one, or any group, to weaken, make ineffective, or should I say, subvert our unions or the movement, for no one knows what tomorrow brings. Those whom we may today trust, those who some may now see as our savior, would not be there forever, and, if the situation continues to be favorable, or to our satisfaction, let us all say - "Thank God For That!" But should it change for the worse, as it sometimes does, let us pray that we could then say: "Thank God For Our Union!"

I have my convictions, my beliefs, and fundamental to them, is that the eventual emancipation of the working man and woman, rest and depends on a strong and dynamic trade union movement, working in their interest and towards their well-being.

Professor Arthur Lewis in one of his publications described a trade union as "the workers solicitor...his insurance company...his political machine." think it is important that we now look at Lewis's statement in the context of my topic - THE TRADE UNION MOVEMENT - A WAY FORWARD.

The trade union must indeed be the workers advocate. It is expected that the union would represent the workers to ensure that justice is meted out to all who work irrespective of race, religious or political beliefs or even age or sex. The Unions must also negotiate the procedures for settling disputes or grievances at the work place, and ensure that we have within the leadership of our unions, not only those who are capable of representing the membership; that is, good advocates; but more so, those who possess the courage to represent those issues affecting the membership, that have political overtones. In Guyana, there are union members, young workers, dismissed from their employment because it was suspected that they did not vote at T.U.C's 1984 election, as they were directed to vote by those who are of the view that for the movement to exist in Guyana, it must take its direction from a political directorate which, it seems, possesses the "divine right to rule.' I speak here of Adonna Joseph & Cheryl Corlett of the G.C.M.F.B.S.A.

Could this be right? Again I know of union leaders dismissed from their employment, because they refused to increase the number of delegates of their unions to the T.U.C's Conference in 1984, beyond what they considered to be their legitimate entitlement. This was all done by political maneuvering, and what could only be described as a blatant misuse of political power and a violation of the 1LO Convention No 87 (Freedom of Association) (2) which states:

"The public authorities shall refrain from any interference which would restrict this right or impede lawful exercise thereof".

The above dismissals strike at the roots of our movement, and in the context of Guyana, it is vital that these issues be not only discussed, but also represented as forcibly as is possible. Such occurrences must cause us to question the movement's continued support for the nationalization process that brought under the control of the state, two thirds of the economic activity of our country, and hence, at lease two thirds of the available jobs. This would be most unfortunate, and should not be overlooked, for it must cause us to question the expressed political ideology of both the party that comprised the Government, and the Trades Union Congress. It gives socialism an evil face.

The state must be the model employer. The citizens must have confidence in those who hold political office, and anything that brings into question the just use of state power, is not good for our country. It introduces fear into the hearts of those who are the producers, and must impact negatively on what is so vital to our recovery effort, and that is - increases in production and productivity. Freedoms of expression, independence of action, and freedom to choose one's leaders, are rights that must be protected by our unions, regardless.

Lewis's second role for the union is that of the "workers insurance company." If a union through the seniority and other provisions in the Collective Labor Agreement cannot protect jobs for whatever reason, it must be able to ensure that at least it could negotiate those conditions of work that provide compensation for the loss of job opportunity. Severance pay legislation has not as yet becomes reality, and must be considered a priority with a timetable set for its promulgation. The same must be said for unemployment benefits from the National Insurance Scheme, for they are both forms of job Insurance.

There are, of course, other issues such as other N.I.S. incapacity benefits, and the right to pensions. Are we, as workers, satisfied that those who now work would be capable of maintaining themselves when they get - "too old to work and too young to die?" In our Pensions Act, the right of a public officer to a pension does not exist. As it now stands, the Act seeks to demand loyalty and compliance through the fear of destitution in old age. How else can it be interpreted? More so, as it has been used as a political weapon. Further the promise of the PNC Govt. "to provide for the establishment of a National Pension Scheme to cater for all workers upon retirement" is yet to be fulfilled.

Young workers may not consider that pensions and job security are their concerns. Let me say this, however. It is everyone's concern, for every time we give a hand out to some unfortunate in the street or some relative in distress, we are impairing our own living standards, and one of the tragedies of life, is that men get old, and so do women.

Lastly, Lewis speaks of the worker's "political machine." This is a very controversial issue and brought to the fore by the President of the Co-operative Republic of Guyana in his address to the Biennial Conference of the Guyana Labor Union in 1984. Comrade Burnham had stated that trade unions could not divorce themselves from politics, quoting a statement made by Hubert Nathaniel Critchlow, that "politics follow us from the cradle to the grave." The quotation was used to justify the affiliation of unions to the PNC.

I must confess that I share Cde. Burnham's view, and so does the T.U.C. I am not too sure, however, if my concept of politics agrees with that of our President. Politics, as I see it, is concerned with the acquisition and use of power towards the achievement of stated goals or objectives. In the context of national politics, this involve the methods used by groups to acquire political power, and the things done by those groups, or the methods they used to achieve the objective they had identified, once elected to office.

In the context of the above, what we must first consider is the objectives of the group seeking political power, and whether their objectives coincide with that of the Movement. Also to be considered, is that if the objectives of the group do not fully satisfy the trade unions, how effective are our trade unions in getting the group to change or expand upon its objectives. Of greater importance, is how effective the trade unions would be in getting the group to confirm, or direct its attention towards the achievement of those objectives it had agreed to pursue, following its acquisition of political power. This I submit is a challenge for the Movement.

The second thing to be considered is the methods to be used by the political group to acquire power and, also, the methods or things they would do to achieve their objectives. One thing that we could be sure of, and that is; what a political group would do to achieve its objectives, very often is determined by what they did to acquire political power.

In a document published under the signature of the General Secretary of the T.U.C. dated 5th December 1980 under the caption - TUC's SUPPORT FOR PEOPLE'S NATIONAL CONGRESS AT NATIONAL ELECTION, the following appears:

"The Executive Council of the Guyana Trades Union Congress on Wednesday, 3rd December 1980 took a decision similar to what the TUC did in 1968 and 1973 to endorse the People's National Congress as the political party which merits the support of the electorate at the National Elections to be held on December 15, 1980.

Before the decision was taken, the Executive Council met representatives of the People's National Congress and the United Force at separate meetings and obtained the reaction of the respective parties to a number of matters contained in the TUC's Policy Statement on which the TUC considered it desirable to have commitments, assurances or decisions by the parties prior to the elections.

It is to the credit of the People's National Congress that notwithstanding its political status as the Ruling Party or the party in Government, it was sufficiently objective to recognize the advantage of accepting the TUC's invitation which provided an opportunity for frank discussion on a number of matters with which the successful party would be expected to deal in its program.

All three of the political parties contesting the elections were invited by the TUC to the discussions. The People's Progressive Party declined the invitation.

The commitments, assurances and decisions given the TUC by People's National Congress covered a number of fundamental issues and matters of national interest and of specific concern to the trade union movement. The party restated its endorsement of the belief expressed in the TUC's 1968, 1973, and 1980 Policy Statements that all political parties and Trade Union Movement should:

I.   pronounce against the fostering of racialism as a means of achieving political power and instead pledge to foster conditions that would lead to the development of a dedicated Guyanese nationalism

II.   denounce any form of totalitarian design or the imposition of any form of totalitarianism on the Guyanese people through misuse of political power:

III.   commit themselves to guard against violations of human rights and fundamental principles enshrined in the Charter of the United Nations and the Universal Declaration of Human Rights, including trade rights, freedom of press, freedom of expression and freedom of association

IV.   commit themselves to be ready at all times to initiate or participate in any action aimed at protecting and preserving these rights and freedom.

ONE PARTY STATE

The Government would not seek to establish a one Party State. The People's National Congress restated its commitment or gave assurances in respect of the following matters

Retention of the country's membership at the International Labor Organization.

1. That the party nor the government will not interfere or try to dominate neither individual trade unions or the Guyana Trades Union Congress.
2. That the government would consult the TUC prior to the introduction of any Labor Legislation, or any Legislation affecting the interest of workers.

3. Guaranteed annual income for sugar workers through adequate out of crop employment or payment.

4. Introduction of legislation: -

    a.   To provide for the establishment of a National Pension Scheme to cater for all workers upon retirement.

    b.   Hire Purchase

    c.   Severance Pay

    d.   Compulsory recognition to Trade Unions.

    e.   Increased Government's contribution towards the Critchlow labor College.

    f.   Commencement of negotiations for a Minimum Wage Package for <u>1980 - 1982</u>

It is important that we now consider what is quoted above as "The People's National Congress restates its commitment or gave assurances in respect of the following matters."

As I see it, the P.N.C. had not honored the assurances given the TUC at (2); (3) (5) (6) and (7) and this must be the concern of the Movement. It cannot be denied that the P.N.C. Government in spite of assurances given by the party had openly attempted to interfere in the election process of the Congress at every election since and before 1980. Further, both overt and covert attempts were made to remove George Daniels as president of the Guyana Public Service Union for having, not only the gumption to contest the Presidency of the T.U.C. against the candidate endorsed or preferred by the party, but spearheaded the effort that resulted in the removal of nearly all the party's supporters from the top positions on the Executive council of the Congress in 1984.

Labor Amendment Act No. 9 of 1984, must also convince the Movement that the promises made by the PNC were merely intended to placate a movement of which it had little or no regard. This is all the more so, when we consider that the bill was not only introduced in parliament without prior consultation with the TUC's Executive Council, but was introduced by the Minister of Man Power and Co-operative who at the time was an

Executive Council Member of the TUC, holding the post of Organizing Secretary. In Guyana, of course, Ministers of Government need not resign the posts they hold in the TUC, when appointed Ministers of Government.

In respect of the Minimum Wage Package for 1980 - 1982 and increased contribution for the Critchlow Labor college, the same can be said, and together raises serious doubts as to the effectiveness of the Movement in getting political parties, once elected to office, to honor their promises. The grant to the Critchlow Labor College was drastically cut in 1982 instead of being increased, and no agreement was reached on the Minimum Wage Package for 1980 – 1982.

Where does this leave the trade unions? There are two options open to the Trade Union Movement and they are as follows:

(a)   Support a political party that subscribes to the thinking of the movement and promises to promote the goals and policies the union advocates or

(b)   Become actively involved in party politics by forming a party of its own and campaigning for political office.

The trade Union Movement of Guyana, represented by the TUC has opted for the first, and I am in agreement with the course that the Movement has taken. This is so, as should we ever decide to move into active party politics, there must come a time when we may find ourselves out of political office, with a Government, pursuing policies directed towards the destruction of the movement. We cannot eat our cake and still have it. Here the Tatcher/Reagan Administrations of the U.K. and USA must be our lesson.

The first option, however, also has its setbacks, for while we lend support to political parties, there is no guarantee that those whom we support or endorse would do the things they promised to do, when they assume office. This is even more serious when the union or movement is ineffective or incapable of getting the political group to honor those promises.

Arthur Lewis, however, says that the Trade Union is the workers "political machine"' and in the context of the Guyana situation, it means the trade union influencing political decisions or getting political parties to agree to implement things the movement considers important. Further, once agreement is arrived at, getting the political party to honor the agreement.

Since 1980, the Movement has not been effective in influencing political decisions or getting the party that comprises the Government to honor agreements arrived at between the TUC and the Party. There may be reasons why the party or government had not honored its commitments to the TUC, especially those agreed to and as set out in the TUC's Policy Statement. Some of the reasons may be valid, but one thing is certain, and that is, the movement would find it more difficult to get the PNC or any other Party to honor those commitments, which it feels, should be honored, whenever the TUC pursues a course of action to which the Party is opposed.

The obvious question to ask is what the movement could do to redress the situation. Must the movement withdraw its endorsement of the PNC and support some other political group? It is my view that such a move may not achieve the results we desire, for as I told a class from my own union in 1983,

"The People's National Congress as a Government will be there for a long time to come and there is nothing that can be done to change that fact, and further, the PNC has no intention of sharing political power with any other group regardless of the consequences."

Many, I know, would disagree with my view. Some may say that the TUC elections in 1984, shows that the P.N.C. can be defeated in an election. I say this, however, in a National Election, many vote, not for a party and its policy, but for a personality, influenced by race and other prejudices. Further, there are many who may not be prepared to pay the price for such a change, and any such change would be costly.

The involvement of the Movement in politics therefore, is something we cannot escape, but how we must be involved is the issue. Must it be that we become, as it is with some unions, affiliated to the P.N.C., or as it is now the case with the TUC, endorse a party that ratified the T.U.C.'s policy statement and then endeavor to ensure that once the party becomes the Government, that they live up to their promises.

Both have their weaknesses. Affiliation cannot bring results unless the union has representation at the decision-making forum of the party, sufficient to influence decisions on issues of concern to the union or unions. Again, endorsement does not guarantee that political parties would live up to their promises.

Hence, I contend, that trade unions must garner and preserve their strength. They must be militant in the representation of their members and never compromise injustice for any reason. Of importance, also, no union could be effective across the bargaining table unless it is capable of bringing its members out on strike. This I know is the contentious issue. But it is the crux of the problem, for strength and militancy must be our strategy for political survival.

Since 1977, the greatest handicap to the Movement was that in bargaining with the government, it was conscious that it was incapable of getting its members, or at least the majority of the members out on strike in support of its demands. For many unions, a strike was something that invokes fear. Fear of the reaction or reprisals of the political administration, since their positions as leaders in their unions very often depended, not on the support of the membership but the whims and fancies of the political directorate. Recent developments in the Movement have brought so clearly to those of us in leadership positions, how tenuous our positions could be, when our support is not firmly rooted in our membership.

CONFLICT OR PARTNERSHIP

So far, we have been discussing the effectiveness or ineffectiveness of the Trade Union Movement today. The second question I posed earlier, however, was - Is it now necessary for our unions to do the things we had to do between 1905 - 1970 to achieve our objectives?

Let me state unequivocally, that I do not believe that we should. Yet, I must confess that the undoubted injustices meted out to several members of our unions over the past years, may suggest that if we are to survive as a movement, effectively representing our members, it is more and more becoming necessary that we should. That is, unless there is significant changes at the level of the political directorate.

The sole problem here, is that the government, in spite of its statements expressing its agreement with the participative approach to Government, has done very little to encourage both meaningful worker participation in management, and trade union participation in those political decisions that affect the economic and social life of the workers of our country.

To me, it is a tragedy that what had promised so much has resulted in so little. H. Desmond Hoyte then Minister of Works & Communication, now President, in a brilliant dissertation titled - "THE TRADE UNION AND THE STATE - IN PARTNERSHIP OR CONFLICT" ably advocated the participative approach, while outlining an expanded role for the Trade Union Movement. So far, they remain pious statements yet to be given effect. And it behooves us to carefully monitor President's Hoyte's future action, so as to avoid the mistakes we once made.

Again, I do not believe that we should revert to the conflict approach in our dealings with Government, but the ball is in the Government's court, and unless something positive is done, trade union/State relations is going to deteriorate, to the continuing detriment of our economy and people.

How can we improve the relationship? Must the Unions and Movement compromise its principles, which eventually would mean its effectiveness, to ensure that there is peace? I think not, for Ronald Reagan, President of the United States of America, has proved that strength is the only guarantee to a worthwhile peace in certain issues. As a result, a strong and effective Trade Union Movement, co-operating with the Government to raise the living standards of our people, must win industrial peace, which would bring lasting benefits to the workers of our country. This should not be difficult, for I could think of no union that differs with the PNC Government or any other major political party, in respect of their expressed objectives. Therefore, strategy, or method, or things to be done to achieve the objective could be arrived at by dialogue; meaningful dialogue.

Unless we could truly establish co-operative arrangements to manage our economy, I can see no real development of a lasting nature, as we would continue to expiate our energy in unproductive pursuits, with a disillusioned and dissatisfied work-force lacking the will to produce. It should not be overlooked, also, that the very name of our country, as expressed in Paper 1, implies the cooperative approach to problem solving.

The time is long past for institutionalized dialogue between Trades Union Congress and the Government, and unless the matter is treated as one of urgency, production would continue to decline, living standards would forever be falling, and inevitably, the Government would have to use repressive measures to control a dissatisfied labor force.

It must not happen. Let us learn from our mistakes, and it is important, not only for the youth of our society, but all who labor, that they understand that the issues I have discussed, have great relevancy to them. A contracting economy, I contend, means less jobs and lowering living standards. Unemployment for those between 18 - 25 years is estimated to be over 35% and retrenchment always affect the young workers the most. Further, unemployment tends to pull wage rates downwards, accelerates crime and prostitution, and dehumanizes those affected.

In concluding the partnership vis-a-vis conflict relationship, let me again repeat that it is important that we avoid the conflict approach in union/state relations, for our economy can ill-afford the costs we would have to pay, and in the final analysis, neither the union nor the state benefits, and definitely not the workers.

It would be observed that in discussing this aspect, I have spoken of union/state relations with no mention of management. This has been intentional, for our industrial relations system has become more a bi-partite one, than tri-partite. In respect of the Public Sector Managers, they have little or no say in the cost issues involved in collective bargaining, and it is doubtful whether their views are consulted when determining personnel management policy. The specialized Government Agency in industrial relations also seems to have had its functions curtailed, and as a practitioner in Industrial Relations, I wonder what is the role of the Ministry of Labor in today's Scheme of things. My views on this, however, were already expressed earlier.

The above adds to the problems of the unions and movement, for if industrial relations decisions are to be made outside of the Industrial Relations System, it is impossible, in seeking to provide solutions to the problems created by those decisions, to have them resolved within the system.

As a result, our Industrial Relations System is in complete disarray. Unions are unsure about who make decisions in respect of Industrial Relations. Managers no longer manage, and even the Ministry of Labor (Manpower) appears to be wandering around in a state of bewilderment. Is there any wonder that our economy is in such terrible shape?

From the foregoing, the time is long past for the Trade Union Movement of Guyana to recognize its social responsibility; first to its members and secondly to the nation.

For too long we have remained silent while our ability to protect our members at their work place became nothing more than mere illusions.

Party politics has failed the working-class. It divided us into opposing camps with too much energy spent; not in furthering the economic welfare and well-being of the masses, but the achievement of political objectives solely concerned with the acquisition and preservation of power, or influenced by what to my mind is much more frightening - FEAR OF LOSING POWER.

The way forward for the Movement, nonetheless, must lead to the forging of lasting working class unity. Yet it must never renege from its mission to maintain and improve the living standards of its members. The two are inter-dependent in the context of the Guyana situation. Further, we must not forget that in a democracy, political power is derived from the people, and there is so much that the people can do, to ensure that the power is used in furthering their interests.

As a consequence, to achieve the two objectives, the following are what I consider to be the urgent necessities if our choice of The Way Forward is to safely take us into the 21st Century and the good life:

1. Bring about real trade union solidarity.
2. Establish a strong financial base for the Movement.
3. Publish a regular newspaper or organ mirroring the views of organized labor.
4. Restructure the Movement by first reducing the number of unions. Next Establish clear cut lines of demarcation, and the elimination of the paper unions that have proliferated.
5. Establish a secretariat within the TUC adequately staffed to satisfy the needs of the affiliates and the expectations of workers.
6. Strengthen the links with our Internationals.
7. Putting into effect an extended education program to produce a knowledgeable group of activists committed to the objectives, philosophy and program of the movement.
8. Establish efficient lines of communication with workers in the several regions.

From the above, it would be seen that what I am advocating is the building of a strong Trade Union Movement, and I am aware that there are those who are fearful of a strong Movement, and to those I must ask - why?

The way forward for the Movement is quite simple. Recent events have convinced me that organized labor can only depend on the strength of the movement to protect its interest. It means therefore, that the leadership of a united Guyana Trades Union Congress, the legitimate voice of organized labor, democratically elected, must at this critical time in our development, consider it a priority that they rekindle that union's inspiration that had once ran through the blood of our workers. Everything else is secondary.

B. Wight Bakke in his Concept of Social Organization referred to the Organization Charter which he described as "The conception held by the participants in the organization of what the name of the organization stands for, its purpose and major policies, together with the basic values shared by the participants."

Here lies the problem. Of late, our members were confused as to what the Movement stood for, and even its purpose. Our policies were conflicting, and it seemed as if we had abandoned those values, which the movement had once cherished. This must change. We must be at one with our members. Our priority must be the rectification of our tarnished image.

The way forward, therefore, is for the Movement to convince the workers of our country that we have not abandoned them, and are prepared to lead the struggle for a better way of life. We can only achieve results, however, with our membership foursquare behind us.

The movement, as I have said, must rekindle that union's inspiration and issue the call for working-class unity, then push those who are fearful along by the sheer weight of our numbers our convictions and our strength.

The last question is, however, where do the others of the working class stand. Let us remember, that as Martin Carter says,

> "Like a jig shake the loom
> Like a web is spun the pattern
> All are involved
> All are consumed.

ROLE AND DEVELOPMENT STRATEGY OF TRADE UNIONS IN A THIRD WORLD ENVIRONMENT

This paper on the Role and Development Strategy of Trade Unions in a Third World Environment is prepared in the context of what I have termed an acceptance of the following truths:

1. There is no single third world environment but several, and anyone attempting to look at the role of Trade Unions in a third world environment must take cognizance of this fact.

2. Trade Unions operate in what we term the Industrial Relations System, which is itself a sub-system of the Total Social System, and the system (I.R.S.) varies with the environment.

3. The Total Social System includes three other sub-systems that impinge on the Industrial Relations System. They are:
   i   The Political System.
   ii The Economic System.
   iii The Legal System.

4.   The function of the Industrial Relation System is to
       make rules – the salaries, wages, hour of work, fringe
       benefits, and other conditions of work governing the
       performance of those, we term the actors within the
       Industrial Relations System. The comprise:

       I   The managers of the several enterprises
             their representations in supervision,
             including also the organizations that they
             create to assist them in their rule-making
             function.

       ii   The workers (non-management) and the
             organizations that they create – Trade Unions.

       iii   The State as represented by some
             specialized agency – The Ministry of Man
             power in the context of Guyana.

5.   The rule making in the Industrial Relations System, to a
       great extent, is influenced by factors external to the
       system. There are nonetheless three givens to the
       actors within the system. That is, things which are
       outside of their control, and they are:

       I   The technology utilized by the individual
             enterprises and the society generally.

       ii   The markets for the products of the
             enterprises and the budgets within which
             the manager is restricted.

       iii   The center of power within the wider
             society and which of the actors have

access to those who wield power
in the wider society.

The paper that follows is prepared with the above in mind.

First, the traditional role of a trade union will be discussed, and extended, to include that of the Trade Union Movement.

Secondly, the things that the union will have to do, so as to ensure that it is capable of enacting its role effectively will be looked at within a framework outlined by E. Wight Bakke in his **"Concept of Social Organizations."**

Finally, the development Strategy to achieve what I term the end objective of the Trade Union Movement will be looked at in the context of two environments that typify the third world and moreso, the Caribbean.

INTRODUCTION

It is my firm conviction that the end objective of the Trade Union Movement can only be the economic emancipation of the working man and women, and if this is accepted, I will argue that this emancipation can only be guaranteed if the workers first strengthen and preserve their unions. Secondly, they must ensure that at all times their unions and the movement is capable of:

1. Protecting them at their work against all kinds of discrimination and victimization.
2. Winning for them the best possible salary, wages and working conditions that the enterprise and/or economy can afford.
3. Ensuring that both the enterprise and the economy are managed in such a manner that it preserves jobs and past

investment, while utilizing the means of production as efficiently as possible.

4. Ensuring that the managers of the enterprise and the economy pursue investment policies that create adequate jobs and further wealth that will continually improve the quality of life of the working man and woman,

5. Ensuring that the fundamental rights of all people, enshrined in the United Nations Charter of Human Rights and the sentiments outlined in the Philadelphia Declaration are preserved and observed.

It, therefore, follows, that if we are to define the role of a trade union, it cannot be limited to the achievement of the five objectives I have set out above, it must also be extended to include those things which I will later outline, and which are necessary if the trade union is to guarantee that it will be an effective instrument to be used by the workers in the achievement of those objective.

I will argue, therefore, that the role of a trade union is to achieve the five objectives I have outlined above and which I will term the secondary objectives. It is, also, the role of the union to do those things, which, as I said, I will later discuss, and which are necessary if the union is to guarantee the achievement of the secondary objectives. Those things will result in what I term the achievement of the primary objective – Preserve and Strengthen the union.

The Primary Role - Preserve and Strengthen the Union:

The definition of a trade union advanced by the International Confederation of Free Trade Unions (I.C.F.T.U.) speaks of – "A continuing, permanent and democratic organization voluntarily created by the workers..."

A trade union, therefore, is an organization, a social organization, and in his book – **The Concept of Social Organizations**, E. Wight, Bakke defines a social organization as follows:

> "A continuing system of differentiated and coordinated human activities utilizing, transforming, and welding together a specific set of human, material, capital, ideational, and natural resources into a unique problem solving whole engaged in satisfying particular human needs in interaction with other systems of human activities and resources in its environment."

It is to be noted, that Bakke speaks of a social organization interacting with other social organizations in an environment, which as I see it, is most relevant to the subject matter of this paper. Bakke further states, however, that there are major features essential to a more specific definition of a particular social organization and they are:

1. The organizational Charter or image of the organization's unique wholeness.
2. The basic Resources, human, material, capital, ideational and natural, utilized in organizational activities.
3. The Activity Processes essential to the acquisition, maintenance and utilization of these basic resources for the performances of the organization's function.

I will now argue that the effectiveness of an organization, greatly depends on its Activity Processes, and that its primary role is to conduct those activities which I will now discuss, as efficiently as is possible. For as Bakke rightly said, unless this is done, the attainment of the secondary objective which I have already outlined, can be "critically imperiled."

A Trade union, therefore, as Bakke also said, will not adequately satisfy the needs of its membership, if its activities are performed ineffectively. Further, their needs will never be satisfied if the activities are not performed at all. Unfortunately, however, the membership will turn to other organizations in their search for need satisfaction, if in their union, there is an inability or a reluctance to conduct those activities that must be directed towards their need satisfaction.

IDENTIFICATION ACTIVITIES

Bakke described this class of activities as those intended to define, make clear, legitimize and symbolize the image of the unique wholeness of the organization, including its function and the main features that distinguish it from other organizations.

This class of activities says Bakke creates the Organizational Charter. That something, that when the name of the organization Is heard, it brings to mind some unique identifying features – What the organization stands for, its purpose and major policies. Together with the basic values shared by those who belong to the organization.

I will advance, therefore, that a part of the primary role of a trade union is to create among its leadership and membership, those unique identifying features that will ensure that both leadership and membership have the same concept of the union. It is also important that the union does such things, that those organizations with which the union interacts, will also understand what it stands for, its purpose, major policies, etc.

It is, however, of importance to note that the leadership of the union assists to a great extent in fashioning and/or preserving the union's Organizational Charter. This is by the way they respond to situations of an industrial relations nature, their utterances, etc., all of which contribute significantly to the effectiveness of the union. Any union in which the leadership and membership have conflicting views about what it stands for, its purpose, etc., must be ineffective.

A trade union, unlike many other organizations, depends on its membership support, to a large extent, for its effectiveness. First, it is a voluntary organization, as there is usually no compulsion to becoming a member. Secondly, the majority of those who conduct the business of the union, offers voluntary service, mainly because they believe that the union is capable of achieving the objects for which it was created and to which they either assisted in determining or to which they subscribe.

I am therefore arguing, that it is the Organization Charter; the image the membership has of the union that attracts them to the leadership positions in the union. It follows that should it ever arise that the membership and the large number of voluntary union workers become unclear as to what the union stands for, its purpose, etc., the effectiveness of the union will be impaired. I further argue, that the leadership by failing to respond to certain situations as would be expected by the membership, also tarnishes the image of the union and hence its effectiveness.

Also important to note, is that a union is a dynamic organization. It grows as it responds to changes in the society and it is necessary that the leadership at all levels, in responding to new situations does not engage in activities which conflict with, or contradict its Organizational Charter as perceived or understood by its membership.

It is not being advocated, that the Organizational Charter of the union, once created, must remain like Caesar – "As constant as the Northern Star." For just as the union is dynamic, it follows that its Organizational Charter must also be dynamic in its concept.

I advance, therefore, that as the need for change arises as a result of societal changes, a new set of activities must take place to either expand or contract the Organizational Charter. The Job of fashioning the Organizational Charter of a union is a continuing one, necessitating continuous activity due to the dynamic nature of the union and the movement.

To be considered, also, is that aspect of the Organization Charter where Bakke speaks of the –"main features, which distinguishes it from other organizations." This aspect is most important, for the I.C.F.T.U.'s definition of a trade union, a part of which I have quoted above, states that it is a "continuing ... organization," which implies something individualistic, if not independent.

I will argue, that if a trade union has created an image of independence or has established traditional relationships with other organizations, such as national trade union centers or political parties, etc., it must, in dealing with those organizations, avoid transmitting confusing signals, especially to its membership. That is, by the things it does or by its utterances, or as said above, by failing to respond to situations when a response is expected by its membership. When this happens, the union distorts its image, confuses its membership, and destroys its effectiveness.

Finally, the Organizational Charter can be limited or extended, and it can also vary between groups within the union, dependent on the activities undertaken by the union, its reaction to specific situations and events, and also, its utterances on specific and general issues confronting the union, or units within the union or the society.

Attached to this paper is a questionnaire that I will ask that you spend some time in answering, for your answers will indicate how you see your union and hence give an insight into the Organizational Charter of your union as perceived by you a female member. It is not necessary that you show what you have done to anyone or return it to me. I will appreciate it, however, if you discuss the failings as you see it in your workshops if the occasion is presented. More importantly, you must endeavor to correct those failings within your union, for your welfare and well-being is inextricably bound to the effectiveness of your union, which itself is determined by how you perceive your union. That is the Organization Charter created by your union.

PERPETUATION ACTIVITIES

Bakke describes these activities as those intended to acquire, maintain, transform, develop and renew the basic resources utilized by agents of the organization in the performance of their work...

In the context of the union, I will argue that we cannot speak of a union as a continuing organization, which suggests permanence, unless the union conducts those activities that are so necessary, if it is to guarantee its continuance or permanence.

Laudable objectives, such as those set out in many union rules, and captured above as the secondary objectives of the union, are not enough. A Union if it is to be continuingly effective in achieving the objective referred to, must undertake the kinds of activities directed towards preserving and strengthening the union, which as I have said, before, must be seen as its primary role.

In discussing the perpetuation activities, Bakke also states that there are sub-classes of the activities, which he listed as follows:

1. Personnel activities to perpetuate people and their qualities.
2. Service activities to perpetuate materials equipment and plant.
3. Finance activities to perpetuate capital.
4. Thought ways activities to perpetuate ideas such as alternative strategies, plan ...
5. Conservation activities to perpetuate natural resources and access to them.

The obvious question is – How necessary are these activities to a trade union? Let us first look at Personnel Activities.

A trade union, like any other organization, needs people to manage the union and do those things that will give effect to the purpose for which it was established. It follows, that if the union is to be managed efficiently, those who are responsible for the execution of specific functions must possess the necessary competence to undertake them.

This speaks of a union personnel management policy, and training to satisfy present needs and, of course, future needs. The future needs satisfaction, termed by some as succession planning, is vital if we are to maintain the continuance of the union as the effective instrument it ought to be.

Already established, is that the union interacts with other organizations. By its objects and the purpose for which it was created, it follows that it must interact with the management of those organizations with which it enjoys recognition rights. If the union, therefore, is to match the management of the work enterprise across the table at bargaining time, those who bargain on behalf of the union must match management in competence, skills, knowledge, and all the other attributes needed to effectively advocate the cause of its membership.

Not to be overlooked is the large number of voluntary workers that must be trained to take up the positions at the branch and shop steward levels of the union, and also the various standing committees. To be included, also, are those who must represent the union on the several boards, commissions, etc., that is now an integral part of union activity.

I contend, therefore, that the union must recognize that an important part of its role is the acquisition and development of the personnel necessary to permit it to operate as an efficient organization capable of effectively pursuing the secondary objectives I have outlined. Unless this is done, the effectiveness of the union will be further put at risk.

Let us now consider the "**Service Activities**". It may be argued that the Union has no need to perpetuate materials, equipment, and plant, but this can only be true if we give a narrow definition to material and equipment.

Let us then consider the material and equipment utilized or should be utilized by the union.

What of the stationary, including the forms, etc., that are utilized in union business? Whose job is it to see that they are there in the necessary quantities and also when needed? What of the equipment to be used in our record keeping. The typewriters, cabinets, etc., and not to be overlooked, the records themselves?

It is important for union officials to remember that everything being done today, whether recorded or not, will become tomorrow's history of the union. If we want to ensure that the history will be accurate and complete, the documentation of today's events becomes important, and more so, the preservation of what is documented.

What also of the equipment utilized in our accounting function? Is servicing left to chance or do we approach it as the organizations with which we interact, approach the servicing of say a $5,000,00 dragline or a $500,000.00 computer?

Next future needs. Are we planning to have them satisfied? How many typewriters, calculators, computers, and cabinets will we need?

These are activities often overlooked by our unions as they appear trivial in nature, but unless the union pays attention to this aspect of its role, its efficiency and effectiveness will be at stake.

I once told my wife that if ever I become the Political Leader of a country, I would appoint her Minister of Finance.

I said this, as it has been my experience that women are more concerned with the efficient spending of money that men and also its safe-keeping. That being so, it would not be difficult for me to discuss with a group of Women Trade Union Leaders the importance of what Bakke terms "**Finance Activities**."

Money they say makes the world go round. The Physicists may challenge this, but no one can refute my contention that without money no trade union can effectively represent the interests of its members. The growth of our local unions since the check-off was first granted to public service unions in 1954 and other unions at a later periods can testify to this. Of course, the first union to acquire the check-off was the Transport Workers' Union in 1949, and incidentally, that was the first union to acquire its own headquarters, and its effectiveness in the 1950s/1960s is unquestionable.

Money is needed to conduct those activities that will define, make clear, legitimize and symbolize the image of the unique wholeness of the union. Money is needed to acquire and develop the personnel necessary to manage the union and service its membership. It is also needed to acquire and perpetuate the material, equipment and building etc., to be used in union activities.

I will argue that unless there are activities directed towards acquiring, protecting and accounting for the finance needed by the union, nothing seriously can be done towards giving effect to the objectives of the union.

It is of interest to note that Bakke speaks of "**perpetuating capital**" and this goes beyond the notes and coins with which we are familiar, as it embodies all the assets of the union – money, land, building, equipment and other property utilized in executing the tasks associated with objects achievement.

I will advance, that a part of the union function must be the acquisition of the funds and other assets necessary for it to manage its business at the level that makes it possible for the union to enact both its primary and secondary roles as outlined. Unless this is done, the union may be no more than a name and a registration number with laudable objectives and nothing more, or what some have termed paper unions.

Bakke also speaks of what he termed "**Thought-ways Activities.**" Activities to "perpetuate ideas such as alternative strategies, plans, organized bodies of data and knowledge, concept of value, self, character of organization, participants position and standing, nature and potential of all the basic resources, the environment, etc. Especially important are rules, codes, and sanctions."

It is my opinion, therefore, that any union that lacks those who can provide what is listed above as thought-way activities, can be nothing but ineffective in its object achievement efforts. I further argue, that any trade union leadership that seeks to curtail the inputs of those who can provide or actuate the above activities does a dis-service to the union.

It follows, that the union must be structured in such a way that the available ideas covering the areas listed by Bakke can be encouraged and developed by discussion, etc. For in the final analysis, they determine the effectiveness of the union.

My experience has been, that the good leader is the one who encourages the contribution of others, can recognize a good idea and develop it; can get it accepted by the majority and put it into effect in the interest of furthering the development of the organization.

Later, when I discuss the Development Strategy this aspect will be further developed.

"Workflow Activities" are those, which are directed towards creating an output. Bakke listed two subclasses of these activities as:

      (a) Production Activities
      (b) Distributing Activities

The first question is – What is the output of a trade union?

The second is – What is it that a trade union produces?

The second question may not be baffling, since for some time now, we have been told that the union provides a service, and so the service is what the union produces.

The first question is at times difficult to answer. This is so, since there is no physical product that we can see. However, students of Industrial Relations will know that the union as an actor in the Industrial Relations System, contributes in the production of the rules settling out the salary and wages, hours of work, fringe benefits and other terms and conditions of work, governing the performance of those we term the actors in the system, as set out earlier when I listed my set of truths.

The rules, it can be said, are what we term the output, and whether the rules will be beneficial to the membership of the union, depends on the effectiveness of the union.

The rules, as mentioned in the truths I referred to in the Preamble of this Paper, are made principally by the Union and the Management through the process of Collective Bargaining, and as all women will know, the outcome of any bargaining is determined by which of the two parties are in the stronger bargaining position.

Of interest to note, nonetheless, is that the strength of the bargaining position of the parties, very often is determined by which of the two parties have access to, or the support of those who wield power in the wider society. Those whom we term the power centers, and they can be a political party, the church, an influential family, the army, etc.

Of course, not all rules are made by the collective bargaining process, for the mechanism for making the rules also include, conciliation, arbitration, advisory Commissions, strikes, wages councils, legislation, etc., and in the context of Guyana, the President of the Co-operative Republic under Labor Amendment Act, No. 9 of 1984 and the Constitution Amendment Act of 1987.

Nonetheless, whether the process is by Collective bargaining or the other mechanisms I have listed the effectiveness of the trade union as represented by its strength, is a factor that will influence in whose favor the rules will be.

To conclude this aspect, I must look at what is termed the "**Distributing Activities**" in the context of the union.

As I see it, this means that the product must reach for whom was intended and then others, by a continuing expansive process. In the context of the union, rules (product) are of no use unless they are observes, and it is the role of the union to see to it that the management lives up to the promises it agreed to honor, and this call for another sort of activities provided for **in the agreement for the avoidance and settlement of disputes**, or the other **legal enactments** governing the welfare of workers.

These activities, production and distributing, when successfully undertaken by the union, very often communication to the membership that the union is satisfying the purpose for which it was created, while at the same time fashioning the organizational charter of the union. These activities are therefore vital for maintaining the union as an instrument to be used in the continuing economic emancipative process of the working man and woman.

"Control Activities" Bakke advanced that "these activities, if effectively carried out, result in work and output of a quantify and quality adequate to sustain the continued contributions to and support for organizational operations by participants and outside recipients of the output."

The sub-class of these activities is listed as:

- Directive Activities
- Motivation Activities
- Evaluation Activities
- Communication Activities

The importance of these activities is self-evident, as they all apply to the union.

There are things, many things to be done by the union, and as such, communicating what is to be done and why, must be the responsibility of someone or some group in the union, and these activities must be conducted effectively if compliance at an acceptable level is to be expected. They can be termed – directive activities.

There are also the "**motivation activities**" directed towards satisfying the needs of those involved In union business, so as to get the best possible performance. The rewards are those that must be offered for diligent performance such as representing the union at conferences and seminars, appointments to boards, etc., and monetary rewards such as honoraria. All must be directed towards achieving better performance.

To be considered also, must be the penalties for behavior inimical to the interest of the union, for where there are no penalties, a drag is placed on increased effort. Foremost, however, is that the leaders must grant rewards when they are justified and penalties when they became necessary, always remembering that an excessive use of penalties discourages contribution or participation when it is voluntary. This is important, for unless leaders approach their tasks with an attitude of justice, fair play and understanding, it leads to factionalism within the union, which lowers performance and affects effectiveness.

Evaluation of the performance is also necessary, if we are to assess not only the performance, but "the state of the whole organization internally and in relation to its environment." This will necessitate both an evaluation of the performance , and the performers within the union against set targets or norms. That is to determine what achievements have been made in advancing the union and the quality of life of its members. Of importance also, are the external or community factors such as the ratio of unemployment, union/public relations and the price/wage ratio. There are other environmental factors, especially those of an economic and political nature, which the union, acting individually, may not be able influence. Yet, collectively, through national trade union centers, they can initiate the kinds of activities to influence decision-making in the economic and political systems directed towards improving the lot of the working man and woman.

Evaluation, therefore, must not be limited to the task and the person executing the task. It must not be limited to determining what was not achieved and who or what was responsible, and then apply penalties. Evaluation is only meaningful, if we also endeavor to assess the areas of good performance and what were responsible. Then looking at the areas of low achievement, a comparative study must be conducted, to be followed by the planning of new strategies and alternative courses of action to improve performance in those areas of low achievement, whether internal or external.

The **"Communication Activities"** as said by Bakke, are "those which supply participants with the premises and data they need in order to perform other activities." This is no doubt true, but communication activities must be conducted with an understanding that - "a relevant flow of Information is as necessary to an organization, as the blood-stream is to a person," as Gordon Lippet says; and how right he is.

Trade Union leaders need the kind of information that can assist them in making better decisions, and so better leaders. It must be remembered, however, that decisions are made, either bases on available information or insufficient or non-existent relying solely on one's experience. Experience, which must never be overlooked, is at times unreliable as a result of rapid changing conditions in the organization or the environment.

Union membership on the other hand needs the kind of information that can make them better understand the need for the union and its purpose, their rights and responsibilities as union members, and how they can become involved in union activity, and why it is so necessary.

Communication activities within the union must be directed, therefore, at both the union leadership and the union membership, all intended to improve the effectiveness of the union.

"Homeostatic Activities" Bakke described as those – "which serve to stabilize and vitalize the organization as a whole in an evolving state of dynamic equilibrium."

This speaks of the dynamic nature of the union and the changes that must be introduced to deal with the changing situations. It involves the activities that must take place to told the union together while it moves from one stage to another in the growth process.

Bakke advances that this class of activities is really a combination of other activities, but with certain specific features. Homeostatic, in medical terminology, says Bakke, is the peculiar nature of the human body, where it tends to automatically adjust to deficiencies developed in the system, as the craving for salt by pregnant women, etc.

In the context of the union, therefore, the homeostatic activities are those, which the union must be capable of performing without difficulty or delay, as it is confronted with changing conditions within and without the union. They must be able to keep the union functioning and preserve its organizational charter, its uniqueness. This must be so whether the conditions created offer advantages to the union or threaten its existence, for what is of importance, is the maintenance of the union as the continuing organization capable of meeting the challenges presented by today's situation, while it preserves itself to deal successfully with those of tomorrow.

CONCLUSION OF THE PRIMARY ROLE

I have no doubt spent too must time in discussing this aspect of my paper, but this is so, as I consider it necessary that trade union leaders develop a wider and more scientific concept of the role of the union. Unless this is done, our unions will be incapable of dealing with the challenges presented by the changing environment of third world countries, as political leaders endeavor to grapple with the development of their economies.

Throughout the world, whether first, second or third, the trade unions are under severe pressure, as many now question their relevance. Living standards are either static or declining and the rules being established or negotiated, impacts negatively on the union membership to a great extent.

It is important that trade unions adjust to these situations while preserving their organizational charter, for new situations lie ahead, which they must be able to confront successfully. If this is to be so, however, the activities I have discussed become tremendously important. Consequently, it is vital that leaders get down to the task of strengthening the union and re-establishing that image it once created as the champion of the rights of the worker at the workplace and the work community.

It is recognized, however, that as a result of the dynamic nature of the environment, the union will have to respond to new situations and as it does so, even its organization change will necessitate change.

Fundamental to the change, must be the preservation of its image as the champion of the worker rights, for without this, the trade union becomes no more than a name, conjuring conflicting images of what it is, confusing the workers, and delaying their economic emancipation.

It is in this context that I will next discuss that aspect of my paper, which deals with The Development Strategy in a Third World Environment.

It will be observed however, that I have declined to discuss the role of the union in achieving the secondary objectives I have outlines. This is so, as I consider them to be very elemental, the achievement of which is dependent on the effectiveness of the union. That is why the pursuit of its primary objective – Preserve and Strengthen the Union, is so vitally important.

THE DEVELOPMENT STRATEGY IN A THIRD WORLD ENVIRONMENT

In the opening of my paper, in outlining what I consider to be a number of truths. I mentioned that there is no single third world environment, but many, and that the environment is always in the process of change.

I also stated that I will be looking at two typical environment of the third world and relate them to the Caribbean scene. These two environments I have termed:

1.   The Multi-Party/Market Economy Environment
2.   The one Party/ Planned Economy Environment

It is now necessary for me to look in more detail at the environment I have identified.

THE MULTI-PARTY/MARKET ORIENTED ENVIRONMENT

These are the societies with a recent colonial past and which still preserves the West Minister Style of Government with a change in political leadership periodically through the process of "democratic elections."

The economy is market oriented, and it is usual to find in these environments private enterprise predominating with the accent being on what is termed foreign investment in the economy. This means that in most cases, capital investment is by way of multi-national corporations, at times in partnership with local investors.

It is also usual that the economy is dependent on either a single agricultural crop such as sugar, cocoa, bananas, coffee, tea, etc., or some base metal such as bauxite, copper, tin, and zinc. It is usual also that the demand for the product is in its raw state and by the developed economies of the first and second worlds of the West, whose economies are also market oriented. In some cases, however, the economy is largely dependent on a tourist industry dominated by private investment.

The type of environment described is, therefore, heavily dependent on the economies of the West. There economic base is very fragile, and this causes many political groups, when in Government, to seek to first strengthen the base, and then expand it by the production of manufactured goods, mainly for export, again to the western markets. This had given rise to the quip –"whenever the United States of America sneezes, the Third World catches a cold."

Another aspect of this environment Is that, as the, markets of the West are very competitive, it forces investors into the Third World Economies, to seek concessionary measures from the Government, very often centering on employment costs, with a view of limiting production costs. This must be considered against the background, that the Third World countries are all competing against each other for what some people claim to be scarce capital. Capital that is becoming more costly as a result of the excessive demand, resulting from the enormous U.S. deficit.

Another feature of this environment is that the several political groups have linkage with existing trade unions, and it is usual to find clusters of unions in opposing camps, determined by which political group they support.

Political rivalry is, therefore, extended to inter-union rivalry, for politics predominate these societies. Further, when it is not inter-union rivalry as mentioned, it is internal-union rivalry resulting again, from political cleavages. This however, has greater consequences for the union and its membership.

Yet another feature of this, and all Third World environments is the high levels of unemployment and under-employment.

This must be the concern of a seminar such as this, for unemployment impact first on women and youth, both of whom have not yet acquired the competitive competence to acquire jobs at times of employment, or to maintain them in times of recession.

This I know may be challenged, but experience shows it to be true, even if not for the reason I have advanced above, but as a result of prejudices, resulting from male attitudes to women in respect of their role in society. This aspect, I know will be fully discussed during this seminar.

Another important feature of this environment and all Third World environments is the predominance of politics as I have already alluded to, and its affects on trade unions.

In the Third World poverty exists, and as a result, it is only the political groups with an appeal to the masses that can hope to become the Government. To maintain themselves in office, therefore, the group must pander to the workers to maintain their support, and this very often have serious consequences for the economy. Failing to do this, they pursue harsh policies while using their influence among the trade union leadership to keep the worker in line.

This is not difficult, for as I have said, poverty is always present and politicians when in Government have the capability of dispensing favors. Either by influencing the granting of recognition to favored unions thus increasing union finance, and/or appointments to political offices where they can wield a certain amount of power.

Let it not overlooked also, that in many cases there is no influential capitalist class seeking political office, and the church is often without influence. At times, of course, the only other group with the capability of changeling the power of the political group, is the army where is exists. This being the case, politics predominate.

It is in this milieu that some trade unions operate in the Third World, and to discuss a strategy for development poses a challenge, as it is seldom that you find a strong national trade union center existing, if one exists at all, since very often, the political divisions negates unity.

THE ONE-PARTY/PLANNED ECONOMY ENVIRONMENT

In this environment, the West Minister style Government is rejected and the one-party/planned system exists. The one-party states are those, where according to the constitution, only one party can exist and elections when conducted are for candidates of the party and who subscribe to its ideology, which is also stated in the constitution, and is usually socialist.

It is usual also, that a party leader who in some cases led the country into independence and becomes a father-figure holding the nation together as he dominates the political landscape.

As a result of its ideology, the economy is state controlled, following a nationalization process, or at times by the joint venture process between the state external multi-national corporations.

It is also the custom that the economy is "planned" and as such prices are state controlled and not left to the "whims and fancies of the market place." Wages are also restricted, as collective bargaining is some- what curtailed as trade unions tend to become integrated into the state or party apparatus, or if not, bogged down by weighty legislation, intended to negative their influence as "disruptive agencies."

It is, again, not usual that when trade unions are not state controlled, they are dubbed as reactionary and accused of being in the pay of external agencies opposed to the system of Government. While this can do doubt happen, especially during times of economic difficulties, it can well be that the unions are only acting in defense of the living standards of its membership in keeping with the Organizational Charter of the union, as the leadership and /or membership perceives it. This is, of course, in taking industrial action.

Another feature of this environment is the dis-illusion created among the workers. Prior to independence and nationalization, the political group campaigned under the banner – "Independence, Socialism and the Good Life."

Workers were led to believe that independence and socialism, where the commending height of the economy is controlled by the state on behalf of the people, would end exploitation. It was this exploitation they were told which was responsible for their state of poverty. A redistribution of wealth which nationalization will make possible is the answer to the question of poverty.

However, after the process of independence and nationalization, the good life is not immediately manifested and another banner is hosted – "SACRIFICE: INCREASED PRODUCTION: SELF SUFFICIENCY." These were the fine print in the political contract between the political group and the workers, and which the worker did not read, hence disillusionment.

Yet another feature of this environment is the massive state sector which often results in the state being the largest, or if not, a significantly large employer of labor. This results in the state now having a vested interest in production cost, which by the very nature of the society, Is usually high when compared with the developed societies.

"If we are to competitive we must lower production costs, "they now say, and as labor costs are the only ones over which they have ready control, wages policies are introduced that lowers the living standards of the workers.

It is to be remembered that the economic circumstances I discussed when I looked at the Multi-party/Market Oriented Environment are also applicable to this environment.

Here, again, disillusionment is created, presenting problems to the political leadership as it affects production, which worsens the problem, that the measures were intended to solve. This so often leads to the introduction of harsher and harsher measures to deal with a problem that progressively gets worse and worse.

STRATEGY FOR DEVELOPMENT

In preparing this aspect of my paper I had to make some assumptions. First, to understand what I was expected to cover in this presentation, and secondly, what the Third World workers expect of a trade union. These assumptions are:

1. When we speak of Strategy of Development we are speaking of the development of the trade union to perform some function.
2. The function of a trade union in the third world, irrespective of the environment, is primarily to improve the welfare and well-being of those who are its members and who, if they did not create the objects of the union, then they sub-scribe to the objects.
3. Workers are concerned over their static or declining living standards and expect that their unions will undertake the kind

of activities that will maintain their standard of living if not improve it.

4. That workers look forward to a society in which all men and women who labor will be able to enjoy the products of the Efforts of all men and women who labor.

It is with the above assumption in mind that I will deal with this aspect of the paper and, of course with the following beliefs.

1. Workers are more concerned with the acquisition and maintenance of jobs and the salary and wages, which will afford them the opportunity of enjoying the best quality of life that the economy can afford.
2. Workers are not generally over-concerned with things like ideology, i.e. socialism; communism; capitalism; imperialism etc.
3. Workers do not like incursions into their leisure hours and would like the decisions in respect of how these hours are to be spent, left to them.
4. Workers would like to entrust the management of their country and the economy in the hands of those in whom they have confidence with the belief that will led them to the good life.
5. Workers, as a form of insurance, join and will support a union so that its leadership will do such things to guarantee that those into whose hands they have entrusted the country and economy live up to their expectations – Deliver the goods.

I further believe that in the light of the Third World Environment:

1. There should be checks and balances against the misuse of political power and that the Church, The Captain of Industry, Trade Unions, The Judiciary, and The Army can provide these checks and balances.
2. The Multi-Party/Market Oriented Society provides greater opportunity for sustaining the checks and balances.

3. The One Party/Planned Economy Environment calls for greater vigilance by those members of the citizenry who belong or work in the institution that must provide the checks and balances if the misuse of political power is to be avoided.

4. It should be of greater concern to workers how efficiently the means of production are used than who owns them.

5. The participative approach to the Management of the country and the economy is best suited for Third World Countries. That is, partnership between the Government, the Trade Unions and Management of the Enterprise, in that of the private companies.

Finally, in the light of the above and all I have already said, my "Development strategy OF TRADE UNION IN A THIRD WORLD ENVIRONMENT" is as follows:

There must be a recognition, that political groups are as much in need of the support of trade unions when they are properly organized, financed, and led, as trade unions are in need of political support. It follows therefore, that trade unions in a Third World Environment, if they are desirous of influencing political decisions they must consider, as a priority, the preservation of their effectiveness and the effectiveness of the Movement.

The effectiveness of a trade union is a measure of the result of the success of the activists undertake by the union, and union activists must accept that – "When the unions inspiration through the workers blood shall run, there can be no power greater anywhere beneath the sun," is no mere slogan, but a statement of fact. The Organizational Charter of the union, however, creates this inspiration, and if the workers are to be inspired by the union, they must perceive the union as an organization capable of championing their rights and also winning for them their economic emancipation.

The workers must, therefore, consciously plan to create a union capable of achieving the kind of successes that develops the much needed inspiration, and for this to be done, as a priority, the following activities must be consistently undertaken:

1.   Identification Activities
2.   Perpetuation Activities
3.   Workflow Activities
4.   Control Activities
5.   Homeostatic Activities

In the context of the movement, however, it is necessary that trade unions which are small, un-financial, and badly organized be gotten rid of by mergers or dissolutions as they are weak links in the trade union chain and a danger to all workers in a Third World Environment. Reducing the number of unions –

a)   Tend to avoid inter-union rivalry, if lines of
      demarcation are outlined, and

b)   Make the union groupings more financial so
      that they can finance the activities necessary
      for their development.

Trade unions in a Third World Environment must also recognize that it is in their interest to have a working-class political group in control of the reins of Government. It is also in their interest to have a united working-class political group with which they can co-operate, so as to hasten the economic emancipation of the workers. Political divisions in the working-class create divisions in the trade union movement, which delay the progress of the workers.

It is, therefore, the responsibility of the unions and the movement to seek political unity among the working class and this must be seen as activities to be given priority.

It is, non-the-less, vital that trade unions in a Third World Environment maintain their independence and effectiveness, as a safe guard to curb excessiveness in the use of political power, especially in the case of these one-party states. To achieve this, trade unions must monitor the legislative process to prevent the right of people, including their members, being legislated away, sometime by well-intentioned politicians.

Trade unions, also, must not permit political excessiveness to develop to the stage where it leads to the seizure of political power by revolutionary groups through undemocratic processes, while claiming to act in the name of the people. Very often they subjugate both the people and the unions in the name of the revolution.

Trade Unions, therefore, must see themselves as the guardians of democracy, and at times the only one, but it must also ensure that democracy exists within the unions themselves. This call for a structure that involves the members in the decision making process. It also places responsibility in the hands of the members to ensure that the union is managed in keeping with its rules. Important to note, however, this is only possible if the membership is knowledgeable of union rules. In as much as the Rule of law must be protected in the society, in similar manner, so must it be protested in our unions? It must not be overlooked that in the Guyana context and that of most third world countries which were once colonies of England, trade union rules, once they are registered, becomes an extension of the Trade Union Act and ipso facts, a part of our laws.

TRADE UNION UNITY FOR PROGRESS - WORKERS STAND UP FOR GUYANA

Permit me first to bring May Day greetings to all workers in this mining community from the Guyana Trades Union Congress under the Theme – "Trade Union Unity for Progress – Workers Stand Up For Guyana".

Today, Comrade Chairman we have marched through the streets of this mining community in unity if not in unison. Workers, Trade Unionists, Managers, Politicians.

I say not in unison, because we do not as yet share that "complete agreement in all aspects", as the dictionary defines unison. It does not follow, however, that our objectives are dissimilar. To the contrary, they are. We may differ somewhat on the thing that must be done to achieve those objectives. Those differences, however, can be resolved by meaningful dialogue. One major problem centers on our concept of a trade union. There are some who believe that a union must be affiliated or associated with a political party and take its policy and ideological direction from that party. With this I have no problem. But there are those, like me, who believe in an independent trade union, cooperating with a working class Government towards the achievement of those objectives that will improve the quality of life of those we represent, and who contribute out of their wages and salary for the services the union provides.

Even here our disagreements are not enormous. All we need is understanding and tolerance.

Today, none-the-less, is the workers day. When we leave here we will be celebrating, as we should. But there is a serious aspect to this workers day. It is the day when the leadership of the organizations created by the workers to protect them at their work; to improve their conditions of work through collective bargaining; to seek to better the conditions of their lives, and to provide a means of expression for their views of problems of society, do some serious stock taking. We endeavor to assess our gains and our losses, so as to determine how far we are from our objectives, which is the creation of a society in which all men will be able to enjoy the fruits of the effort of all men who labor.

This May Day, however, has a greater significance. It is one hundred years ago today when the tragic event occurred that gave birth to this day that we now celebrate. May 1, 1886, was the day set aside by the workers of the United States of America for a general strike to press their demand for the eight hour day, and it was at the McCormick Harvester plant in Chicago, where police intervention, after clashes between strikers and strike-breakers, led to four workers losing their lives.

The riots that followed two days later resulted in seven policemen being killed and sixty wounded when a bomb was thrown into the ranks of the police. The response of the police accounted for four workers being killed and fifty or more being injured. It was a sad day for the World Labor Movement.

There is a lesson here for us. It was disunity in the ranks of the labor class of the USA that conditioned the clashes and the riots, and set back the cause of the labor movement. These are not things of which we in Guyana are unfamiliar.

Comrade Chairman, I have said that May Day is a time for stock taking by the Trade Union Movement. Our Movement is now sixty-seven years old, and there is no doubt that over those years there have been significant gains. However, for us to make a meaningful assessment, we must assess our gains and our losses relative to others who enjoyed a comparable standard of living with ours, when Critchlow founded our first union in 1919.

It is my contention that today, 1986, the standard of living of the Guyanese worker no longer compares favorable with that of workers in our sister Caribbean states, and there are reasons for this, and all of the reasons could be summed by one word – Disunity - Disunity among the ranks of the Guyanese workers.

Some I know may attempt to disapprove this, but I will say, let us not waste time in meaningless accusations or attempt to defend the indefensible, but direct our efforts towards correcting the situation, for Guyana possesses the potential to afford its people a much better standard of living. None can dispute this.

I have said that disunity is the cause of our problems. Some again, may question this, advancing that even in the ranks of the Trade Union Movement of our sister Caribbean states, there was and is disunity. That argument cannot be faulted. I will advance, however, that what sets Guyana apart from our sister Caribbean states, is the levels of disunity that exists within the ranks of our individual unions, unfortunately, that bred the disillusionment that exists among the trade union membership over the ability of our unions to protect them at their work; to improve the conditions of their workplace through collective bargaining.

At another forum, I expressed the view that within our society, there are those who wield considerable influence and who seem afraid of a strong Trade Union Movement. I may be wrong, but I will advance, however, that a weak trade union is of no use to its membership, a barrier to communication between management and worker, and of little use to a Government which is serious in its pursuit of raising the levels of productivity within our country and, hence, the quality of life of our people.

There is, Comrade Chairman, a kinship between trade union militancy and productivity. Here in Guyana, the "union's inspiration" that we so lustily sing about is dead, and so is the will to produce. At the management level, there seems to be the belief that trade union militancy is a stumbling block to the achievement of managerial objectives. The situation here in Linden belies this, for I am advancing that trade union militancy has been on the decline in this industry over the past fourteen years, resulting from repeated efforts to manipulate the trade union leadership, commencing from Verbeeke and Benjamin to Lewis and James. These figures are taken from the 1983 Bank of Guyana Report and, therefore, should be accurate, and while we accept that market conditions may have influenced our output, I am sure that even the management of this enterprise would say, our performance should have been better.

I am, none-the-less, aware that there has been an improvement over 1984 and 1985, but let me advise, that aggressive marketing is a waste of time unless matched by greater effort to improve morale at the production levels of the enterprise. In an article titled – "Change – A Challenge to Management by Gordon L. Lippet", the then President of the Leadership Resource, Inc. of Washington, D.C. had this to say- "The success in accomplishing improved productivity, greater efficiency, better service depends on management's mastery of the human resource to cope with the changing demands of an organization".

Comrade Chairman, it is my argument that the mastery of the human resource of this Guyana Mining Enterprise, especially at this time, cannot be achieved without the full involvement and cooperation of the unions in the management of the enterprise. I must however, advance that the unions themselves must realize that they will have a greater responsibility when that day comes. You, the representatives of workers, cannot, therefore, sit by and wait for that day to come before you start equipping yourselves to meet the changing demands and challenges, for as the People's Poet, Martin Carter prophesizes,

> Like a tide from the heart of things
> Inexorably and inevitably
> A (that) day will come".

Comrade Chairman, I will urge that the union leadership at all levels, and the membership of the two unions in this industry, have the tasks of preparing themselves for the rightful role that they have to play in getting this enterprise that is so vital to our economy, back on a sustained growth path, more so, as the industry now has the additional responsibility of providing the product that will be used to satisfy the energy needs of our country. This, I submit, must have serious implications for the industry.

In this effort, however, the management has a part to play, for they must honor those conditions in the collective agreement between Guymine and the Unions that have been held in abeyance for so long, especially those in respect of management's contribution toward the education program of the unions. I am aware that the fault does not all lie with management, but as I said, the time is past for leveling blame.

New Union/Management relationships must be established here at Guymine, for without this, all efforts at the mastery of the human resource will be futile. What I am advocating is the participative approach to management, the meaningful involvement of the workers, through their unions, in the decision making process of the enterprise.

Let me state, however, that those of us from the Trade Union Movement, do not see meaningful involvement of the workers, through the unions, in the decision making process of the enterprise.

Let me state however that those of us from the Trade Union Movement do not see meaningful involvement as having meager representation on some board, which, in any case, makes little or no decision of a significant nature. Participation as we see it, must be an extension of the collective bargaining process, where workers, through their unions, have already earned the right to participate in those decisions that determine their salary, wages and working conditions. It is a tragedy that the management of so many enterprises, public enterprises, do not recognize the vital role the unions can play in strengthening communication between management and the worker. The union is an important channel of communication and can contribute meaningfully towards improving the efficiency of both capital and labor if it is adequately utilized, and if, at the same time, the unions are conscious of their expanded function and the attendant responsibilities.

The involvement of the workers in the decision making process of the individual enterprise is however not enough in the content of the Guyana situation. The expanded public sector, embracing 80% of our economy, makes it necessary for the process to be extended to include the Cabinet. I strongly advocate that there is tremendous need for continuous dialogue between the Trades Union Congress and the President of the Cooperative Republic of Guyana, for it is vital that he acquires as much feedback as is possible, on the decisions made by the importance decision making forum over which he presides.

One writer, in speaking of this important aspect of the communication process, feedback, expressed the view that without adequate feedback, false perceptions creep in. Even small errors that go undetected may become magnified into major distortions. Communication, he said, gains in speed and efficiency as more and more feedback is employed – C.P. Prahalis – Crossing the Communication Crevice.

Comrade Chairman, there is need for the relationship between the Government and the TUC to be improved, for there are too many false perceptions and distortions resulting from the absence of dialogue. I advance, that at too many important decision making forums in our country, decisions are made on hearsay, which by the very nature of our society can be very dangerous, as there are so many with their own axe to grind. There can be no dispute that the relationship between the Government and the TUC has deteriorated considerably, attested to by the two May-Day rallies we had in 1985 and the frustration of the TUC's Annual Delegates Conference last September. Even as I write this address, uncertainty hovers over our being united on this 100th Anniversary of the event that inspired the founding congress of the Second International Conference held in Paris in 1889, to designate May 1st as the Workers Day. How tragic, but I urge that we put those things behind us.

There is however, another reason for us to institutionalize dialogue between the President of the Cooperative Republic and the TUC, for our Industrial Relations System has been transformed, to the extent that many industrial relation decisions are being made at the level of the Cabinet, and many of those decisions put serious restrictions on the managerial function, thus impairing the Union/Management relationship since the restrictions frustrate the collective bargaining process.

In this industry alone, there are several issues still lying at the Union/Management level or at conciliation, and which cannot be resolved without intervention of Cabinet, due to this new development. The fact is that our industrial relations mechanisms for resolving disputes do not provide for this recent phenomenon.

While at the level of the individual enterprise, difficulties are experienced; it is at the level of conciliation that the greatest handicap exists, for conciliation and arbitration are the mechanisms used for averting strikes that disrupt production. Conciliation, however, is meaningless when the root cause of a dispute lies in a Cabinet decision in which the Chief Conciliator, the The Minister responsible for Labor, was a party in the decision making process. The hands of the Conciliator are tied, be he a mere Labor Officer or the Chief Labor Officer, when the obstruction is rooted in the Cabinet. We cannot overlook the fact that a well-intentioned Conciliator knows that should he offend the Cabinet, not even his Union is capable of protecting him at his work.

Comrade Chairman, the situation is froth with danger and we must therefore address these problems, for unresolved grievances, even if they do not cause strikes, create the frustration that impede production. The question I must necessarily ask is - "Has bad Union/Management relations contributed to this decline? If I must provide the answer, I will say "Yes". Let us therefore proceed with the task of correcting this. We need trade union unity and the setting up of the mechanisms that will utilize that unity in the achievement of progress.

Comrade Chairman, I know that some of my colleagues, my friends, must feel left out since most of my remarks were directed at the workers of Guymine, both management and non-management, and the two unions in the industry.

This has been deliberate, for unless the smoke continues to belch from those chimneys we see over and beyond us to the south, there would be little need for the thousands that now comprise this community. It is the $45M (approximately) in wages and salaries paid by Guymine that sustains this community. Withdraw it, and we can well have a ghost town, similar to those that once littered the American West.

It is important however for us to note that the services you provide here at Linden impacts the quality of life of those who sustain this community, the Bauxite Workers, hence, the productivity of the Guyana Mining enterprise. This is so, whether you are employed in the Regional Office, the Town Council, the Hospitals, the Schools, the Police Service, the Shops and Stores, the Market, the Bus Company, as a taxi driver, a boatman, a farmer, or even as trader who provide the outlet for your much sought after merchandise. You all have a part to play and a stake in the success of this most vital industry, for finally, as my friend Martin Carter says:

Like the jig shakes the loom
Like a web is spun the pattern
All are involved
All are consumed

TRADE UNION FOR PROGRESS! YES! We need unity, and we need a strong, well-led and responsible Trade Union Movement. Yes! We can all stand up for Guyana and I will urge that you do, but if we can rekindle that union's inspiration that we sing about, in standing up, we will be Standing Tall.

Greetings again on behalf of the Guyana Trade Union Congress, Happy May-Day! Long Live the Trade Union Movement! Long Live the Cooperative Republic of Guyana!

TRADE UNIONS: WHAT THEY ARE AND WHAT THEY DO
1998

The definition of a trade union, quoted below, is that adumbrated by the International Confederation of Free trade Unions and used in developing this paper: Trade unions, What They Are and What They Do:

> A trade union is a continuing, permanent and democratic Organization, voluntarily created by the workers, to protect them at their work, to improve their conditions of work through collective bargaining, to seek to better the conditions of their lives and to provide a means of expression for the workers' views on problems of society.

ORGANIZATION: WHAT IT IS.

Before proceeding to discuss the continuing, permanent and democratic characteristics of a trade union, it is necessary to first note that a trade union, as stated in the above definition, is termed an organization. This is what results when persons who share common concerns and problems, align themselves in a group with an objective of satisfying common needs. In the process, they functionally group activities where like-problems, questions, and decisions tend to come together. It can be said, then, that workers join or create the organizations we call trade unions, because they share common concerns and problems and they hope to satisfy many common needs. It can be said, also, those organizations created by workers, share common characteristics.

None would deny that those who work for a wage or a salary do share many common concerns and problems, and through the trade unions they created or joined, they seek to find the solutions to their problems and seek to satisfy their many common needs. It is how trade unions endeavor to solve the many problems of workers and seek to satisfy their many common needs that this paper will address.

A CONTINUING, PERMANENT & DEMOCRATIC ORGANISATION
(a)   Continuing & Permanent

If the Trade Union Movement is to survive, the continuity of which the above definition speaks must be reflected at the workplace. This means that it is there where the presence of the union must be continuously felt. In other words, the Union's presence must be visible in the workplace.

Now if the union is to make a continuing impact at the level of the workplace, the branch, local or whatever name the smallest unit of the union is called, must see itself as a microcosm of the larger body, the union. This means that the branch, like the union of which it is a part, must be doing such things, directed towards giving effect to the objects of the union, as set out in its Rules or Constitution.

The objects are important, for they are in truth a "shopping list" of the things that the union was voluntarily created to accomplish. Here, it is important to note that the importance of the objects lies in the fact that the law mandates that the Funds of the union be only spent "in pursuit of the objects of the Union." Consequently, it is necessary that those at the workplace be made knowledgeable of both the objects, and rules of the union in which the objects are adumbrated.

The rules are important, for apart from setting out the objects of the union, they also embody the rights and obligations of the individual members. They also list the responsibilities of the leadership of the union, including those of the branch and the constraints imposed on them.

Yet another aspect of the continuing nature of a trade union centers on that of problems. No one can deny that the problems faced by workers are continuous. Acknowledging this, it must follow that since the problems are continuous, the union, if it is to successfully address the continuous problem, must itself be a continuing organization. More importantly, however, is that the problems mostly occur at the workplace. Therefore, it is at workplace where the continuous nature of the trade union must be most visible. That visibility is found in the shop stewards and branch officials, hence their importance.

In respect of the permanent characteristic of a trade union, it is advanced that the permanence is an "off-shoot" of its continuing feature. The question that arises, therefore, is how to recognize that permanence at the workplace?

The permanent records kept by both the union and branches relative to their activities should recognize the permanence. Especially those directed towards giving effect to the achievement of the objects of the union. This speaks of records of meetings, correspondence received and dispatched, reports on activities undertaken. Included also, must be the records of financial transactions and membership, together with that of the property belonging to the branch and union, and into whose hands the property has been entrusted. It need not be mentioned why this is important.

The importance of proper record keeping cannot be over stressed. Everything that the union is doing today, especially at the workplace, will become the history of tomorrow. That is, of course, provided that those who would document the history are provided with the records of what is being done today. Unless the historian can have access to what is being done today, the history would be subjective and very often filled with inaccuracies. It is in the union's interest to avoid this.

The final aspect of the permanence of the union is a statement attributed to Ray Gunther, a Minister of Labor in the Wilson Cabinet of the 1960's. As Gunther then said:

> "Trade Unions are not eternal, they will continue to exist for as long as they remain compatible to the society in which they seek to exist".

It is important for unions to ponder upon what Gunther had then said. This is so, for the permanence of a union is not guaranteed, as history attests, by way of the number of unions, earlier established, but no longer exists. The most notable being the Manpower Citizens Association registered in 1937. That permanence would be determined by the effectiveness of the union in satisfying the needs of its membership as dictated by changes in both the world and the environment in which the union functions.

(b)   A Democratic Organization

A great American President in speaking of democracy in his famed Gettysburg Address had this to say:

> "and that this nation under God will have a new birth of freedom and that   Government of the People, by the People, for the People shall never perish from this earth".

Abraham Lincoln

President Lincoln's views of government, must also apply to the trade union. It is advanced, therefore, that those who must speak for the union at all levels, must do so with the authority of the membership.

Further, those who must speak must be elected from among the membership. Lastly, whenever they speak, whatever they are proposing or advocating must be in the interest and /or well-being of the membership, and with their consent.

To conclude this aspect, unless democracy is present in the union, especially at the workplace, the continuity and permanence adumbrated in the definition of a trade union to which reference has been made cannot be guaranteed. Equally, the need for the union's existence and even its relevance may soon be under challenge as Gunther had stated. However, there is yet another aspect of democracy, which will be, discussed later, when the issue of "Justice at the Workplace" is discussed, and that is the Rule of law.

2. TO PROTECT THEM AT THEIR WORK

There are three distinct aspects of the Union's obligation to protect the worker at the workplace. They are:

a. Protecting the job of the worker
b. Protecting the physical being of the worker
c. Protecting the worker against injustice

a. Protecting Jobs

In a publication titled – The Dynamics of Industrial Democracy – Clinton, S. Golden and Harold Rotenberg posited that in as much as a worker works for a salary or wage and with the accumulation of a year's salary/wage he can purchase a plot of land which no one can take away unless he sells it, in similar manner the worker with some years of service should have ownership of his job "unless he voluntarily gives it up or forfeits it by the infraction of a rule agreed upon by his union and management".

It is the view of many, that the protection of jobs must be the first responsibility of the union at the workplace. Unfortunately, especially in the context of today's Global Economy where profits become the overriding factor, the attitudes toward jobs held by management and union are changing rapidly, to the extent that they are becoming irreconcilable.

Today's manager, ever conscious of the "bottom line", sees the worker as a unit of labor-cost to the enterprise which must be monitored to ensure that it does not have an adverse effect on the "competitive edge of the enterprise in the Global Market Place".

What is important here, is that "employment costs" in the Guyana context is always of great significance to management. This is so, since it is the one factor of production over which they have most control.

It is now important to consider a slide in the Guyana dollar and its likely consequences for companies utilizing a large amount of foreign inputs. Now, every movement downwards of the Guyana dollar relative, to say, the $US, is likely to push upwards the cost of imports into our country. This mean that if the $G continues to slide, companies to which I have referred will be seriously affected due to the kind of inputs utilized in the production process, including, of course, the refurbishing and maintenance inputs.

What follows from this, is that so often when market forces, influenced by the above, impact negatively on total production cost, jobs are likely to be put at risk. This is so, since the only recourse that management may have to maintain its   competitiveness, is to cutback on employment cost by way of reduction in staff levels or wage/salary cuts.

However, while the declining value of the G$ can seriously affect the "bottom line" of the company as stated above, its effects are mainly on the expenditure side of the Budget Statement. This speaks, of the "Planned Expenditure" of the company.

Notwithstanding that, there are times, nonetheless, when the income side of the budget statement is affected, i.e. its "anticipated income." This occurs when market forces impact negatively on the price of the commodity produced by the company, be it gold, bauxite, sugar, rice, or rum, all of which are produced mainly for export and are subjected to the varieties of the markets for the respective commodities.

In similar manner to the adjustments that must be made to protect the company's "bottom line" when the expenditure side of the budget is being affected, measures will have to be introduced to protect the bottom line when the income side (anticipated income) is threatened.

This is in no way suggesting that at times when market forces affect the bottom line, the only resource that management may have, is cutbacks on employment costs. This is so, since there are alternatives such as more efficient use of both the existing labor input and other inputs.

Here it is important to note the views of E. Wight Bakke about the manager's job in a publication – Mutual Survival, the Goal of Union and Management." As Bakke states:

> "The job for which he is immediately rewarded or punished is promoting the welfare, not of the world, not of the National Economy, not of the industry, but of his own company."

Mention has already been made of the differing attitudes of management and labor towards the thorny issue of jobs. Also identified were some of the factors that tend to condition the attitude of management towards jobs. It is now necessary to look at the attitude of the union towards the same jobs, and some of the factors that condition the attitude of the union's leadership.

First to be looked at, is perception. Now while a manager in looking at a worker may only see a unit of production with a cost to the enterprise, the union official, looking at the same worker is likely to see someone working for wages or salaries which will enable that worker to provide food, shelter and the other necessities of life for both the worker and the worker's family. In other words, the worker meeting his/her social responsibilities.

Here, it is necessary to comment on the specific case of the female worker, especially the female heads of households. They must be of great concern to the union due to their vulnerability, which will not be discussed here. Suffice it to say that job loss for those workers can have serious social consequences. Important to note, it was the job-loss of female workers during the difficult period of the late 1970's - 1980's, which was a major contributing factor to many of our current social ills.

There is yet another important aspect of job-loss that must be of importance to the union. It must not be overlooked that every job that is lost, if not matched by a job created, pushes up the rate of unemployment, and if a negative trend persists, it eventually threatens wage levels. This is so; since high levels of unemployment increases competition amongst workers for the scarce jobs, while it decreases competition amongst employers.

Earlier, while discussing the effects of market forces on the profitability of the enterprise, mention was made of the effects it can have on jobs. It is therefore important to discuss the impact of job-loss on the bottom line of the union's budget, i.e. its "anticipated income" and "planned expenditure." This is necessary since job losses mean fewer dues hence less income for the union.

Unfortunately when union and management are discussing job-loss, the discussion is usually centered on management's efforts to counter the negative impact on it finances by the market forces, which has already been alluded to. Often overlooked is how the measures to be introduced, will affect the union's finances. Yet, though seldom ever discussed, it is always an underlying issue, and most often, it tends to influence the union's behavior whenever the issue of job-loss is under discussion.

Job-loss is fast becoming a major issue in union/management relations. Daily, the need to "down-size", to be "lean and clean." is being put forward by both management and government as the way to counter the threat posed by globalization. From what has already been said, the impact of the Global Market Place is presenting, and will continue to present tremendous challenges for both union and management at the workplace, (the micro industrial relations system of the enterprise). As already advanced, both union and management are being affected. It is submitted therefore, that union/management confrontation is not the way to go. What is now needed, is for, as Bakke suggests, union and management to sit down on an ongoing basis and reasonably and rationally discuss their "mutual survival, in the face of the enormous challenges being posed by the Global Market Place, a context, a given to their collective relationship, over which they have no control.

b.   Protecting the Physical Being

It was the advent of the industrial revolution on or about 1750 that ushered in the need for safety at the workplace. The motivation of the early capitalist was profit and more profit. People were an expendable commodity and in the greedy pursuit of profit many were being mangled or killed in the production process.

At that time, the view of the employer was that accidents were the result of carelessness by the workers, no matter the long hours they had to work, and the "hell-house" that was the early factory.

The first efforts of the workers in those days to address the issue of industrial accidents were to obtain legislation that would provide compensation for those injured or killed. Here in Guyana, our first effort was when Ordinance # 21 of 1916 – Accidental Deaths and Workmen's Injuries (Compensation) – was enacted, with Amendment in 1940, 1963 and 1972. Then in 1947 came the Factories Ordinance, which for the first time addressed the causes of accidents. The factories ordinance, however, did not become fully operational until June 1953. We had arrived at recognition that "accidents do not happen, they are caused." In 1968 came the National Insurance Scheme and Act # 21 of 1972 and Regulation, 1974. Finally, in 1997 – The Occupational Safety and Health Act.

Accepting therefore, that accidents are caused, it becomes the responsibility of the union to ensure that accidents are eliminated from the workplace.

Training therefore becomes important, for while there are legislations enacted to offer protection to the worker at the workplace, the effectiveness of the legislations will depend on how knowledgeable are our workers and their leaders at the workplace, about the rights and obligations of both workers and management, as set out in the legislations. Therefore, the educating and informing of workers about the things mentioned above must be seen as an important function of the Union at the workplace.

c.   Protection Against Injustice

There are many who claim that Guyana's return to the democratic fold on the 8th October 1992 when the PPP was returned to office after 28 years of the PNC, was no more than a return to political democracy and some may question even that. As some see it, while Guyana may have returned to political democracy, that democracy has not "trickled down" to many workplaces.

Fundamental to democracy is the Rule of Law, where the laws are sacrosanct, inviolable. It also implies that just mechanisms must exist for making the laws. Fundamental to the making of the laws, however, is that they must be done with the consent and approval of the people. What is needed they argue, are not laws per se, but Just laws.

The question that now arises is whether industrial democracy as it relates to rules, rulemaking and mechanism for making rules, do exist at the level of the workplaces of our country.

Fundamental to the rule of law is the "right to natural justice." This implies that discipline should only be instituted after "due process." This means that the worker, if suspected of the infraction of some rule (law), he should be charged with the committing of an offence and afforded the opportunity of defending himself against the charge leveled. In other words, he must be afforded "due process."

What must be next considered is to whom must the worker be answerable for the charges leveled against him. Must it be to those who have leveled the charge, i.e. management, or as it is in the judicial system of the country, before his peers in the form of a jury or an impartial magistrate. Similar to the judicial system, in matters of discipline at the workplace, it must be a jury of his peers by way of a disciplinary committee. Those who must comprise the committee must meet with the approval of both management and the worker.

Cognizance must be taken nonetheless of the complaints by many managers of the difficulties they experience in instituting discipline. They complain of the "long drawn out procedures" which inhibit their right to manage and its negative effects on production and productivity. The union's response to that, must be, it is the price we have to pay for democracy. As it is so often said, it is better for five guilty men to go free than for one innocent man to be convicted.

It must not be overlooked; that what is being advocated is justice at the workplace. What is being advanced, therefore, is the establishment of an industrial judicial system at the workplace. However, if such a system is to be effective, it places responsibilities on both union and management. First, in the processing of a grievance, it must not be an issue of winning, i.e., union defeating management or management defeating union, but a process for determining the truth, so that Justice will prevail.

Unfortunately, winning is most often the objective of both union and management hence the conflict relationship experienced at the workplace.

There are both advocates and opponents of the grievance procedures trade unions have been able to establish at the workplace. Yet, if there is to be justice at the workplace, there can be no substitute. John

Dunlop and James Healy in their "Collective Bargaining: Principles and Cases," had this to say about the grievance procedure:

> "Any statement they make will be subject to check by the other side before a superior officer. In this way the grievance procedure as a channel of information may be expected to be less subject to self-serving statements of facts than most chains of command within an organization."

What Dunlop and Healy seem to be suggesting, is that those who dispense discipline, knowing that their acts would be under scrutiny by both union and those higher up the managerial chain of command, would be more prone to avoid decisions centered on "self serving interest" which so often is the cause of industrial disputes. Further, knowing that disputes via the grievance procedure, would likely reach the stages of conciliation and arbitration, those higher up the chain of command may tend to be more just in their decision—making when reviewing acts of their subordinates. Important here, is the confidence both union and management must have in the impartiality of the conciliators and arbitrations if the process is to be effective.

Here, mention must be made of the many violations of grievance procedures that seem to be escalating. This is by both union and management. Experience has shown that whenever they occur, it is usually due to the violating party, knowing that their acts relative to the issue in dispute would not stand up to scrutiny at either conciliation or arbitration. To use a Guyanese colloquialism – "they prefer to be wrong and strong." There is a disturbing situation arising in both the private and public sectors however, and that is the refusal of managements to go to arbitration and challenging unions to take them to the courts. This seem to imply that they are suggesting that the courts would be friendly to the managerial hierarchy, recalling the statement of Justice Scrutton in 1920. As he had said:

> "The habits you are trained in, the people with whom you mix, lead to your having a certain class of ideas, you do not give as

> sound and accurate judgments as you would wish...How can a labor man or trade unionist get impartial justice? It is very difficult sometimes to be sure that you have put yourself into a thoroughly impartial position between two disputants, one of your own class and one not of your class."

As said earlier, democracy comes with a price tag. Justice and the rules of law impose a restriction on the excessive use of might by the mighty. It is a leveler, since before the law, all are said to be equal. Yet, one must not be blind to the fact that in spite of equality before the law, some are more equal than others since we still live in an imperfect world. It is for this reason, the trade union is so necessary at the workplace, for it is, itself, a leveler.

This raises the issue of the disciplinary code, which must be operable at the workplace. The code ensures equal treatment, since it removes subjectivity and prejudice from decision-making in respect to allotting penalties as a measure of discipline. This is so, since the code matches penalties to the offenses.

To conclude this aspect, if justice is to prevail at the workplace, it places a responsibility on both union and management. First there must be a functioning Industrial Judicial System present, where the rule of law is a fundamental constituent. It is also necessary for mechanisms to be in place for the making of Just rules. Finally, if I.J.S. is to be effective, it is necessary for those who must comprise the disciplinary committee, to be always conscious of their responsibilities. They sit not as union members or management's representatives but as jurors whose responsibility it is to make decisions based on facts supported by evidence.

Here, mention must be made of a statement by Justice Cummings in hearing an injunction filed by a member of NUPSE against the principal officers of the Union. As Justice Cummings had said - "it is not whether it is right or wrong, just or unjust, moral or immoral but what the law says." In the case of a member of the disciplinary committee, it is advanced that in arriving at decisions, the law will be the relevant rule(s) as set out in the collective labor agreement, and rules or regulations governing work performance of the employee as stated or implied in his contract of service, or upheld by the common law. In respect of the common law the obligations of the worker are:

i. To work and to co-operate
ii. To obey orders
iii. To take reasonable care and
iv. To be trustworthy

Equally there are obligations placed on the employer. They are:

i. To pay wages and salaries
ii Not to make unauthorized deductions
iii. (In some cases) to provide work.
iv. To provide a safe system of work
v. To obey the law, and
vi. To allow time-off

3. IMPROVING CONDITIONS OF WORK...

The definition of a trade union to which reference has been made, speaks of improving conditions of work through collective bargaining. It is contended, therefore, that if the union is to improve conditions of work, those who must bargain on behalf of the workers must be knowledgeable of the conditions of work that are in need of improvement and those which must be added. This can only be obtained from records of the grievances of the workers at the workplace and not what some leaders may think are the grievances.

If we are to remove subjectivity from decisions relative to what must be included or excluded from the C.L.A., it becomes incumbent on the branch leadership at the workplace to ensure that there is an up-to-date, accurate and well structured grievance register kept by the branch. The same, of course, must also apply to the union headquarters where a composite of all grievances must be kept.

In discussing the permanent characteristic of the union, earlier, the need for accurate record keeping was mentioned. The grievance register is one such record. Another is the minutes of meetings kept by the branch, for it is at the branch meeting where problems are aired and recorded for use when decisions are to be made about inclusions and exclusions needed in the C.L.A.

However, if trade union leaders at all levels are to be prepared for their task in improving the conditions of employment of their members, it is imperative that they are knowledgeable about what is collective bargaining and, also, what are the objectives of the union in collective bargaining. Equally, the members must be made aware of the process, which impacts so much on their living standards.

In the Taft/ Hartley Act of the United State of America, Collective Bargaining is stated as:

> the performance of mutual obligation of the employer and representative of the employees to meet at reasonable times and confer in good faith with respect to wage, hours and other terms and conditions of service or the negotiation of an agreement or any question arising thereunder, and the execution of a written contract if requested by either party, but such obligation does not compel either party, to agree to a proposal or require the making of any concession.

In the Employment Protection Act of 1975 in the United Kingdom, collective bargaining is stated – "as negotiations related to or connected with any of the matters listed in section 22 of the Trade Union and Labor Relations Act." They are:

a) allocation of work or duties of employment as between workers or group of workers.
b) matters of discipline
c) membership or non-membership of a trade union on the part of a worker.

d) facilities for officials of trade unions; and

e) machinery for negotiation or consultation, and other procedures, relating to any of the foregoing matters, including the recognition by employers or employers' associations of the right of a trade union to represent workers in any such negotiation or consultation or in the carrying out of such procedures.

The above two definitions clearly set out what collective bargaining is all about. In summary, it is the process in which the employer represented by a specific team of managers, meets with the workers, represented by their trade union within the frame-work of an agreed set of procedures to negotiate an agreement which will set out the salaries, wages, hours of work and other terms and conditions of employment that will become operable in a particular enterprise, from an approved date. The said agreement also includes provisions for setting disputes that may arise out of the agreement, and the negotiation of a new agreement on the termination of the existing agreement.

The definitions, though important, are not enough for an understanding of the importance of collective bargaining. For of equal importance, is an understanding of the sacrifices workers had to make so as to have a say in the determination of salaries, wages, hours of work, fringe benefits and other terms and conditions of employment. It is therefore the obligation of the trade union and the TUC to ensure that its education arm, the CLC, educate our workers and their leaders about that aspect of our trade union history.

To conclude this aspect, to obtain a better understanding of what collective bargaining is all about, a knowledge of the Objective of the Union in Collective Bargaining, and how it relates to the role of the union will be of assistance. The objectives are:

i.   To preserve and strengthen the union

ii. To improve the economic well-being of the members

iii. To acquire more control over jobs

iv.   To promote broad social and economic objectives

v.   To promote the personal ambitions of the union leaders.

(i) To Preserve and Strengthen the union.

It is unfortunate that today's young workers are either unappreciative or ignorant of the contribution of trade unions to the living standards they now enjoy. Truthfully, had it not been for trade unions, the condition of work now enjoyed by workers would not have been possible. It is imperative; therefore, that workers be made conscious of the contribution of the Trade Union in this regard, for this is the best way of ensuring the preservation of the trade unions created by workers.

Consequently, the history of the Trade Union Movement must be a prerequisite in every course run by our unions and CLC. For the long courses of the CLC, it must be an analytical history, clearly setting forth cause and effect. It is important, however, that in presenting the history of the Movement, every effort be made to identify those who contributed to the development of the Movement - the heroes and heroines who made possible that which is now taken for granted. Sadly, for most workers, there is but one hero – CRITCHLOW. This must be changed, and it is the responsibility of our unions and the Critchlow Labor College to be the instrument by which this is achieved. Research must be done to bring to light the other Heroes of Labor, for this will in no way diminish the brightest star of all, Hubert Nathaniel Critchlow.

The other aspect is that of strengthening the union. Strength, it is posited, will result from strengthening the finances of the unions. It is here where an adequate dues structure becomes necessary, and a guaranteed source of income, a necessity.

Collective bargaining necessitates research and the manpower necessary to present the information obtained, which speaks of the ability to analyze and utilize the information to advance the well-being of workers.

The guaranteed source of income will come from the check–off and agency shop. It follows that knowledge of the check off and agency shop and their contribution towards preserving and strengthening the unions, is most important. Therefore, courses ran by trade unions and the Critchlow Labor College should also include as part of the curriculum, the concept of the check–off and agency shop together with the benefits they have brought to the workers.

Notwithstanding the above, an important aspect of trade union finance is that of accountability. It is definitely an area in which trade unions are most deficient and this is a matter, which both unions and the College must address as a matter of urgency.

(ii) To Improve the economic Well- Being of the Members

The need for a strong union is primarily to improve the economic well-being of the membership. It is important to restate however, that strength is derived from the financial capability of the union. This is so, since it is out of the union's financial resources will come the ability to develop or employ the skills necessary to prepare the union's case for salary, wages, fringe benefits and other terms and conditions of service.

The other aspect of improving the well-being of the members, apart from the skills necessary to prepare the union's case for presentation to the employer, is the ability to articulate the union's case. Unfortunately, however, under 5 percent of the participants who have benefited from courses in Communication and Effective Speaking ran by the Critchlow Labor College, are bona fide trade unionist. This is a shortcoming that the College's administration must address, and also a challenge to our unions to reduce the imbalance. Nonetheless, this does not preclude trade unions from introducing such training courses on their own.

(iii) To acquire more control over jobs.

Trade unions have always questioned management's claim of having "the right to hire and fire." Over the years, trade unions have been whittling away on this right to hire and fire, to promote and demote, and to transfer. Today, unions have been able to have an industrial judicial system established at the workplace. Conditions of service are no longer determined solely by the employer but by collective bargaining, already discussed. Further, discipline, resulting from rule violation is not unilaterally dispensed but via a grievance procedure that affords the worker "due process". Important, also, penalties inflicted on workers found guilty of rule violation are not subjectively done but in accordance with a "disciplinary code" negotiated with the employer, as already stated.

Notwithstanding the above, trade unions have nonetheless obtained more control over jobs by way of the seniority provisions they have managed to get included in the Collective Labor Agreement, such as:

1.   Management's obligation to keep a seniority list for every category of employee.

2.   Downsizing to be done in accordance with the principle of first in last out.

3.   Promotion, training, etc., to be done in accordance with seniority. However, seniority status for an employee can be lost due to poor performance and/or challenge through the grievance procedure.

Many have questioned the union's intention in seeking to have more control over jobs via the seniority provisions in the C.L.A. especially that of seniority in promotion. They claim, that in doing so, the union is seeking to promote inefficiency. The union's response to this has always been that seniority avoids subjectivity, favoritism, racism and even nepotism, all of which contribute to industrial conflict, which have a negative effect on production and productivity and so greater consequence for the work organization.

(iv) <u>To promote Broad Social and Economic Objectives</u>

It is said of today's trade unions, that their concern goes beyond such issues as wages and salaries, protection of jobs, and that of the physical well-being of their members. Also of concern are such issues as education, health care, housing, access to potable water and electricity, and equally important, good Governance.

It can be said, therefore, that the concern of today's trade unions is all aspects of the workers lives. It is this all embracing characteristic of a trade union that has brought trade unions into repeated conflict with varying governments.

The reason for the conflict stems from a belief held by political parties, that once they are elected to office, the responsibility for issues such as education, health care, housing, access to potable water and electricity, etc., are their executive domain and attempts by trade unions to "meddle" in such issues, they tend to see as anti-government activity and even subversive. This is even, more so, if a trade union should question the attitude and conduct of those entrusted with government and administration, towards those issues stated above, i.e., education health care, etc.

In the 1950's – 1960s, the then Civil Service Association, now the Public Service Union, developed a piece of land into the housing estate known as Lamaha Gardens. Later The TUC was instrumental in developing what is known as TUCVILLE in the Georgetown district. In the Berbice area (Region 6), another trade union housing estate, TUCBER, was developed.

In the field of education, many unions offer scholarships/bursaries to the children of their members for studies at the secondary and tertiary levels. In the field of health care, many trade unions provide such benefits to their members, either through their own health plans or such health care providers as insurance companies. Further, through the collective bargaining process, trade unions have been able to get employers to provide sickness and health benefits for their employees.

Yet another contribution to the promotion of broad social and economic objectives is the number of credit unions established by trade unions with savings in excess of a billion dollars. The saving is done through salary deductions by the employer, which is paid to the credit union in similar manner to the check off of union dues. The credit unions have contributed in no small measure to the improvement of the economic well-being of the Guyanese workers.

It can be said, therefore, that trade unions have moved beyond the "bread and butter" issues of the past, to those concerned with the total livelihood of workers who are their members.

(v) To Promote Personal Ambitions

Of the five objectives of the union in collective bargaining, "the promotion of the personal ambitions of the union leader" has been the most controversial. This is so since the human side of the bargaining process if often overlooked, and with disastrous consequences.

The union leader, like the union itself, must have his/ her own needs, and it is at the bargaining table that the union leader will seek to have some of those needs satisfied. One such need is what A.S. Maslow termed Esteem Needs – "the desire for reputation or prestige, defining it as respect or esteem from other people, status, dominance, recognition, attention, importance or appreciation". These desires are important to trade union leaders who, when they are baulked in their efforts to satisfy those desires, the resulting frustrations cause them to react negatively. The end result being various forms of industrial conflict.

It should not be overlooked that trade union leaders function within a democratic structure and so the retention of office is often dependent on how effective they are in satisfying the needs of the membership. Further, if a leader has ambitions to move further up the union structure or aspire to positions on the National Trade Union Center such as the Executive Council of the TUC, success at the bargaining table can earn those trade union leaders the recognition, prestige and respect which will serve them in good respect.

Yet another aspect of the human problem is that as it applies to those representing management at the bargaining table. Like the union leader, management representatives also have needs to be satisfied. Unlike the union leaders, however, the management negotiator does not function within a democratic structure. Consequently continuation in office is dependent on how the management negotiators satisfy those to whom they are answerable. Further, the management negotiations.

It is this kind of relationship that can frustrate union negotiators at the bargaining table. Management negotiators most often adopt positions that deny union leaders the opportunity of satisfying their esteem needs while they seek to satisfy their own. This is so, since the satisfaction of the management esteem needs can only be obtained by their satisfying the expectations of those to whom they are answerable.

It must be said, nonetheless, that it is not being advanced that conflict is inherent in collective bargaining. Conflict results from the bargaining process only when those involved in the process, turn a blind eye to the human factor in collective bargaining.

4.   TO SEEK TO BETTER THE CONDITIONS OF THEIR LIVES

In discussing the objectives of the union in collective bargaining, the Promotion of Broad Social and Economic Objectives were addressed as one of the objectives. However, apart from the industrial role of a trade union, then discussed, it must not be overlooked that the union also has a political role.

The political role of the trade union is often misunderstood as previously discussed. Yet, in-spite of the misunderstanding, it must not be overlooked that political decisions of a governmental nature, impact on the lives of trade union members. It is the responsibility of trade unions, therefore, to ensure that political decisions do not impact negatively on the conditions of their members' lives. It is also the union's responsibility to use its influence, to make sure that budgetary and fiscal decisions are implemented, so as to better the conditions of the workers' lives. The union's influence in this respect must be expanded to encompass, working in cohort with other trade unions or through national trade union centers such as the Guyana Trade Union Congress.

This aspect of the trade union function is important and far-reaching. Apart from issues raised while discussing the promotion of broad social and economic objectives such as education, health, housing, etc. already commented upon, there are other issues that impact on the workers live in the work environment and beyond. They include such issues as:

(i)   the purchasing power of the workers' dollar,
(ii)   the distribution of the national income. i.e. who gets what and in what proportion,
(iii)   the levels of unemployment, vis-a-vis investment,
(iv)   good governance and the preservation of workers' rights.

(i)   Important in determining the purchasing power of the worker's dollar, is the Consumer Price Index published by governmental agencies such as the Bureau of Statistics. In the compilation of any such index, the trade union national center must be involved. This is so, since unless workers can have confidence in the published data; the resultant lack of confidence creates an attitude of suspicion, which will have negative consequences at the bargaining table. Not to be overlooked is that for every increase in the Consumer Price Index (CPI) without a concomitant increase in salary and wages, the real wage of the worker declines. This is so, since the salary or wage cannot purchase the same amount of goods as could have been purchased prior to the increase in the CPI which is an index showing the movement up or down in the prices of consumer goods.

(ii)   Similarly, is information relative to the distribution of the national Income which   is the sum total of the money value of the goods and services produced over a stated period, usually one year. The distribution at a minimum should show the amounts received by the three categories-Land, Labor and Capital. Equally important is information relative to the payment of revenue to the national coffers by the three groups via taxation.

(iii)   Relative to unemployment figures, its importance lies in the fact that high incidents of unemployment tend to pull down wages. Further, rising levels of unemployment reduce expendable income (total take home pay) which will likely affect the country' economy.

(iv)   Good governance and the preservation of workers' rights, speak of the respect shown by a government for the democratic principles such as the rule of law, the strict adherence to the United Nations Charter of Human Rights, especially those set out in the country's constitution. Not to be overlooked is the ILO conventions ratified by the government and those which trade unions will like to have the government ratify since they all are intended to improve the life of the worker.

5.   TO PROVIDE A FORUM OF EXPRESSION

A trade union, if it is to be effective, must be seemed by its membership as their advocate. Important, however, the views the union will be advocating must not be the perceived views of the membership. To ensure that this is so, the structure of the union must be as such that forums are in place whereby the union's leadership can be informed of the problems its members are experiencing, not only at the workplace but as members of the wider society away from the workplace.

In discussing the Role of the Union in Seeking to Better the Conditions of the Workers' Lives, mention was made of the type of problems to be addressed by the union. It should be recognized, therefore, that the problems stated, could only be represented if the union is first made aware that such problems do exist and there are forums for that purpose, provided for in the union structure. However, providing the forums is not enough. Members must be encouraged and equipped with the ability to utilize the forums for their advantage.

The question that arises, however, is what are the forums for the expression of the workers' views on problems of society? Internally, the forums can be said to be:

(i)   The Branch Meeting
(ii)   The Executive Council of the union
(iii)   The General Council (In some unions)
(iv)   The General Members meeting or Delegates Conference.

It follows from the above, that the views of the members of the union, expressed at the branch meeting, can move from the branch meeting, on to the supreme authority of the union, the Annual General Meeting or Delegates Conference. It is important to mention however, that while the branch meeting is the best forum for the expression of the views of the rank and file members of the union, they may not, by themselves, utilize the forum for varying reasons. Nonetheless, they can do so through the shop stewards who are the day-to –day union representatives and spokespersons of the rank and file membership in the shop, office or whatever constitutes a worksite.

It does not follow that it is only within the union that there are forums of expression. This is so, since collectively, unions have created other forums of expression for the workers views, such as the Executive Council of the National Umbrella Organization (TUC), its General Council and Delegates Conference. Further to those, are the Regional Forums such as the various organs of the Caribbean Congress of Labor and those of the Inter- American Regional Organization of Workers (ORIT).

Internationally, there are the organs of the International Conference of Free Trade Unions (ICFTU) to which the union is affiliated through its affiliation to the TUC and the International Trade Secretariats (ITS) to which the individual trade union may be affiliated.

Lastly, and probably the most significant forum of expression for the workers views on problems of society, is the International Labor Organization, an organ of the United Nations.

UNITY TOWARDS IMPROVED WORKERS WELFARE
1982

"Trade Unions are not eternal, they will continue to exist for as long as they remain compatible to the society in which they seek to exist…".

These are not my words but those of a former Minister of Labor in the 1960s Wilson Cabinet in Great Britain.

The words nonetheless are worthy of note; for as trade unionists we seem to believe that our unions are here for all time. We blindly accept that definition of a trade union which speaks of "a continuing permanent organization created by the workers ..". The fact is our unions will continue to exist for as long as they continue to be relevant to the society within which we operate.

It is the above context that we must consider the theme of your conference 'UNITY TOWARDS IMPROVED WORKERS WELFARE', for our task, the real task of the trade union is to improve the welfare of those whom we represent, and if we fail to do, we lose our relevance and become nothing more than an anachronism.

Your theme speaks of unity, and no one can gainsay that fact that every union, and the very trade union movement itself, needs unity if it is to function effectively.

I am hereby reminded of the first stanza of the borrowed anthem of our trade union movement, Solidarity Forever, and I quote-

> When the unions inspiration through
> The workers blood shall run,
> There can be no power greater anywhere
> Beneath the sun,
> Yet what force on earth is weaker?
> than the feeble strength of one,
> But the union makes us strong.

The questions I must now ask of you are:

1. Does the Union's inspiration truly run through your blood?
2. Does your Union and the Trade Union Movement have any power?

The answers to these questions are important to the leadership of the Trade Union Movement, for how you perceive your union and the trade union movement will determine how you would react to your union and the movement.

Without the inspiration flowing through our blood, there is no unity. There must be a sense of commitment, the belief that it is through our unions that our welfare would improve. It is when we have this commitment, this belief that our unions are strong, and all things being equal, that we are able to sit around the bargaining table and negotiate those conditions that can improve our welfare.

PREREQUISITES FOR UNITY
Cde. Chairman, we need unity in our Unions and in the Movement that we have created for unity would give us power, but I must warn that

such power must be used wisely as there is always the temptation to use our power to improve the welfare of our members at the expense of others in the society. Power carries with it responsibility and there are those who being fearful of the use of power by our unions have deliberately set out to ensure that power is denied us by creating disunity among our members and even between individual unions.

It is important that we consider this development for there is a crisis of production and productivity and the appeal has been made to the leadership of our unions to get our membership to double their productive efforts.

I would like to submit that the response of our membership to the call for increased productivity would depend on how they perceive those of us who are leaders. If they see the leadership as a group of self-seekers as I think they do, not interested in their welfare, and further mouthpieces of other groups within the society, it is my view they will not respond positively to our call.

Further I submit, if they see their unions as being incapable of protecting their interest and advancing their welfare, there can be no inspiration and without the inspiration there can be no unity and this lack of unity makes the unions weak and ineffective.

In our culture workers expect certain things from their unions and their leadership. What they expect is conditioned by historical development and included in their expectations is the relationship that should exist between the union and the employer and his managers, and also, the relationship between the employer, his managers and the union leadership.

It is imperative that we consider these relationships if we are to concern ourselves with unity, for I submit that here lies the root cause of the problems confronting our unions today, and I am sure that you will agree with me that there are problems, tremendous problems.

Let us consider the relationship between the trade union and the employer and his managers. Traditionally the employer and his agents, the managers, were those classified as the exploiters, those who amass great profits or wealth at our expense. Those we had to fight to wrest from them what we needed to advance our welfare

The interplay between the employer and his mangers on the one hand, and the workers and their unions on the other created a type of relationship that is described as antagonistic. In this relationship, the managers are looking at the union as a source of coercion and the union is looking at the management as a force of exploitation. This relationship bred suspicion and misunderstanding, but nonetheless, in the struggle between the two groups, the best interest of the two groups were served. This I know will be questioned.

It is important that I repeat this statement, "in the struggle between the two groups, the best interest of the two groups were served". There was however a proviso – provided that there was unity among the ranks of the workers and that the conditions that existed dictated there was unity.

Daily we hear the chant that our unions are not as strong as they used to be. There is no militancy among the leadership it is said and the same applies to the membership. Why is this so?

The truth is that since independence and the process of nationalization, the relationship between the two groups has changed. We have moved from the antagonistic to the partnership relationship, and here lies the trouble.

The changes seem to have taken place at only two levels. First at the level of the employer who for the most part is the government and I speak here of the political administration, and second, the level of the leadership of many of our unions. There has been little or no significant change among managerial hierarchy and also the membership of our unions.

I know that managers will challenge this statement. They will tell you that they accept or believe in worker participation in management. They will tell you of the innovations they have introduced at the level of the office and shop floor. They will also tell you that they accept trade unionism but the second tier leadership of our unions will tell you of how they frustrate their efforts and make it so difficult for them to function.

The managers challenge is not difficult to understand since for the most part they are products of the antagonistic environment and change is not easy especially at this period when all enterprises are experiencing great difficulty in maintaining economic buoyancy. The lack of change among the membership however requires a little more explanation.

Since independence the relationship between the employer, the political administration, and the union leadership has changed to that of a partnership. The relationship was generally accepted by the membership of our unions for at one time they were reaping the benefits of that relationship. There was nothing that seriously affected their welfare, but some doubts were created in the late 1960s among workers in the traditional public service over the attitude of the political administration to their pay claim of a 25% across the board increase in salaries. "The Government is interested in development and now when we are amassing money for development, the civil servants are asking for more money. What do they need with more money, some only to buy a second motor car"? Those words, or words to that effect came from the Prime Minister in an address to the nation.

The euphoria of the period triumphed nonetheless for it was "we government" and the same feeling continued into the 1970s bringing a closer and closer relationship between the Trade Union leadership and the Government.

There was however not full acceptance of this relationship especially in the traditional public service but the gains accrued by the salary and wage revision of 1973 allayed the fears of those who benefited.

In the bauxite industry rumblings were heard shortly after nationalization and the repatriation of pension funds and since then the membership were critically observing the relationship while assessing how it was affecting their welfare. In other sectors of the economy affected by the nationalization process the same uneasy feeling existed but since no serious damage was being done to their welfare the workers were hesitantly going along with the change.

All of this must be considered in the light of what was taking place at the worksite for the only changes the workers were seeing were those emanating from their trade union leaders with little or no corresponding change from the managerial hierarchy. As the economic bite started to be felt, the problem was compounded as the managers were getting the backing of the political directorate in their efforts to enforce what was termed Discipline.

As I said, the workers were apprehensively going along with the change. Then we arrived at 1977 and the Minimum Wage Agreement.

The agreement was negotiated by the Trade Union Congress and was binding on all public sector enterprises. It was hailed as a significant achievement - the progeny of the new relationship. It specified that the minimum wage would move from $5.50 per day in the public service to $8.40 in 1977, then to $11.00 in 1978 and $14.00 in 1979.

The agreement also provided for the adjustment of salaries and wages for all employees above the minimum wage by the formula of $x + (x - 600) * .08$, where x = monthly salary as of 12/31/1976. The 600 increased to 920 in 1978 and 1200 in 1979. This change was primarily intended to benefit the worker in the lower rungs of the salary/wage pyramid and to achieve a salary/wage differential ratio of 1:6 by 1979. The existing salary/wage differential in the traditional public service was 1:10 as of 12/31/1976.

There was an aftermath to the agreement however for no sooner than it was implemented for 1978 there followed redeployment of personnel, increases in National Insurance contributions, and an extension of the contributions to the Dependents Pension Fund to include teachers, police and all workers employed in the traditional public service and also the teaching and police service. That was followed by increases on almost every consumer item, which caused the consumer price index to rise by 55% over 1977 and 68% over 1976 as reflected in the table below.

Year	Index	Year over Year % Increase	% Increase Over 1976
1976	157.5	9	-
1977	170.5	8	8
1978	196.4	15	25
1979	231.4	18	47
1980	264.0	14	68

The TUC did not bargain for what transpired after the signing of the 1977 agreement and so the leadership of the movement was soon under tremendous pressure from their membership to do something.

The welfare of the workers was now being threatened. What transpired after however is now history and I must say that the trade union leadership did not come out unscathed. As far as the workers were concerned their fears were justified. As leaders we were tried and found wanting. Our unions were found to be ineffective and as far as our members were concerned the blame was placed on the new relationship.

Following events did nothing to change the opinions of the workers. The failure of the government to implement the $14 per day minimum wage in 1979 only strengthened their belief that their unions were weak and ineffective and their leadership, as they described them, were in the pockets of the political administration.

This belief has serious consequence for our Trade Union Movement, for as long as the belief exists, there can be no "union's inspiration flowing through the blood of our members", and without this inspiration there can be no unity; unity that is so vital to the mobilization of the workers of our country to meet the tremendous challenge that confronts us as a nation. A challenge that is imperative to achieving the acceptable levels of production.

There is a dire need for us to get the much-needed inspiration rekindled so that it can again flow through the blood of the workers. Without it our unions will continue to be ineffective and incapable of protecting or improving our members' welfare. The longer it continues the worse it would be for the Movement for soon our relevancy would be challenged, not only by our members, but by those who look to us to mobilize our members towards achieving national economic objectives. THIS MUST NOT HAPPEN.

There is a great need for unions today as there has always been. It is in the interest of our workers to have a trade union movement capable of improving their welfare. Similarly it is also in the interest of the state to have a trade union movement capable of mobilizing its members towards the achievement of agreed on economic objectives. Only a strong trade union movement can accomplish this. Let this be clearly understood.

The change however from the antagonistic to the participative relationship is not something that we could or should change. The new society that we have conceptualized demands this. It is therefore important that we get our trade union membership to accept this. They must be convinced that the changed relationship has nothing to do with the problems they are experiencing. What's more, they must be made to understand that were it not for the new relationship, their lot could have been much worse.

How are we to achieve this? We must first get our trade union membership to understand that the country is in the midst of a serious economic crisis that necessitates measures that will affect their welfare. Further it is also imperative that the leadership themselves understand

and can articulate the nature of the crisis to their members so that they can accurately communicate the fact that the measure may affect the welfare of our members but in the light of the prevailing circumstances nothing better could have been done.

Secondly, at the workplace there must be visible signs of change. The workers must no longer feel that the new relationship is working against their interest. It is not enough for management to speak and write of their changing approach to management. Their words must be matched by deeds. Here, let me advise, workers are not easily fooled.

Thirdly, the political administration must realize that it is in their interest and the nation's interest to have a strong trade union movement led by those in whom the workers have confidence. I have already expressed the view that there are some who are fearful of a strong trade union movement and deliberately set out to curtail its influence. Some even attempt to foist a movement on the workers and equally on the leadership and unless that inspiration that I spoke of is generated such a movement is incapable of executing the tasks for which it was created and as result becomes irrelevant. When that occurs the Movement will be useless, of no use to the workers and of little, if any, to those who created or fashioned it.

So far we have considered the relationship between the union and the employer represented by the political administration. It is now left for us to look at the relationship between the union membership and the leadership.

Historically the leadership of our trade unions was in close contact with the membership. They identified with the membership. They were often seen at the worksite and were familiar with the membership. Their standard of living was almost at the same level as those whom they represented and that brought about a feeling of oneness, unity.

The membership of our unions was not then as large as they are today and as a result, the unions were not as financial. That meant that the leadership had to be committed. There was little hope of financial reward. All they could have looked forward to was a meager honorarium at yearend if the funds were available.

The leadership of the unions also served part-time. Few unions could have afforded fulltime officers and those that were adventurous enough to accept fulltime appointments knew that compensation, while far from attractive, was also not guaranteed. As such, very often, the only fulltime employee of the union was a typist and even that depended on affordability.

The conditions as they existed compelled both the membership and the leadership to be militant. As a matter of fact, the leadership had to be militant for most often they were the ones against whom the wrath of the employer was directed, for, let us remember, trade unions were not accepted as they are today. They had to struggle for their existence and as I have said, very often the trade union leader was an employee working for the same employer as the member.

The relationship therefore between the leadership of our unions and the membership was of a personal nature, for as the saying goes, they were all in the same boat. It did not follow however that is was all smooth sailing between the leadership and membership for very often, the membership meted out their frustrations and anger on the leadership. In other words they "cussed them out".

We must remember that the leadership was always at hand, so whenever the membership wanted to let off steam, the leadership was the target. They well knew that it was dangerous to tackle the employer or the managers for that led to serious consequences, of which they were well aware.

The above relationship typifies our culture for it had set norms of behavior between the leadership and membership of our unions. With the passage of time however, things have changed and so have the relationships.

Today trade union membership has expanded and as a result of better wages and salaries the dues are higher. The unions of today therefore are more financial and this is witnessed by the many unions that now possess their own headquarters and a sizeable full time staff.

The activities of the unions have also expanded. Collective bargaining is now well entrenched in the union/management relations and this consumes a lot of the time of the leadership. This means that the leadership now mainly fulltime has been removed from the workplace and their activities make if difficult for them to maintain the close contact with the membership as it was in earlier times.

There is yet another dimension of the problem for the activities of the Trade Union Congress have also expanded as a result of the greater involvement of the Movement in national life. Not to be overlooked also is that collective bargaining in the public sector is becoming the responsibility of the TUC and this in itself poses additional problems for the union leadership.

Fortunately your union is an exception, for being a small union with a restrictive membership, it is still possible for our leadership to be in close contact with the membership and this conferenced attests to this fact. There are few unions that can today find it possible to hold half yearly conferences involving the general membership, for the norm now seems to be, biennial and triennial delegates conferences. Of course, finance dictates this.

This does not mean that your union would have no problems, for being a small union it follows that your financial resources would be slim and it may not be possible for you to offer the benefits and services that are now expected of a union at this point in time. More of this later, however.

As I have said, the leadership of our unions is today removed from the membership. The membership can no longer see them as often as they would like, even if it is just to "cuss them out", and this poses problems for the unions and the Movement as the membership seem not to be able to understand the new development/relationship.

How are we to solve this problem? My contention is that we will have to strengthen our branch system. More responsibility and authority must be given to the branch leadership and what is of greater importance, the finances of the unions must be decentralized so that the branch can execute programs directed towards satisfying some of the needs of the membership. The branch must be more involved in looking after the welfare of the membership.

What I am advocating is the strengthening of the second tier leadership of our unions. The members must see the branch leaders as important persons in the union's administration. This is only possible however if we, the top leadership, make them feel important and what's more, treat them as being important

The membership needs leaders with whom they can relate and respond to. They do not see the present branch leadership as important union leaders. The fact is that they do not see them as leaders at all.

In strengthening the branch we will be doing two things. First, we will strengthen the union for the old adage still holds, "The strength of the union lies in its branches". Secondly, we will be developing a cadre of leaders at the workplace with whom the members can relate, leaders wielding influence, who will fill the void created by the removal of those leaders who have now taken up fulltime positions in the union administration, or engaged in the expanded activities of the Union and the Movement.

It is not necessary for me at this time to indicate what some of these expanded activities can be. They are:

1. Members of the Executive Council of the Union and also members of the many standing committees of the union.
2. Members of the TUC Executive Council and/or members of its many standing committees

3. Representatives of the TUC or the Union on the Board of Public Corporation or other public sector agencies
4. Representatives of the TUC on regional or other international trade union bodies or participating in their activities.

I am therefore contending that if the union is to function effectively and the movement to effectively advocate and advance the welfare of the worker, these activities, which can be time consuming, yet important, must be undertaken.

Let it be understood however that I am not advocating that the top leadership of our unions should remove themselves entirely from their membership. They must get out and meet their members as often as time constraints permit. But let me advise, whenever they go to meet the rank and file, they must do nothing to belittle the branch leadership in the eyes of the membership. On the contrary, it is important that they do everything to enhance the image of the branch leadership.

Cde. Chairman, I have so far been discussing the changing relationship between the union and the employer and their managers, or what we can call "The State". I have also discussed the changing relationship between the union leadership and the membership.

In discussing these relationships I have endeavored to establish that there are many aspects of the relationships that affect the unity that is so vital if we agree to strengthen our unions. Earlier, I have also endeavored to establish that it is through unity that we can rekindle the union's inspiration that is so necessary if our unions are to mobilize our membership to grapple with the serious problems that confront our society, and foremost among them are the problems of increased production and productivity.

WHAT WE MEAN BY WORKERS' WELFARE

The theme of your conference is "UNITY TOWARDS IMPROVED WORKERS WELFARE", and while I have endeavored to establish that unity in our unions is necessary if we are to improve the workers welfare, it is necessary for me to take a look at the term "workers' welfare".

The dictionary describes welfare as "good health, happiness and prosperity". In trade union terminology, we describe our unions as:

"Continuing permanent organizations created by the workers to protect themselves at their work, to improve the conditions of their work through collective bargaining, to seek to better the conditions of their lives..."

As I see it, it is through trade union action that the workers can enjoy good health, happiness and prosperity, for that is what trade unionism is all about.

The definition of a trade union which I have quoted above speaks of "protecting themselves at their work", and this is important, for without a job there can be no "good health, happiness ad prosperity" for the workers. Job protection therefore must be seen as an important aspect of the trade union function and it is so important that we do not lose sight of this aspect of our function as I am afraid seems to be happening. However, it is necessary that while we seek to advance the welfare of our members, we do not do so at the expense of others, for that would make a mockery of the right to work as enshrined in our constitution.

This I know must require some explanation. What I am advocating is that our unions while they negotiate those conditions that will offer their members the job protection they need, must at the same time ensure that in doing so, they do not condone inefficiency and the other malpractices that adversely affects production, for that can jeopardize the continuing existence of the enterprise and also the jobs of all the those who work for the enterprise. In the context of the Guyuana situation, such malpractices impact negatively on the economy and can affect the welfare of thousands of workers in the public sector by the retrenchment process with which we are all so familiar

The definition of a trade union I have advanced also speaks "to improve the condition of their work". This must be taken in the context that the workers spend the majority of their waking hours within the walls of the work enterprise and in work related activities such as dressing for work, and travelling to and from work. It follows therefore that if the workers we represent are to enjoy any happiness out of life, the workplace must contribute to the sum total of their happiness. This, our unions must give serious consideration.

There is however another aspect of the working conditions that is important and that is those conditions that tend to remove the frustrations that affect production and productivity. Trade unions must see this as an important part of their function, for the frustrations that result from such things as insecurity, long working hours, inadequate vacation, and of course, the work environment which in itself impede the productive efforts of those who work. Here lies a challenge for our union leadership.

Important for us to consider now is salaries and wages and its impact on workers welfare.

It is said by some that the worker works for a salary or wage and with that buys a standard of living. Accepting this, we can extend it to say that to a great extent, the welfare of the workers could be purchased. Good health to a great extent is determined by the foods we eat, the environment within which we work and live, and access to the best possible medical attention. Our salary and wages therefore can be used to ensure that we eat foods with the necessary nutrients, and what is more important, that which affords us some enjoyment or pleasure; in other words, some happiness.

In a publication titled "Poverty and Basic Need" by Guy Standing and Richard Szal, in speaking of Guyana and the inadequate intake of protein and other nutrients, they made the following comment, "Thus rather than availability being the problem, it appears to be more one of waste, and most importantly, the distribution of the available supply and the ability of certain groups to afford many items of food that were available".

I would therefore advance that it is our unions' responsibility to ensure that the salary and wages paid to our members are such that they can purchase the foods with sufficient protein and other nutrients so as to guarantee their good health.

Now in considering the environment and its contribution to good health we must take into account such things as proper housing, portable water, electricity and sanitation, etc. and there is no doubt that adequate wages influence where our members will live and hence their environment.

The above of course also speaks of the conditions of the lives of the members of our unions as mentioned in the definition of a trade union I have advanced above.

In considering the environment and its effect on the health of our members we cannot overlook occupational safety and health. This is an area which has been sadly neglected and has been responsible for the undue suffering of many of our members in the later days of their lives, and for some, even before. Inadequate lighting, harmful noise levels, lack of safety-wear and guards, dangerous materials such as cement, asbestos, chemicals, pesticides, etc. have had devastating affects on the health of so many, and what is so much worse, has cut short their work-life without any compensatory benefits.

We must also not overlook the health services at the disposal of our members. I would advance that our unions have the responsibility to make certain that whenever our members fall sick, they have access to the best possible medical attention and this can be done through the collective bargaining process.

Many charges have been leveled against our health services and it is for our unions to ascertain whether these charges are justified and if they are have them remedied.

In the final analysis however it is our responsibility to create an environment within which if our members fall sick they not only have access to the best possible medical attention, but also as I see it, either free of cost or within the financial capability of our members. This must be so to avert unnecessary hardship being placed on the households of those whom we represent. Failing to do this will affect the welfare of our members adversely.

Cde. Chairman, I will hereby advance that if our unions can guarantee the good health of our members and pursue the activities that will bring this about with the involvement of the membership through their branches the happiness we all look forward to can be assured.

It has always been my contention that the creator intended man's existence on this planet to be a happy one, and if our trade unions should work towards the acquisition of happiness for our members, then we will be doing the creator's work as he intended.

I contend therefore that if our unions can acquire for our members pleasant tasting and nutritional foods, a healthy and safe environment, both within and without the work enterprise, access to adequate medical attention, and the salary and wages that can afford the workers the opportunity of beneficially utilizing their leisure hours, then the unions, through the process of collective bargaining would therefore have acquired another facet of the workers welfare, happiness.

The third facet of the workers welfare is prosperity. As I see it, prosperity refers to the continuing increases in economic well-being. That state where the worker is getting as he moves through life, a reasonable amount of happiness, comfort and satisfaction and can also continuously look towards the future without undue fear.

I am sure that none here assembled will disagree with me when I say that the vast majority of workers in our country has not as yet reached that state in man's development, but I submit, that here in /Guyana, it is the goal towards which we are working. However, our trade unions have a responsibility, for ours is the task of convincing our members that the current efforts being made will lead them to prosperity. But for us to do this, as leaders, we must first be convinced ourselves, and herein lies the problem.

I say this as I am convinced that the workers do not believe that the efforts now being made will lead them to prosperity. I do not believe that the majority of our workers are as yet convinced that the future holds anything good for them. This is why there is a general atmosphere of frustration and where for so many it seems as if our people have lost the will to produce.

It is for the union leadership to convince our membership that the new society in the making has something to offer them. Every man and woman look forward to prosperous days and it is towards that objective that they work. However to gain prosperity, some amount of sacrifice is needed and most workers are aware of this. It is however important for us to know that people will only make sacrifices if they know that the sacrifice made will lead to something better for them.

There are some I know who advocate the concept of the sacrifice generation. A state where one generation makes the ultimate sacrifice so that the following generation can enjoy the prosperity denied the former. I do not accept this. It is my view that every man and woman is entitled to the best possible living standard in his or her own lifetime and as I see it, this is what trade unionism seeks to ensure. Should we as leaders ever accept this concept of the sacrifice generation there would follow a disintegration of our unions for our membership will no doubt consider us as not being relevant to the advancement of their welfare.

This I also advance must not happen. We must convince our members that prosperity lies ahead and mobilize them towards its achievement. To do this however we need a strong trade union movement with a committed leadership capable of convincing our member that their welfare is our concern. It is when we get our members truly believing this that the union's inspiration will once more flow through their blood and we will have the kind of unions capable of doing the things for which they were created.

Cde. Chairman what we need at this time is a trade union movement concerned with the total life of the workers. This means from the time they awake in the morning to the time they go to sleep at night. The union should even be concerned with where and how the workers sleep at night.

If the unions are to improve the workers welfare, I advance that they will have to go even beyond what I have so far advocated. Our unions must plan and execute such programs that will satisfy those needs of the worker that cannot be satisfied during the hours when they are in the employ of the work organization. I must now ask what is the Local Government Officers Association doing towards satisfying the recreational needs of its members? Their cultural needs? Their need for socialization?

Cde. Chairman I know that it may be advanced that the finances of your union does not permit you to consider such programs that can satisfy the needs I have listed above, but I must ask whether you have thought of using your right to bargain so as to satisfy those needs.

The employers as I see it must be made to understand, especially those in the public sector, that they have an obligation to contribute towards the satisfaction of the needs of our members for recreation, cultural development, and socialization. As I said earlier on, their words must be matched by deeds. We cannot speak of partnership if management is going to continue to operate as they did in the past. The time is long overdue for the Georgetown Municipality to erect a building and put it at the disposal of their employees so that programs could be mounted to satisfy those important needs which if satisfied can advance the workers welfare.

Cde. Chairman this aspect is important. We are in the midst of a crisis that makes it difficult for trade unions to negotiate the level of wages that can satisfy the aspirations of our members. Our members are frustrated and this is because our union programs are limited. There are a number of needs that we can satisfy in the short term and which can end the frustration or most of it that now exists. By doing this, we can rekindle that inspiration that is vitally necessary.

It is our task to produce a happy worker but this can only come about if we have a workforce that is contented. This is not going to be easy but the challenge is ours. We must earn the confidence of our membership and to do this we must communicate to them by the things we do that we are truly committed to the advancement of their welfare.

Finally your theme I found to be most fitting and interesting and permit me to extend my congratulations to your conference committee. It is however necessary for those of us who hold leadership positions in our unions to recognize that our members are beginning to question our relevance. The reasons for this, I have endeavored to outline. It is therefore left for us to do the things that are necessary to rekindle the union's inspiration that one flowed through the blood of our workers. No one else will do it for us. Our unions are today as needed as they have ever been but to achieve for the worker those things for which we had created our unions, we need unity first, and then and only then, can we proceed with the task of improving the workers welfare.

Cde. Chairman, I wish you a successful 27th Bi-Annual Conference and sincerely trust, or should I say implore, that coming out of your deliberations would be measures that can truly create the unity that is necessary to improve the welfare of the workers whom you represent.

LET US NOT FORGET "THE UNION MAKES US STRONG"!

ABOUT THE AUTHOR

My Dad, Leslie Melville, was born on the 16th of April 1925 in New Amsterdam, Berbice, in British Guiana, a colony of England.

My dad was a born fighter. While still a toddler my Dad slipped from the arms of the Nanny and fell through a window to the ground floor twelve feet below. He was not expected to survive. At the age of ten he contracted typhoid fever causing him to loose an entire school year. In spite of that setback, Dad completed his primary education in 1940 and moved on to graduate from Berbice High School in 1945. While in High School, my Dad represented his school at both Cricket and Football and shared the high jump record with another long-standing friend.

At the insistence of his Father, upon graduation from High School in January 1946, my dad and his father left New Amsterdam for Georgetown, the colony's capital, for what he thought at the time was compensation for successfully completing his Senior Cambridge Examination, a British International Examination. Dad spent the majority of his visit meeting friends and family from Berbice, most of which he was meeting for the first time since most of them had earlier migrated to the Capital.

The afternoon of the second day of the visit proved to be a life changing experience. My Dad was taken to visit Mr. J.C. Nurse, the Clerk-in-Charge of Pure Water Supply Scheme (PWSS). Mr. Nurse previously worked with the PWSS in New Amsterdam. This organization was responsible for the drilling of Artesian Wells, the laying of pipelines and the construction of overhead tanks necessary for the provision of potable water to the Colony's rural community. The end result of the visit was one my Dad nor his Father expected, or at least that was assumed by my Dad. Instead of returning to Berbice as expected, my Dad was told to return at 8 am the following day to begin working as a Junior Account Clerk for a salary of $17.60 per week. According to my Dad, the offer thwarted all his plans made by his father for spending the first six months of 1946. I often wonder whether my Grandfather was fully aware of the outcome of the visit long before leaving Berbice.

It was seven years later in October 1953 while working as a Technical Assistant that my Dad would commence his long career as a Trade Unionist. One afternoon while leaving work William Baveghems and Hugh Erskine, President and Vice President of the Public Works Pure Water Supply and Sea Defense Workers Union approached him with the beseeching request "Man! Come with we, the union needs someone who the Administration would respect. Come with we!"

As my Dad noted in his book, at that time he was not a member of the Union and was unaware of the functions of the trade union and therefore wondered why he was approached as opposed to the other members. However, having developed a close relationship in his new position as a Technical Assistant with Bavie and Skins, as they were known, he was moved by the appeal and promised that he would discuss the offer with my Mom, his new wife of one year. He committed to them that should she agree, he would attend their conference scheduled for the following day.

My Dad went home that day and discussed the offer with my Mom. Surprisingly, as my Dad describes it, she casually offered no objection. I often wondered, knowing the years of sacrifice in time and effort dedicated to this Movement by my Dad and at times the concern for his safety, whether it was the distractions of being a new wife and Mother that resulted in the casual response, or whether like my Dad, she we unaware of the life changing journey upon which he was about to embark.

In keeping with his promise, my Dad arrived at the Negro Progress Convention Hall the following day to attend his first Trade Union meeting. It was at that meeting that he was elected Treasurer of the Public Works Pure Water Supply and Sea Defense Workers Union later renamed the National Union of Public Service Employees (NUPSE). Thus began my Dad's career as one of Guyana's most illustrious Trade Unionists, one which would take him to the Executive Council of the Guyana Trades Union Congress, serving in the positions of Principal Assistant Secretary from 1976 – 1984; Registrar of the Critchlow Labor College from 1976 – 1986; then as Committee Member, Assistant Secretary, Education Officer and General Secretary of the Guyana Public Service Union over the period of 1967 - 1989. In 1972 Dad obtained a scholarship from the American Institute of Free Labor Development to study Industrial Relations and Labor Economics at the Front Royal College in the US.

In addition to being a Trade Unionist, my Dad is also well known for his eloquence in speech delivery. Like the leaders of his time, he possessed a natural ability to communicate with all levels of society oftentimes using language as his weapon of choice. Dad served as a President of the Georgetown Toastmasters Club, an organization that was very special to him. While teaching a course in Communication and Effective Speaking at Critchlow Labor College, my Dad was awarded second place in an International Taped Speech Contest sponsored by the Toastmasters International.

In the years following his entrance into the world of Trade Unionism

Dad has written extensively of his service to both the Movement and his country as the demonstrated in the fifteen essays embodied in this book, A Voice Crying in the Wilderness. Whereas his concern over the plight of the working people of his country earned him many negative experiences, as he often written and spoken, it was the price he was willing to pay for championing the cause of those who, due to no fault of their own, lacked the ability to adequately articulate both their plight and its cause.

It was in 2004, fifty years after dedicating his life to the betterment of the workers in Guyana that his journey in the land of his birth as a Trade Unionist, a Defender of his people would end. My Dad left Guyana that summer to vacation with his family as normal. My mother had migrated almost 20 years earlier mainly due to the nightmare that life in Guyana had become, joining the exodus of the Guyanese middle class which was dubbed by many as the worst brain drain in history. Within a week of his arrival, while preparing the necessary blood work for a scheduled lens transplant in his right eye, it was detected that his blood count was extremely low. To quote the nurse, "I have never seen anyone physically walk into the hospital with such a low blood count". My Dad was diagnosed with stomach cancer and the family decided to go ahead with the surgery ignoring concerns shared by the doctors of his age. Remarkably, my Dad completed the radiation treatment with very minimal hair loss and nausea, once again to the amazement of the hospital staff.

In 2007 my Dad made his first return trip to Guyana after accepting an appointment from the International Development Bank (IDB) as the Public Service's nominee to the committee appointed to revive the Public Service Rules. To my Dad's dismay, it was both a fruitless and shameful exercise for the committee never met, but instead included in the redrafted rules a clause permitting the fining of errant employees, a position which was contrary to the laws of Guyana.

It was my Dad's view that the Chairman of the Committee seemed to have bowed to the dictates of the Administration in power. To further add to his frustration and to confirm his belief of the Administration's involvement, his salary as a member of the Committee was withheld and was only released after complaining to the IDB.

My Dad returned to the US extremely disheartened, finally accepting the reality that the country of his birth, his beloved Guyana, was still not ready to respect the well-being of the working men and women that his Movement had toiled so hard to achieve. When asked for his opinion on what saddens him the most of the current state of affairs in Guyana, his major complaints were the closure of the Critchlow Labor College and the self-destruction of the Guyana Trades Union Congress.

Early 2013, after leaving a very stressful job of over twenty years in Corporate America, while visiting my Dad I came upon these essays and was amazed at the relevance to today's society. I remember equating their application to the current political challenges of our time, almost as similar as one could apply Paul's Letters to our current day morality challenges. For example, I was impressed that in 1964 my Dad had the foresight to discuss the preparation of society for women entering the workforce, environmental challenges on worker output and hence compensation, the impact of the minimum wage on society and terms such as a worker's value add. Most importantly and one which resonates today globally is his argument that for the Union to be successful they must also understand the cost aspect of their demands on the employer. He encouraged the workers to educate themselves so that they can better partner with the employer. Whereas he supported the rights of the workers, unlike most Trade Unionist of his time and of today, he realized that in order for the union to succeed in its quest for worker participation in management, not only must the workers of the enterprise be trained for their new roles, but more importantly so must the Union's leadership.

After reading these essays I encouraged my Dad to publish his works. As you read these works, as an exercise, I implore you to consider the period in which they were written and decide for yourself exactly how much progress has been made by the worker of today. Are we better off with or without unions? Did the unions cause their own decline and/or demise? Could unions work in today's global environment?

On the Monday before Thanksgiving of 2014, while in the midst of Christmas preparations, my dad's favorite time of the year, he tripped and fell after having been recently declared cancer free. My dad survived the required back surgery, but unfortunately did not survive the rehabilitation process. On February 9th, 2015, in a country that in 2004 snatched him from the jaws of death, The United States of America, my Dad passed surrounded by his wife of 63 years, Bebe Lila, his children, grandchildren, in-laws and cousins, most of whom he raised as his own.

As we watched our Patriarch, our gentle giant, take his last breaths, memories of conversations about his beautiful Guyana where he spent his final days in the travelling phase of the dying process flooded my mind. As we all hugged and kissed him, wanting to deny the fact that his time had come to go Home, wanting to keep him with us just a little while longer so we can hear one more story about Guyana, have one more political argument about world politics just to have his blue eyes light up with the challenge, I recalled one of our last conversations with guilt where he expressed concern about his work that would be left uncompleted. All I could think of was the pain in his eyes as he made this statement knowing full well that I was responsible for one of his uncompleted works, the publication of this book which ultimately represents his life struggle to effect change in Guyana.

My Dad often wondered whether had he stayed in Guyana he could have averted the destruction of the Movement or prevented the closure of the Critichlow Labor College, a place where he touched so many young, hopeful lives. My elder sister Ferial along with my two brothers, Patrick and David, together with my Mom often begged him not to focus so much on a country that he could no longer be a part of and instead awake to the realities that the closing stages of his life will be spent in this Land of the Free and the Home of the Brave enjoying and nurturing the future of his children, grandchildren and great grandchildren as they chart a life of their own in this land that has been their refuge.

Even as I write this, I must admit that I myself often think of what ifs, like what if we hadn't left, could he have made a difference. The reality is that we will never know. The only thing we can be certain of is that we each must chart our own course, think of what we want our legacy to be and work towards it. My Dad fought for the well-being of the worker in Guyana and had many successes. I carry as my life's motto, one of his favorite quotes, "Stand on your feet before man, and on your knees before God, and only God". Don't stop fighting for what is right wherever you call home!

Gillene Nelson nee Melville

The Entrepreneur's Publisher

RICHTER
PUBLISHING

.

www.ingramcontent.com/pod-product-compliance
Lightning Source LLC
Chambersburg PA
CBHW060330200326
41519CB00011BA/1887